Liberating Economics

Liberating Economics

Feminist Perspectives on Families, Work, and Globalization

Second Edition

Drucilla K. Barker
Suzanne Bergeron
Susan F. Feiner

UNIVERSITY OF MICHIGAN PRESS

Ann Arbor

Copyright © 2021 by Drucilla K. Barker, Suzanne Bergeron, and Susan F. Feiner
All rights reserved

For questions or permissions, please contact um.press.perms@umich.edu

Published in the United States of America by the
University of Michigan Press
Manufactured in the United States of America
Printed on acid-free paper

A CIP catalog record for this book is available from the British Library.

Library of Congress Cataloging-in-Publication data has been applied for.

First published February 2021

ISBN: 978-0-472-07473-0 (Hardcover : alk paper)
ISBN: 978-0-472-05473-2 (Paper : alk paper)
ISBN: 978-0-472-12842-6 (ebook)

Contents

Digital materials related to this title can be found on the Fulcrum platform via the following citable URL: https://doi.org/10.3998/mpub.10048520

Tables

Preface to the Second Edition

The genesis of this book lies in the year 2000 when Susan F. Feiner and I decided it would be a good idea to write a book about feminist economics. The bulk of the writing took place a couple of years later, although due to the vagaries of the publishing world the first edition of Liberating Economics was not published until 2006.

Slightly more than a decade has now passed and the world has changed dramatically. Globalization has tied the economies of nation-states more closely together; climate change, which was then only on the distant horizon, is a stark reality; and class divisions among women have widened, particularly those stemming from North/South differences.

Feminist economics has also changed over this period. When we began it was an upstart field, fighting for recognition and legitimacy in economics. That fight is over. Feminist economics is now well established as a subfield of the discipline in which using gender as a category of analysis is fairly commonplace. It is time for a second edition of our book.

Our lives have also changed. Writing the second edition corresponded with Susan Feiner's retirement from the University of Southern Maine, at which time she turned her attention from teaching and scholarly writing to other interests, most notably feminist political activism. Much of the writing from the original book remains as do her political and intellectual vitality.

Revising this book is not a task that I could have taken on alone. I am grateful that Suzanne Bergeron was able to join me, bringing her expertise in gender and development and care work to the project. In addition, she brought fresh eyes and new perspectives.

Although some of the original book remains, there is much that is new as well. The global North/South remains as one organizing principle. The intersection of gender with race, class, and other categories of social difference is another. The importance of social reproduction to economic well-being is a third. Chapters 1 through 5 were updated with new data and concepts. In the first edition, development and globalization were discussed together in one chapter. This second edition separates them, devoting a chapter to each. Once that change was made, other changes followed, including a stand-alone chapter on the global labor market that focuses on global supply chains, transnational care, and informalization. The other significant change was that due to the enormous significance of the 2008 financial crisis on people's lives, we added a stand-alone chapter on gender and debt.

Finally, we need to note that this book went to press just as the Covid-19 crisis began. The multiple crises of care and social reproduction thus revealed have engendered a host of new scholarship, while bringing renewed attention to existing feminist work on this topic. We look forward to engaging with this rich body of work in our future endeavors.

DKB, 2020

Acknowledgments

We would like to thank all of the institutions that supported this project in its original and now second edition. These include Hollins University, the University of Southern Maine, The Hawke Institute at the University of South Australia, the University of South Carolina, and the University of Michigan-Dearborn. We would also like to thank the academic organizations that have supported our work connecting feminist theory to economics. These include the International Association for Feminist Economics, the Association for Economic and Social Analysis, the National Women's Studies Association, and the Feminist Theory Section of the International Studies Association. We are grateful for the many invaluable conversations, debates, and friendships that have been nurtured in those spaces. Many colleagues offered thoughtful comments on earlier chapter drafts. Thank you. We also thank our students, whose questions and interests helped us shape our ideas. Thanks also go to Danielle Coty, Elizabeth Demers, and the team at the University of Michigan Press; to Athena Sargent and Peter Wissoker for their careful copyediting and insightful comments; and to the anonymous readers for their valuable feedback. Finally, we gratefully acknowledge the loving support of our families, who encouraged us even as our work spread over dining room tables, family rooms, and vacations.

1 | Introduction

We think that most people will agree that there are significant problems with the economy today. Gender inequities immediately come to mind. Globally, women continue to lag behind men in access to paid work or resources such as land. Their wages are 24 percent lower on average.[1] Their employment conditions are more likely to be unstable, precarious, and lacking in benefits or safety protections. This situation is worse still for those who face multiple, intersecting forms of discrimination by race, caste, citizenship status, sexual orientation, gender identity, and the like. In the United States, for instance, white women earn 81.5 cents for every dollar that white men earn, but for black women that figure drops to 65.3 cents per dollar.[2] In the United States and over most of the world, migrant domestic workers with insecure visas often find themselves in difficult and abusive working conditions because they lack legal recourse. Gender non-conforming persons face significant labor market discrimination, resulting in higher rates of poverty than the rest of the population.[3]

Meanwhile, women around the world continue to shoulder a disproportionate amount of the unpaid care work—at least two and one-half times more than men.[4] This work is essential for human well-being, yet it is all but invisible in economic policy. The stereotypes and gender roles that cast women in the caretaker position at home contribute to a segregated labor market. Paid care and domestic work are seen as a natural extension of women's roles at home, and thus undervalued and underpaid. Women today may have the kind of access to credit that their grandmothers could not have imagined, but they are also more likely to be burdened by chronic indebtedness than men. Given the forms of discrimination they experience and their lower wages and higher care work burdens, it is not surprising to find that the majority of the world's poor are women. And poor women are the most vulnerable to the droughts and natural disasters created by climate change.[5]

Mainstream economics provides at best a distorted explanation for these inequities. To a large extent, it justifies them as reflecting people's individual choices and abilities. For instance, it argues that the gender wage gap is largely due to women's voluntary occupational choices and lack of investment in human capital, not to structural inequalities.[6] To the extent that gender discrimination is recognized, it is only in the very narrow terms of the barriers that keep women out of paid work. The labor market itself is assumed to be a sphere of mutually beneficial voluntary exchange and long-run harmony between workers and employers.

The failure of mainstream economics to adequately account for the value of unpaid care and domestic work also contributes to a distorted picture of the economy and the role of women and gender within it.[7] Care work is at the heart of what is now referred to as social reproduction, the many quotidian activities—cooking, cleaning, childcare, eldercare, and care for the community and the environment—that are necessary for the functioning of any economy. This work, associated with the private sphere, which is typically viewed as the domain of women, goes unrecognized and unvalued even though it is essential for human life. Neglecting social reproduction leads to policy failures that often increase the workload of women and girls to the breaking point, while reducing the quality of life for all. Further, mainstream economics measures the success or failure of an economy by market efficiency, profitability, and growth of gross domestic product (GDP) per capita. These measures significantly limit space for addressing goals such as poverty reduction, security, equity, human flourishing, or the health of the planet.

Feminist economics, in contrast, recognizes that power and privilege play an important role in determining what is produced, who produces it, and who gets it. It examines the structural inequalities that are a central force behind the dynamics that create the wage gap and many other gendered economic outcomes. Consequently, conflict and power are as likely to characterize economic processes as are harmony and mutually beneficial voluntary exchanges. Markets are as likely to reflect and contribute to social disparities by gender, race, citizenship status, and sexual orientation as they are to resolve them.[8]

Feminist economics also emphasizes the importance of measuring the value of unpaid care and domestic work. Work done by feminist economists over the past few decades has made the enormous amount of labor that goes into care work and domestic work visible, which, when taken seriously, improves policy outcomes. In addition, feminist economics offers an alternative evaluative framework, emphasizing the goals of providing an acceptable standard of living to current and future generations, equity, decent work, human security, and environmental sustainability as crucial to our economic well-being.

What Is Economics?

Wait a minute, feminism and economics? Is not a price just a price? A market just a market? Do not people feel the ups and downs of economic activity equally, regardless of gender, race, ethnicity, or sexual orientation? Will a change in interest rates affect everyone the same way, regardless of gender? To all these questions feminist economists answer a resounding "no." Gender—like race, ethnicity, class, sexual orientation, nationality, and other markers of social location—is central to our understanding of economics and the functioning of economic systems.

But what is economics? Let us begin to explain this by asking a simple question: how do we get our daily bread? As individuals we only produce a tiny fraction of the commodities we consume each day. We buy the rest. How is it that ordinary goods and services like bread, soap, and electricity are available for us to purchase, providing we have the cash? A loaf of bread, like a bar of soap or a kilowatt of electricity, requires the coordinated activities of thousands of people, in dozens of occupations, scattered around the globe. Farmers grow wheat expecting to sell to millers. Millers process flour to sell to bakers. Bakers produce bread to fill orders from large supermarket chains. And grocers sell us bread so we can make sandwiches for ourselves, our families, and our friends.

Our daily bread depends on all of these activities, plus those involved in manufacturing farm equipment, transportation, newspaper advertising, and supermarket staffing. Each of these must take place at approximately the right time, in roughly the correct sequence, and in sufficient quantity to keep grocery store shelves stocked. As we widen the scope of our vision to encompass the enormous array of commodities available today—education and health; computers and cell phones; art and music; childcare and eldercare; Barbies, books, and bombs—the complexity of modern economies becomes apparent.

All economies must produce, distribute, and consume goods and services. What is the mechanism by which individuals come together to do this? For Adam Smith, the father of modern economics, it was the market. The competitive market functioned as an "invisible hand" or mechanism through which the activities and practices of self-interested individuals are guided to bring about economic outcomes that benefit the larger society. As Smith famously stated, "It is not from the benevolence of the butcher, the brewer, or the baker that we expect our dinner, but from their regard to their own interest."[9] In market economies, many goods and services are produced in anticipation of profits that may be realized when commodities are sold. The focus on commodity production, sales, and profits has been central to economic analysis since Adam Smith first wrote those words in 1776. What happens to all those loaves of bread once they are sold? Adam Smith and most of the economists who followed him have largely ignored this question.

What they were unable to see was that much of what happens in markets relies on the vast amount of unpaid labor that takes place in the home and the community. When we begin to acknowledge this unpaid labor, a whole host of previously hidden economic activities and motivations becomes apparent. As the feminist economist Nancy Folbre has argued, not only do the goods and services produced outside the market come into our vision but a different set of values and practices behind many of these activities must be reckoned with, such as care, obligation, and reciprocity.[10] Thus feminist economists extend the horizon to analyze the economic activities that take place in families, households, and communities without assuming that these activities parallel behaviors found in markets. It is important to note that Adam Smith himself believed that there were multiple values and motivations that made up the economy. While he wrote in *The Wealth of Nations* of benefits of individual self-interest and competition for achieving economic goals, he also analyzed the importance of human benevolence in *The Theory of Moral Sentiments*. Mainstream economics has largely evolved, however, to celebrate the pursuit of self-interest and to push values associated with care, altruism, and obligation to the margins.

The focus on markets, self-interest, and the mutually beneficial nature of voluntary exchange remains a cornerstone of what is known today as neoclassical economics. For most economists—and much of the general public—neoclassical economics is the mainstream, the standard against which all other schools of economic thought are compared. Neoclassical economists start from premises about the state of nature and the nature of human beings. Nature is parsimonious, so resources are scarce. Human wants, in contrast, are unlimited and more is always preferred to less. Neoclassical economics is further defined by its reliance on rational choice theory. By rational choice, economists mean that individuals can (and do) arrange their preferences (their likes and dislikes) logically and consistently. Then, given their preferences, and the constraints of time and income, individuals make choices that maximize their well-being. Given this specification of rational choice, the mathematics of constrained optimization can be used to solve many problems, all of which take the same logical form: economic agents maximize their well-being by engaging in activities up to the point where marginal (additional) benefits just equal marginal (additional) costs. The economics literature is rife with examples: childbearing, marriage, surrogacy, prostitution, drug addiction, and even suicide are said to result from this rational, maximizing behavior. These assumptions allow neoclassical economists to define economics as the science of choice: the study of how societies allocate scarce resources among alternative uses. In this view, economics is an objective, gender-neutral, and value-free science that articulates the laws of economics in the same way that physics articulates the laws of physical phenomena.

We, on the other hand, agree with the feminist economist Julie Nelson that economics is better understood as the study of provisioning of human life than a science of choice.[11] To focus on the provision of material well-being also draws attention to the social nature of the economy. It is not governed by a set of laws determined by abstract individual preferences. Rather, social norms and institutions play a role in determining the myriad ways—market and nonmarket, competitive and cooperative, and so forth—that material provisioning is carried out in any given context.

Rethinking Economic Man

The mainstream economics framework described above contains many difficulties. From a feminist perspective one of the most serious is its assumptions about human behavior.[12] In neoclassical economics, the economic agent is commonly referred to as *Homo economicus*, or economic man, an autonomous, rational, and self-interested agent whose goal is to maximize his own well-being without accounting for the needs of others. Further, his decisions are assumed to be made in isolation, not influenced by other individuals or social factors. *Homo economicus* is theorized as a universal subject, defined absent gender, race, class, or any other markers of social location. Indeed, neoclassical economists see the universality of the economic agent as a triumph of their paradigm.

In contrast, feminist economists argue that there is no universal economic agent. They ask questions about the production of individuals: Where do these so-called rational agents come from? Do they spring from the ground fully formed? Or are they created by the societies in which they live? Recent research has shown, for instance, that those taking economics 101 classes—with their emphasis on the positive outcomes that derive from individual self-interest—actually come out being more self-interested and less cooperative, even when cooperative behaviors would lead to better personal outcomes.[13] Feminist economists also ask questions about the neoclassical assumption that all exchange is voluntary. Is all economic activity, absent a gun to the head, voluntary and mutually advantageous? If so, conflict, power, and exploitation are ruled out apriori. In contrast, feminist economics interrogates these questions, investigating the ways that gender, race, class, and other categories of social difference work to structure power and privilege in economic contexts, rather than viewing these categories as mere descriptors attached to rational agents who are in all other regards identical.

The Problem with Economic Science

Neoclassical economists do analyze issues that are central to feminist economics, such as male-female wage gaps and women's role in development. However, such work does not use gender as a category of analysis.[14] This means that it fails to interrogate the implicit assumptions about gender, race, class, and so forth that justify gender differences in the first place. Thus many mainstream economists continue to offer explanations of differences in economic outcomes that rest on troubling assumptions about race and gender that are not noticeably different from those that circulated during the Victorian era in the nineteenth century.

During the Victorian era, in emerging capitalist industrial societies, the doctrine of "separate spheres" emerged. Men's place was in the competitive arena of the economy and leadership of the home, while women were relegated to the private sphere of the household, expected to be subservient to their husbands and to devote themselves to the care of their children and husbands. Laws, editorials, sermons, and scientific research endorsed the view that any woman whose behavior even hinted at autonomous action in the worlds of commerce, politics, religion, or education risked her sanity, her femininity, her fertility, and her health.[15]

While only upper- and middle-class women could achieve this ideal of separate spheres and "true womanhood"—working-class women of all races had to participate in paid labor in order to survive—all women in these societies were subject in some way to the doctrine. Upper-class women who did not marry well or receive an inheritance that would enable them to live independently had to find employment as governesses, teachers, or lady's companions. A fortunate few found employment as writers, often using a male alias. Jo, from Louisa May Alcott's novel *Little Women*, is an example. The range of occupations for working-class women were those that mirrored "women's work" in the household, such as domestic service, laundry, food production and cooking, and textile and garment production. Women marked by differences of color, ethnicity, or class—black women and Irish women, for example—although excluded from the same standards of feminine virtue as white women due to the legacy of colonialism and slavery, were still expected to live by the codes of obedience and subservience that characterized the Victorian era.[16]

An equally important, self-evident truth of the nineteenth century was encapsulated in the racist euphemism "the white man's burden." This expression rationalized the exploitation of the peoples of Asia, Africa, and the Americas that took place during the colonial era. Ideas of racial inferiority came to be an integral element of the ideology of the Victorian era, and race was seen to be as determining of one's station in life as biological sex. Today, many scholars, men as well as women, realize that when views such as these are at the foundation of a discipline's approach to its field of study, the knowledge that results is likely to be one-sided and biased against gender equity and racial justice.

Feminist economists, following this idea through the labyrinth of over two centuries of economic scholarship, have discovered that gender and race bias are woven through the theories, empirical investigations, and policy prescriptions put forward by today's mainstream economists. These economists, not coincidentally, have historically been almost exclusively white men.[17] The homogeneity of the economics profession is not without consequence. As feminist philosophers of science have shown, science is not produced by isolated individuals. It is produced in science communities. Theories, hypotheses, and patterns of reasoning—paradigms—are shaped and modified within such communities. To the extent that implicit assumptions and values are shared among the members of a community, they will not be questioned.[18] This has been a persistent problem in the economics profession, which has historically been a bastion of white, upper- and middle-class men from the global North. While more women and people of color are entering the profession today, graduate training socializes them to accept the overarching values and norms of the profession.[19]

Economics became a formal, academic discipline, complete with professional societies and journals, in the last decades of the nineteenth century. The men who conducted economic research, measured economic activity, and formulated economic policy were all thoroughly wedded to the Victorian ideology that defined women solely in terms of their childbearing, domestic capacities. This, of course, shaped their views regarding women's proper economic roles, the features of the economy worth studying, and the correct direction of economic policies aimed at women. In the writings of the most influential economists of that time period, men—but not white women or people of color—were viewed as autonomous, rational human beings. In contrast, white women were seen as passive and economically dependent wives, mothers, and daughters.[20] Because the culturally and ideologically accepted view of separate spheres equated "woman" with "dependent" and "caretaker," and since the realm of the home was deemed to be "not the economy" (as neither monetary exchange nor commodity production took place there), economists developed their theories without taking women's productive but unpaid roles into account.[21] The view that women's proper place was in the home led economists to advocate restrictive workplace legislation, unequal and lower wages for women, and outright prohibitions on women's employment.[22]

One of the practical effects of this was to mask the very real and adverse conditions facing women and children in the labor force, an effect that continues in economics to this day. Many leading economists of that time also believed in the racial inferiority of African Americans. This led them to endorse racial apartheid in the US South. For example, through the decades of the 1880s and 1890s the American Economic Association and many of its members provided active support for the Jim Crow laws that so profoundly affected every sphere of African American life and death.[23] Though most economists today may not know it, racism and sexism are an integral part of the "repressed history" of the discipline.

Feminist Approaches to Social Science

The discussion above makes clear that a social science field can pay attention to women's role in society, but not be necessarily feminist. Specifically, *feminist* social science questions existing gender inequalities, rather than viewing them as optimal or natural. In fact, it asks what made certain ideas about gender seem natural or ideal in the first place? Rather than taking men and women as obvious and timeless categories, feminists examine the ways that gender relations structure systems of privilege and power in different historical and contextual contexts. Take for instance the traditional and still widely held view that women and men are "opposite sexes." The resulting dualisms through which we make sense of these opposite sexes—aggressive versus passive, rational versus emotional, detached versus caring, leader versus follower, strong versus weak—are assumed to be given, universal. The characteristics associated with women suit them to lives of domesticity and the care of others, while men are viewed as suited to competitive achievement in politics, business, and the professions. When these ideas about male and female characteristics are applied to the labor market, for instance, some types of work get coded as masculine, while others are coded as feminine. The former is almost always accorded more status and pay than the latter.

This gender coding is often projected forward and backward in time with the effect that gender roles are seen as unchanging and unchangeable. Feminist scholarship has, however, demonstrated the enormous variation in how societies have organized and made sense of gender difference, as well as the enormous variations among people within a particular gender themselves. Thus feminists argue that the behaviors, attributes, strengths, and weaknesses of women and men are not determined purely by biology, nor do they follow some overarching design. With other feminists we take Simone de Beauvoir's famous remark, "One is not born, one becomes a woman," as a bedrock commitment. We look to the social construction of gender to understand both the causes and the consequences of women's subordinate economic status.

We also take seriously another of de Beauvoir's insights, this one into the possibility of women as a coherent group with shared interests. In the 1949 introduction to *The Second Sex* she says:

> [t]hey (women) have no solidarity of labor interests; they even lack their own space that makes communities of American blacks, the Jews in ghettos, or the workers in Saint-Denis or Renault factories. . . . They live dispersed among men, tied by homes, work, economic interests, and social conditions to certain men—fathers or husbands—more closely than to other women. As bourgeois women, they are in solidarity with bourgeois men and not with women proletarians; as white women, they are in solidarity with white men and not with black women.

Accounting for different interests among women requires thinking about the ways that power relations among women play out along a variety of intersecting social categories. Thus we need to be attentive to when we can and cannot make categorical statements about "women's experience" or claims about what is good for all women. Discussing gender absent its intersections with race, class, and other markers of social difference results in a distorted understanding of the way that power operates in the economy and marginalizes the experiences of many.

Consider, for example, the notion, popular in liberal feminist circles in the United States in the 1960s and 1970s, that the path to women's liberation is through paid employment. Liberal feminism, with its emphasis on integrating women into the public sphere in order to be equal to men, saw expanded job opportunities for women as fostering gender equality and freedom from familial, patriarchal constraints. What it did not recognize was that paid employment's liberatory potential differed significantly depending on one's class, race, or migrant status. Among middle- and upper-class white women who had previously been confined to the home, having access to paid work in professional fields where they could earn a decent wage might have indeed been a liberating option. But working-class women, women of color, and migrant women—many of whom already held positions in the labor market often characterized by low pay and poor working conditions—had a very different perspective on the liberating potential of paid work.[24]

Further tensions between the groups arose when middle- and upper-class women entered professional fields through the 1980s, 1990s, and into the new century, and poor and migrant women increasingly provided the lower-paid domestic labor and care work that make those careers possible. As feminist scholars Cinzia Arruzza, Tithi Bhattacharya, and Nancy Fraser put it,

> The aim of liberal feminism is meritocracy, not equality. Rather than abolish social hierarchy, it aims to feminize it, ensuring women at the top can attain parity with the men of their own class. By definition, its beneficiaries will be those who already possess considerable social, cultural and economic advantages . . . [L]iberal feminism enables professional-managerial women to "lean in" only because they can lean on poorly paid, migrant and working-class women, to whom they subcontract caregiving and housework.[25]

It is not that solidarity is impossible, but that it must be created and sustained through alliances and ethical commitments, rather than through shared interests. Differences among women arise from hierarchies of race, class, ethnicity, nationality, gender identity, and sexual orientation. Further, we cannot comprehend these differences by simply adding up, say, one's oppression as a black person with one's oppression as a woman, but rather by making sense of how these identities intersect to create specific experiences of oppression for black women.[26] These differences create systems of privilege and disadvantage among women that are antithetical to feminist aspirations for social justice. The tension between talking about the interests of women as a group and recognizing important differences among them is as acute in feminist economics as it is in all other branches of feminism. Women occupy multiple and often contradictory social locations that challenge simple notions of common interest.

Feminist Economics

While there were a handful of economists calling for a more gender-equitable economic system in the late nineteenth and early twentieth centuries, the foundation for feminist economics as it exists today can be traced back to the 1970s and 1980s. During this period, scholars began to question the received ideas about women and gender in economics, engaging with the different theoretical traditions such as neoclassical economics, institutionalist economics, and Marxian political economy. Efforts to critique the treatment of women in the neoclassical and institutionalist traditions at first focused on their flawed understandings of women's labor force participation, the gender wage gap, and occupational segregation. Also key were challenges to the limited role accorded to household production and women's unpaid domestic labor. Much of this early work was published in mainstream journals such as *The American Economic Review*. Feminists working within and against the Marxian political economy tradition highlighted its failure to acknowledge the oppression that women faced due to the sexual division of labor between paid productive and unpaid reproductive work. The publication of a number of special issues on women and economics in the *Review of Radical Political Economics* during this period supported and disseminated this critical scholarship.

The emergence of a distinct school of thought organized under the banner of "feminist economics" did not, however, occur until the 1990s, a decade that saw the creation of the International Association for Feminist Economics, the organization of the first international conference on feminist economics (which all three of us attended), and the launch of the journal *Feminist Economics*. Julie Nelson's account of the emerging field, written in the middle of the 1990s, highlights its critique of the masculinity of mainstream economics on a number of different fronts. These include the mainstream's failure to acknowledge the gender biases in its assumptions about human nature, its attachment to mathematics and logical purity as a way to prop up a false standard of scientific objectivity, its failure to consider activities outside the market such as care and domestic work as valuable, and the ways that preferred methods of economic education create a chilly climate for women.[27] Since then, feminist economists have continued their critique and reformulation of economics, tackling issues at the core of economic theorizing, such as how to make sense of economic behavior and the functioning of markets, as well as particular questions that arise in subfields such as development, household economics, and labor. The field is no longer fledgling but is an established alternative within the discipline of economics. Still, the entry-points and perspectives of feminist economists remain diverse. Some adhere more closely to neoclassical visions of the economy, calling for an integration of women into the market as the key to their empowerment. Others, including ourselves, are more skeptical of this approach. Given the range of methodological commitments, interdisciplinary engagements, and political leanings of those who label themselves as feminist economists, there is no one overarching feminist economic theory. In the chapters that follow, we draw on the insights of a wide variety of perspectives and literatures in this field.

Evaluating the Economy

How feminist economics evaluates economic success is a key distinction that differentiates it from the mainstream. Textbook neoclassical economics teaches that the success or failure of an economy is measured by market efficiency, profitability, and growth of GDP per capita. Feminist economists question the narrow focus on these goals as indicators of what an economy should strive for. For one, this focus measures only what is produced in the market, leaving out the value of the enormous amount of goods and services produced in households and communities outside the market, as we discussed earlier. The emphasis on GDP growth in particular rests on the assumption that such growth benefits everyone—"a rising tide lifting all boats." However, there is significant evidence that the gap between the wealthy and those with so little they can barely survive widens as economies grow, thus challenging this "lifts all boats" assumption. The laser-like focus on growth in mainstream economics also fails to consider the ways that our voracious use of natural resources is destroying environments and communities.

The emphasis placed on efficiency and profitability as central goals of the economy is also troubling because it is based on the belief that there is an underlying logic that guides the economy, in which we cannot interfere—even when current economic approaches are not working for most of us. Ethical questions about issues such as poverty, gender inequality, and environmental degradation are pushed to the margins of mainstream economics.

Such narrow, bottom-line thinking sometimes leads economists to make deeply unethical policy recommendations. For example, a leading economist once suggested that the United States ship its toxic waste to Africa because Africans in general do not earn as much as Americans, making the economic loss from toxic waste less since the income loss due to deaths in Africa caused by toxic waste would be less than income loss due to deaths in the United States. There is an impeccable market efficiency logic in this recommendation. However, the ethics of such a policy recommendation are obviously unacceptable.

Yet even in the absence of ethical implications, we find mainstream "market logic" arguments wanting because they fail to present the economy as it is: something that humans create, that strives for outcomes based on our shared goals—not some idea about the "machine logic" of efficiency—and in which ethics would be a big part of the picture. In this concern, feminist economists join a growing chorus of nonmainstream economists who reject strict market criteria to focus instead on outcomes related to human well-being and shared ethical futures. One widely known example of this is the movement to reframe social well-being outside of growth and GDP with new goals and indicators. Feminist economist and Nobel laureate Amartya Sen, for example, helped to launch an alternative indicator for the United Nations, called the Human Development Index, which makes human development the criteria for assessing the economy. Others have come up with alternative measures of social and environmental well-being through tools such as the Genuine Progress Indicator and the World Happiness Report. There is also a "beyond GDP" effort led by leading economists to rethink the criteria for evaluating economic systems beyond efficiency and growth to focus more on human thriving.

The United Nation's Sustainable Development Goals for 2030, which feminist economists also had a hand in framing, center related ethical indicators associated with provisioning, security, fairness, peace, and sustainability alongside growth. Other efforts to reframe the goals of the economy away from strict efficiency include social movements around the world such as "Buen Vivir"—loosely translated as "living well"—in Latin America, which is focused on reducing the exploitation of nature and humans through community-centered economic practices, and "Eco-Ubuntu" in South Africa, focused on similar principles. The global Solidarity Economy Network also places an emphasis on economic outcomes of equity, security, and sustainability over profits. Social movements such as these provide evidence that people are working to "take back the economy" for human provisioning, security, equity, and sustainability.[28]

As you read this book, we urge you to keep the following in mind. Any economic system should be evaluated with regard to how well it meets people's abilities to enjoy a socially acceptable standard of living and a good quality of life, now and for future generations. Obviously, the specifics of what constitutes an acceptable standard of living and quality of life will differ from culture to culture. A few universals that we would include are an egalitarian division of labor, an egalitarian division of income and wealth, decent working conditions for all, and environmental sustainability. We will return to these issues in the conclusion and reflect on what this book adds to understanding the complexity behind them as well as suggesting avenues for change.

Mapping the Terrain

The potential scope of feminist economics is enormous. In writing this book we had to establish priorities and set some boundaries. It was important to go beyond topic areas that were simply "about women." At the same time, we needed to retain the relevance of the under examined economic conditions that women face, while centering gender as a key category of analysis. To accomplish this, we decided to focus on topic areas where the economic consequences of the gender divisions of labor are of particular salience.

We begin in chapter 2 with an examination of the history of the Western family to show the economic, political, and cultural effects of the male breadwinner–female homemaker model of domestic life. In the nineteenth century, feminist economists like Charlotte Perkins Gilman, Harriet Martineau, and Josephine Butler recognized the many ways that the increasingly rigid gender division of labor disadvantaged women. In the twentieth century, feminists began to make a direct connection between the subordinate status of women and the assumption of a gendered split in the economy. Standard economic theories take this gendered production-consumption divide as a given, and in so doing they reproduce and reinforce the gendered dualisms that shape our understanding of social relationships. In this chapter we also examine recent changes in the household divisions of labor in different-sex households as well as labor divisions in same-sex households.

Our discussion in chapter 3 builds on this history of the gender division of labor to analyze caring labor. While the care work performed in households is at odds with mainstream economics' notion of what counts as work because it is unpaid, the emotional aspect of care work is also something that sets it apart. Thus even care work that is performed in the paid labor force is often understood and valued differently than other kinds of occupations. In the chapter, we trace out a number of debates about care work in economics. We also highlight the ways that race, ethnicity, and citizenship status intersect with gender to influence the valuation of care in the paid labor market. Our feminist analysis of caring labor challenges many long-held views about women's work by recognizing its importance, on the one hand, and its socially devalued status, on the other. In this chapter we also discuss a range of workplace and government policies and community initiatives that address work/life balance and support care work.

In chapter 4 we turn to a discussion of gender, work, and policy in the United States with a focus on labor force participation, the wage gap, and occupational segregation. The clustering of men and women into different kinds of jobs, and the devaluation of "feminine" occupations, helps to explain persistent disparities in women's earnings, wealth, and career achievements. Many nations have programs and policies aimed at reducing gender segregation in paid employment. Chapter 5 examines the relationship between gender and poverty in the global North, along with a discussion of how well poverty alleviation strategies, such as social welfare, are addressing this problem. We examine some of the main factors that place women at higher risk for poverty, including the ways that mothers' care work responsibilities constrain their labor market choices, as well as the overrepresentation of women in low-wage and precarious work. This chapter also examines the rhetoric and realities of welfare reform in global North countries and the impact of these reforms on women's lives. As always, the chapter is attentive to the ways that gender intersects with race, class, sexual orientation, migration status, age, and other identities and power relations to structure poverty and inequality.

Chapter 6 explores the uneven impacts of globalization on people's lives. It traces through the colonial power dynamics upon which contemporary globalization has been constructed to contemporary projects of neoliberal globalization through restructuring, privatization, and transnational movements of capital. It also outlines globalization's effects on poverty, overall labor market conditions, climate change, and health. Chapter 7 builds on the analysis of the previous chapter to show the impacts of globalization on women's labor market experiences in the global South. It provides a close-up view of gendered global supply chain production, care labor migration, labor informalization, and transnational sex work, with significant attention to the interplay between gender and race, ethnicity, class, and citizenship status in determining women's labor market experiences in these contexts. This chapter is a new addition to the second edition. Chapter 8 is also a new addition. It examines the evolution of the subfield of gender and development from 1970 to the present and the challenging work of tackling women's poverty and inequality in global South contexts.

Chapter 9, on debt, gender and crisis economics, is also a new addition, inspired by the global financial crisis of 2008 and its persistent negative impacts on the lives of people around the world. This chapter examines some of the causes of the crisis and also engages many gendered facets of finance and debt. The book closes with a chapter on feminist futures that lists our feminist aspirations for securing stable, fair, and sustainable economic outcomes for all. Chapter 10 briefly sketches our vision for creating a feminist economics that works for all of us.

2 | Family Matters

Reproducing and Challenging the
Gender Division of Labor

A catchy restaurant slogan cheerily proclaims, "When you're here, you're family!" We ask, is our dinner free? Can we wash the dishes instead of paying the bill? Of course not—when you patronize a restaurant, you are a customer, not a family member. Families are social units made up of people joined by marriage, birth or adoption, or mutual consent to offer each other economic, social, and emotional support. From an economic perspective, families are places where many of the economic activities relating to production, reproduction, and redistribution occur.[1] Cooking, cleaning, caring for children, making household repairs, eldercare, and providing for family members without access to market incomes are some examples of these activities. Determining who will do this work and how family resources will be allocated to different members often generates tension and conflict. Indeed, economic relationships within families are characterized by inequality, conflict, and exploitation as well as by support, caring, and cooperation.

Historically, mainstream economics has rarely examined the inner economic workings of the family, viewing these activities and decision-making processes as "outside" of the economy.[2] Feminist economists, in contrast, examine gendered patterns of resource distribution, domestic labor, and consumption that take place in families. While the amount of production that occurs inside the household has decreased over the decades, today, as in the past, many of the economic relationships and activities constituting family life occur outside the market. Children do not ordinarily pay parents for the meals they eat, nor do adult family members charge each other for their help and cooperation. For these reasons feminist economists analyze the family without assuming a direct parallel between the family economy and the market economy.

Understanding the historical development of the family is important because the male breadwinner–female caretaker model of family organization is often held up as a universal and eternal ideal. Demonstrating the historical and geographical contingency of this model, the gender division of labor it promotes, and the ideologies on which it rests is essential to a feminist critique of contemporary economics. It is not too strong to say that many feminist social policy positions rest on a critical understanding of this family form.

Families Then and Now

While relations of love have undoubtedly played an important role in family life historically, family relationships have only recently been defined almost exclusively in terms of the emotional ties among family members. Throughout most of Western history, for instance, people married to consolidate power (especially among the ruling classes), to connect families to each other, to improve chances for survival, and/or for other economic, social, or political reasons. Love had little to do with it.[3] Further, the ways that families were organized were influenced by the broader economic systems in which they were embedded. Feminist scholars have long recognized that the domestic sphere has significant economic functions. As economic systems changed, so too did the organization of the family and the ideologies surrounding it.

One telling example of how changes in economic systems changed families is the transition from feudalism to capitalism in Europe. In much of Europe, from roughly the sixth through the fifteenth centuries, the predominant form of economic organization was feudalism. The majority of people were peasants who lived in self-contained manorial villages controlled by feudal lords. The lords—not the people themselves—often decided who would marry each other, and their decisions were based on custom, as well as social and economic considerations within the manor.[4] The organization of production in the manors was determined by custom and tradition. For instance, a peasant family's use of a plot of land to farm was determined by customary rights, with further customary rights to use the common lands of the manor for grazing animals and other purposes. While there was some market exchange, families were largely self-sufficient in the feudal system. Peasant families typically grew most of their own food, made their own clothes, and crafted the items used in daily life. Where a family lived was where that family worked, and what a family consumed was mainly the result of household labor. Economic activity was primarily for use, not for exchange.

Because households were not perfectly self-sufficient, trade and barter existed. Important items like baskets, barrels, nails, plows, and shoes required specialized labor. Goods not produced locally were sold by traveling merchants. Families traded their agricultural products for these goods. Artisan and peasant households delivered a portion of their output to the feudal lords and religious authorities, who often, in turn, traded these goods for luxuries or the needs of war. But in general, households produced what they needed, and most surpluses above household customary needs were accidental. When such surpluses occurred, they would be taken to local markets where they were exchanged for handicrafts. Although the sexual division of labor existed, men and women often worked side by side in the production of foodstuffs and handicrafts. The self-sufficiency of agricultural villages required that all able-bodied people work at most all of the necessary tasks.

In the middle of the fourteenth century, feudalism reached a turning point. The Black Death, or bubonic plague, spread across Europe, killing more than a third of the population. The share of production and wealth to which the feudal lords had grown accustomed diminished because of the labor shortage. Their attempts to restore their economic status by working the remaining peasants harder was met with revolt and resistance. However, the English ruling classes prevailed, and peasant rebellions were violently suppressed.[5] In the English countryside the collective use of the land was slowly displaced from the fifteenth century to the mid-nineteenth century. The conversion of customary, feudal titles to land into formal, contractual private property rights allowed landowners to make sweeping changes in the organization of agricultural production. Whereas before peasant farmers had grown subsistence crops on small parcels of land and grazed their animals on common fields, feudal lords and wealthy farmers were able to enclose these common lands and convert them into sheep pastures, large farms, and deer parks. Peasant farmers were violently forced off their land and deprived of their livelihoods.[6] Agricultural unemployment soared, as did rural poverty. As more and more families lost their traditional right to work the land, they became dependent on money wages to purchase the goods they needed to survive.[7] Although some found employment in the mines and textile mills across England, many, perhaps most, were transformed into vagabonds and paupers. Not surprisingly, it was women who suffered the most when their livelihoods vanished and their communities fell apart. Pregnancies and caring for children meant that they were less mobile, and nomadic life exposed them to male violence.[8] In other areas of Europe the enclosure of formerly common lands proceeded with similar effects.

This period also saw the rise of a new powerful merchant class focused on promoting and expanding trade. Over the course of the nineteenth century, mass-produced, machine-made goods and large-scale and imported agriculture, especially cotton and sugar, replaced artisan and home production. Household necessities ceased to be items produced by family labor; they became instead commodities to be purchased with money. In many ways the economic history of the transition from feudalism to capitalism is a history of firms producing things that were once made in households and then selling them back to households. As factories, markets, and the wage labor system eroded traditional economic relationships, the unity of production and consumption was sundered. As feminist theorist Silvia Federici points out in *Caliban and the Witch*, it is also a history of the transition to labor, not land, serving as the primary source of wealth. The separation of the peasantry from the land was necessary for the development of a wage labor that could produce a surplus—a level of production greater than the worker was paid—for the capitalist who hired that worker. Further, Federici argues, the separation of production from reproduction was absolutely crucial to the transition to capitalism. It confined women to the supposedly noneconomic domestic sphere and devalued and cheapened their reproductive labor—which reduced the wages needed to keep workers able-bodied and productive, adding to capitalist profits. As Federici argues, this transition did not occur without considerable struggle on the part of women, who were disciplined through various methods meant to condition them to the new order, including the witch hunts that characterized Europe during this turbulent period.[9]

These changes obviously had huge ramifications for the economic and affective organization of families. As industrial production became increasingly important, the productive activities of the household came to be defined as unproductive, consumption-oriented activities.[10] In actuality, however, important productive economic functions continued to take place in households, as Federici argues. The household is, to this day, the place where the labor force and much else is produced and reproduced. Many household activities—shopping, planning, meal preparation, and cleaning—are as much *work* as they are *consumption*.

There is considerable controversy regarding the effects of the transition from feudalism to capitalism on women's well-being. Some have argued that these changes made women increasingly dependent on men and men's wages since it limited their income-earning possibilities, which were traditionally tied to collective access to the commons where they gathered the leftover grains, picked up wood for fuel, and kept small farm animals.[11] Others, such as Federici, argued that the transition led not only to dependence but also to the confinement and exploitation of women's unpaid labor. Others argued that the transition to capitalism and emergence of new economic family forms freed women from domestic drudgery.[12] One point of agreement is that although some women did find avenues for income earning, the general trend during the nineteenth century was to relegate women's productive activities to the domestic sphere, contributing to the idea that women's work was not work at all.

The Cult of Domesticity

Feudal society had been shaped by the hierarchical economic and political relationships between peasants and landed nobility. The emerging capitalist society was shaped by the hierarchical relationship between wage workers and the capitalists: the owners of the factories, shops, farms and mines who employed wage laborers. The capitalists accumulated economic resources and came to wield tremendous political power. In the cultural sphere, its members sought legitimacy for their privileged status in the new social hierarchy by emulating the behavior of the feudal nobility. During the eighteenth and nineteenth centuries, one way that capitalist families were able to distinguish themselves from workers (and show their similarity to the nobility) was by systematically withdrawing the labor of their women and children from the workplace. While the entrepreneurial men of this era engaged in the cutthroat competition of early capitalism, women in this class were expected to be properly occupied with duties that were increasingly seen as natural to their sex—housework and mothering. This arrangement reinforced the patterns of separating production from reproduction and work from family life that were already in motion during this time.[13]

As these patterns of domestic and industrial life became accepted markers of social status, the ideology of the "cult of domesticity" emerged in the nineteenth century to justify them.[14] This ideology defined families and households exclusively in terms of nurturing, endearment, and affection. That labor and exertion are needed to maintain households was largely ignored, while relations of economic dependence were cloaked in flowery sentiments regarding women's true calling and men's duty. This ideology has a number of important effects, not the least is that it reproduces the now-familiar gendered dualisms of production-consumption, public-private, labor-leisure, and competitive-nurturing.

The cult of domesticity rationalized the belief that unpaid household labor was women's work and that women's work was not work at all. In consequence, the ideal of the Victorian housewife became a norm for all women, and the housewife came to be called the "woman of leisure."[15] But despite ideology, many women needed paid employment. Women need jobs when they are not married, when the earnings of the men on whom they depend are too low to support the family, or when they are the sole support of children due to death, divorce, desertion, or choice.[16]

There is a long history of women expressing dissatisfaction with their relegation to the domestic sphere and dependent status. For instance, the fiction authored by women in the eighteenth and nineteenth centuries often details women's oppression and the emotional consequences of their disenfranchisement. Charlotte Perkins Gilman—feminist, economist, and social critic—offers an insightful feminist analysis of the cult of domesticity in her short story "The Yellow Wallpaper." Facing tremendous social opprobrium, women sought education, employment, and financial and legal independence. The struggle for women's rights generated intense opposition. An incredible amount of intellectual, cultural, and religious energy was deployed to convince people that a woman's proper place was in the home.

Of course, living in a manner consistent with the Victorian ideal depended on the success of one's husband or father since women could not spend their time in unpaid activities unless they had access to income from someone else. Only the upper classes were able to realize the ideal of the dependent housewife. For many women, the market economy of the Victorian era was a harsh place. Some poor and immigrant women worked in sweatshop conditions in factories in Europe and North America, while many others worked as domestic help to keep wealthy and middle-class Victorian households running. In this latter group we can include formerly enslaved African American women in the southern United States, who had few other options open to them.[17] But as the cult of domesticity shaped the social vision of gender, the oppressive economic realities of these working women's lives were obscured, and the tightly constrained opportunities for upper-class women were cast in terms that belied the stifling narrowness of women's appropriate gender role.

The cult of domesticity was an integral component of the economic and social relations of the period, casting women in the role of full-time homemakers and consumers, while men were cast in the role of full-time wage earners and producers. Proponents of the cult of domesticity sought to root this dichotomized vision of gender in religion, biology, natural law, psychology, and economics. The development of this essentialist view of gender led to a system of laws, conventions, policies and social customs that ensured the subordinate status of women in the family, the church, the state, and the economy. It also led to the development of key ideas in economics about women's place in the economy. For example, the father of modern microeconomics, Alfred Marshall, divided the world into market and household, the first characterized by production and cut-throat competition, the other by nonproductive housework and acts of love. Marshall was adamant in his belief that women should be focused on their duties in the "true home" of the household, taking care of others and investing in their children. He argued that paid employment would cause women to neglect these duties to the detriment of societal well-being. William Stanley Jevons, another leading economist of the late nineteenth and early twentieth centuries, adopted a similar binary view of the market and family, arguing further that the very economic theories he was producing—focused on abstract rights and freedoms for people to choose and bargain in markets—should be ignored in the case of women, for it would cause the "destruction of the comfortable home" where men could expect to be nurtured—an evil that no theory, he argued, can mitigate.[18] The ideas that these two key economists generated about women's proper place would have lingering effects on economic theory and policy for many decades.

Women, Property, Employment, and the Law

That women are full human beings with equal rights under the law is a revolutionary concept. Until the middle of the nineteenth century, women—whether or not they were married—had no independent legal existence. In the West, where central governments enforced national legal codes, the laws of coverture governed virtually all aspects of women's lives. These laws established man and wife as one, and that one was the man. It did not matter how women contributed to the livelihood of the family; under no circumstances did she have independent rights to any sort of property or wages. Wives were the property of husbands who were legally entitled to any income they earned or wealth they inherited. Even when women's labor was essential to the success of family farms and family firms, they had no legally enforceable right to allowances, their own wages, or their own property. Similarly, on the sale of property (and they had no legal right to block such a sale, even when property came to the family as an inheritance from their relatives) they had no right to any of the proceeds of the sale, even if there had been an increase in the property's value. In fact, there were circumstances under which family property could be sold, leaving widows and children homeless and destitute. In addition, women could be forced to give up their jobs upon marriage. By the middle of the nineteenth century, many women, and some men, began to question the fundamental unfairness of these practices.[19] Social reformers like Barbara Leigh Smith Bodichon, Elizabeth Barrett Browning, Harriet Martineau, John Stuart Mill, and Harriet Taylor Mill in the United Kingdom worked to change these oppressive laws there. One of the most significant achievements of these reformers was the passage, in the late 1880s, of the Married Women's Property Act, "which allowed wives to gain control of their personal property and income."[20] The radical idea that a wife had a right to property acquired in marriage, and to wages she earned in the market, was initially received with favor by the revolutionary socialist movements that swept through Europe and the United States in the second half of the nineteenth century.

The view that women should earn wages ran counter to the dominant ideology of the day. For instance, the revolutionary socialists Karl Marx and Friedrich Engels repudiated women's demands for full economic equality and higher wages as a threat to worker solidarity.[21] Their position does not surprise us: by the last decades of the nineteenth century the notion that women were naturally suited to lives of domesticity was just common sense. When women's roles are defined in relation to home and family, their paid employment seems frivolous. Consequently, firms are justified in paying women less than men.

The economist Alfred Marshall went so far as to argue that women's wages should remain low to induce them to stay home and tend to their domestic responsibilities. He added that men should be paid a wage that reflects the subsistence needs of the family as a further disincentive to women's work outside the home. Throughout the mid-nineteenth century, the British enacted legislation (the Factory Acts) that expressed Marshall's views about women's wages, since these laws restricted the hours women could work and the wages they could earn. Regarding the family wage, however, policymakers were more stinting, and it took labor movement action to eventually secure it, which we discuss further below. Since

18 to 20 percent of British women were heads of households who depended on their own earnings for survival, restricting women's wages and hours had the direct result of increasing women's poverty.[22] Similarly, in the United States during the late nineteenth and early twentieth centuries, reformers advocated gender-specific protective legislation to restrict the occupations and hours of women's work.[23] Here, protective legislation aimed at women was based on the idea that their wages should not be too high because high wages would jeopardize women's economic dependence. At the same time women's wages should not be too low since extreme poverty could force women into prostitution.[24]

Legislators, clergymen, and newspaper editors argued that the public interest would be best served if policy aimed to preserve the morals and character of the "mothers of the race." As feminist economists Deborah Figart, Ellen Mutari, and Marilyn Power show, femininity, whiteness, and motherhood were linked in public opinion, and laws were enacted to reinforce these links.[25] Legislation protecting Anglo-European women helped to ensure white women's economic survival. In contrast, such protections were not sought for work done by women of color: the few jobs that were open to African American, Latina, Asian, and Native American women were not covered by the new laws. Racism underscored the view that there was no public interest in preserving their moral character. Women of color were not included in labor legislation as either mothers or workers.

In both Britain and the United States, this type of legislation reflected and reproduced the ideology of the male breadwinner–female caretaker family. This ideology had significant negative consequences for the material circumstances of women since it prevented them from becoming economically independent. Indeed, until the 1960s it was legal for firms to pay women less than men for the same jobs. Today, women are still a long way from economic equality. Women's lower earnings continue to keep them dependent on and subordinate to men in many cases. That men's wages are greater than women's is due, in part, to the legacy of the family wage system that was the material basis of the ideology of domesticity. Earning a wage sufficient for one adult male to support his family was an important goal of working-class organizations. Sadly, improvement in working-class men's earnings came at the expense of women's economic opportunities regardless of their class.

A Brief History of the Family Wage

Male-dominated working-class organizations of the nineteenth and twentieth centuries sought allies in the upper classes by tapping into the ideology of domesticity. Working-class men sought the exclusion of women from the higher-paying male occupations to protect the family wage in those occupations. Upper-class reformers sought the exclusion of women from paid employment because of their view of women's nature. Indeed, the notion that women are too fragile to be subjected to the rigors of industrial life emerged as an important theme in the labor history of this period. As noted, achieving a family wage was an important goal of unions in Britain, the United States, and the rest of Western Europe. Male unionists actively campaigned for legislation that would bar women from particular industries and specific occupations to limit competition for jobs and raise wages. As a result, by the end of the nineteenth century the top several echelons of workers in key industries, and the managers of the new corporate bureaucracies, had succeeded in winning wages large enough to purchase the food, clothing, and shelter needed by a middle-class family.

A wage of this magnitude was called a family wage since it enabled a worker to support a family largely without a second worker taking a job outside the home. Even today, when more than half of all women work for pay outside the home, many people continue to believe that married women—especially those who are middle class and have young children—should work outside the home only if the family needs the money. The persistence of this collective myth that designates women as the special, almost mystical, source of childcare testifies to the power of ideology. As the ideology of the bread-winning husband and domestic wife became a social truth, the gap between male and female wages was reinforced. Since popular sentiment regarded women as wives, daughters, or mothers, but not workers, their wages were considered "pin money," destined for incidentals rather than necessities.

This perspective ignores the fact that for many, male wages alone were not adequate for the maintenance of the family. In addition, the belief that women's wages were merely "pin money" meshed neatly with the need for a ready supply of low-wage factory, mill, and domestic workers. That is, as long as many people, including women, saw their wages as secondary to the wages of the primary breadwinner, women could be paid less than men. As the family wage system became the expected norm, economic pressure mounted for women to specialize in unpaid household labor. Because women's wages were substantially lower than men's, it was economically rational for women to remain outside the paid labor force. Their wages would be too low to replace the work of childcare, housecleaning, and cooking that they would not be able to do if they were employed outside the home for wages.

It is important to realize that achieving a family wage was always restricted to a small share of the working class. In the United States it was standard practice to exclude particular ethnic groups from good jobs. Native American, African American, Latino, and Asian American families, for example, were dependent on the income generated by women and children since racism was often used consciously and deliberately to exclude men of color from jobs that paid a family wage. This not only divided workers but also helped create different interests for white women and women of color, since these women had quite different relationships to the processes of paid employment, fertility, child-rearing, and family formation.

The economist Deirdre McCloskey has argued that women unambiguously and uniformly benefitted from the spread of markets and the development of industrial capitalism.[26] This argument rests on the view that the machine production of goods, and the attendant decline in consumer prices, led to a rising standard of living that was widely dispersed. But this claim is hotly disputed in economics, sociology, and history.

The onerous work and harsh discipline of factories in the nineteenth and early twentieth centuries were principal costs of the industrial revolution. Under these labor conditions, it was a privilege, indeed a benefit, to escape into the home. Protecting women and children became the shared aim of upper-class social reformers, working-class men, and some working-class women. Part of this involved removing children from the labor force and making child-rearing a major economic activity in the household. The ideology of feminine domesticity made children's upbringing the exclusive domain of women. This vital economic function has received scant attention. Simultaneously, protective legislation forced women out of many types of paid work, regardless of women's needs for earned income or their desire to hold a job. By casting the male breadwinner–female caretaker model of the family as natural, the cult of domesticity also obscured the divergent interests that shape family life.

The Changing Forms of Contemporary American Families

During the twentieth century, in much of the Western world, families aspired to a form in which husbands and fathers would focus on income-generating activities, while wives and mothers specialized in homemaking and child-rearing. Ironically, this is often referred to as the "traditional" family even though it is very modern. Moreover, this mode of organizing domestic life was never a real option for many families. But despite its relatively short history, and the rather narrow cross section of the population to which the definition applies, its impact on society in the spheres of culture, politics, economics, and even psychology has been strong.

In traditional families, men work full-time outside the home to earn income and women work full-time in the home to sustain the family. Today, among families with children in the United States, this family form is in decline. Approximately 20 percent are made up of traditional married stay-at-home mothers with working husbands, down from 40 percent in 1970 and 65 percent in 1960.[27] In economics, the male breadwinner–female caretaker model of the family was exalted as an ideal for many decades. Gary Becker, whose work on the economics of the household revolutionized the field in the 1970s, proposed that this was the most efficient and natural arrangement because of human biology. For an efficient household in which each member contributed their comparative advantage, husbands, he argued, should specialize in earning, while wives should specialize in care work because of their biological function of reproduction.[28] Further, he argued that this division of labor was the outcome of harmonious decision-making within the family, rather than the product of power and conflict. As we have demonstrated in this chapter already, however, there is nothing natural, inevitable, or even necessarily efficient about this arrangement. The division of labor in which men are relegated to the public sphere of paid work and women to unpaid domestic work is a socially, historically, and politically determined outcome, and one for which there has been considerable struggle. That this arrangement is currently becoming less appealing to adults in much of the world today also points to its historical and social contingency.

There are certainly women and men for whom this family form is worth emulating. For poorer families the prospect of having one person exempt from the harsh conditions of low-wage work undoubtedly has great appeal. For other families, a full-time homemaker is an important status symbol. And for yet other families, assigning the woman to full-time homemaking is a reasonable response to the high cost of quality childcare and the scarcity of jobs with decent pay and benefits. The structure of traditional households, however, also contains gender power dynamics.[29] In traditional households, women have no independent access to income. They are therefore dependent on the generosity and sense of fairness of the breadwinner, who, as a result, has a great deal of power in important household decisions. Indeed, feminist sociologist Arlie Hochschild's pathbreaking study of the relationship between work and family found that a major factor contributing to the breakup of traditional households involved women seeking additional avenues for achievement and fulfillment and becoming less willing to submit to patriarchal authority.[30]

Another family type, one that is increasingly becoming the norm, has both partners working for incomes outside the home and sharing household tasks. In the United States, about 60 percent of adults say that they prefer this type of arrangement, with almost three-quarters of adults under the age of thirty being in favor of a sharing of paid work and tasks. Currently, half of all married and cohabiting different-sex households in the United States are made up of dual earners.[31] Many of these households aspire to be egalitarian households, where gender is not the key variable determining who works outside the home for pay and who does the household labor, and both housework and market work are shared. Yet while the gap between male and female hours spent in unpaid household labor is shrinking, even among dual-earner different-sex families, housework and childcare are still, on average, largely the responsibility of the female partner. The division of tasks within the household is often gendered, with women working in frequent, time-consuming, indoor and care-related tasks such as cooking, cleaning, and childcare, and men doing infrequent outdoor-related tasks such as taking out the trash and mowing the lawn.[32] Researchers have found that for dual-career different-sex couples, men spend only 35 minutes in unpaid care work for every hour that a woman spends.[33] These households are prone to conflict as parents struggle to balance work and family life without much outside support, often placing the greater burdens on women's shoulders. Women in particular feel dissatisfaction with this division of tasks and feel their burden is driven by restrictive gender roles.[34]

One way that families resolve these conflicts is by hiring outside paid help. Author Barbara Ehrenreich's interviews with people in two-earner households who hired maid service workers in the United States found that many did so to restore the family peace. However, bringing in paid household help raises its own set of ethical issues. The people who are hired to help with housework are generally poor women at the bottom of the social hierarchy because of their race, class, migration status, or ethnicity. The pay is often low, and the working conditions are poor. Many cleaning services are highly exploitative. For those who work as live-in domestics, many are not covered by labor laws.[35] Increasingly, these women workers are immigrants and refugees who leave their own families to care for families in the rich nations. In the United States, domestic work was often the only option for African American women, and until the 1960s a high percentage of employed African American women were domestic workers.[36] Today, the racial and ethnic composition of household employees reflects both the gains that African American women have made in the workplace and the different face of poverty in the United States. Now, domestic workers in the United States are likely to be poor women from the Philippines, Latin America, or Eastern Europe.

Feminists argue over whether it is ethical to hire household workers. Some point out that we have no problem hiring other types of help at home (e.g., plumbers and gardeners). Others argue that hiring cooks, housecleaners, and nannies is inherently exploitative. Our position is not that it is wrong or immoral to pay for housework, childcare, or cooking. Rather, the problem stems from the conditions of work. These low-status jobs are almost always the province of poor, disadvantaged women who often have families of their own. Bringing these jobs into the formal sector and providing legal protections to all workers regardless of gender, race, or immigration status will improve the status, pay, and security of this work.

Much of the recent attention to family needs and policies by politicians, think tanks, scholars, and activists has been prompted by dramatic changes in the composition of families. In addition to the shift from male breadwinner to dual-earner households as the dominant household form, single-parent households are becoming increasingly common. In the United States, approximately 20 percent of all children are living with a solo mother, and 3 percent with a solo father.[37] Because workplace structures and social policies typically presume that people with children live in partnered families, heads of solo households often find themselves struggling even harder to balance paid work and care responsibilities.

Another important change in family structure concerns the rising number of same-sex couples, either with or without children. Almost all of the existing research and policy discussions on families and household care burdens have incorrectly presumed different-sex coupling only, reflecting a heteronormative bias. However, the growing recognition of same-sex coupling, including the legalization of gay marriage in many countries around the world, has placed more attention on same-sex household labor. A key question is whether same-sex couples have more egalitarian relations than different-sex couples, given that they are not unencumbered by gender role expectations. Many studies show that, in fact, same-sex couple households are more egalitarian in their sharing of paid and unpaid labor. However, once same-sex couple households have children there is a shift. Due to high time demands in both paid work and care work responsibilities, often one parent will take on more of the paid work and the other more of the care work. However, because these decisions are based on deliberate decisions rather than reliance on gender role expectations, same-sex couples typically express more satisfaction with these arrangements than different-sex couples.[38]

Many feminists advocate a change in social and economic policies to support and encourage the formation and reproduction of egalitarian households. Nancy Fraser posits three idealized visions of the family in social policy—the universal breadwinner model, the caregiver parity model, and the universal caregiver model—in order to systematically think about which policy frameworks will best encourage gender equity in the division of labor.[39]

The universal breadwinner model focuses on equal labor market opportunities for women and men based on current labor market expectations. In this model of gender and paid work, the cooking, cleaning, childcare, and eldercare services that are today mostly provided by women in the household would instead be provided by the government (e.g., subsidized day care) or purchased on the market. The caregiver parity model aims to enable caregivers (usually women) to care for their families. Such policies would provide generous family allowances and paid employment leaves for new parents or those with other significant care obligations. Under this model, women's lives would be different from men's lives, but women would be less overworked. On their own, Fraser finds both these strategies inadequate for the realization of full gender equity. On the one hand, the universal breadwinner model is androcentric in its exclusive valorization of paid work and maintenance of "unencumbered worker" employment expectations that do not build in flexibility for caring labor requirements; on the other, the caregiver parity model fails to promote women's economic independence and maintains a gender division of labor.

In contrast, the universal caregiver model is predicated on families characterized by equal divisions of labor outside and inside the home. In this model, both women and men participate in both paid and unpaid labor. Child and dependent care, along with housework and working for pay, would be shared equally between adult householders. For this division of labor to become a reality, several things need to happen. As in the universal breadwinner model, women's earnings need to be equal to men's so there will be no economic advantage to female specialization in childcare and housework. Further, work for both women and men will have to be restructured so there will be no economic disadvantage to those adults who take responsibility for children and other family members. While these changes may be slow to come, these goals should inform national and international public policies.

Cooperation, Conflict, and Divisions of Labor in Families

Providing for the material well-being of family members by redistributing resources like cash, goods, services, and assets is an important economic function of the family. The social norms that guide the uses to which resources flow vary across and within cultures. While disagreements among family members over what kind of cereal to buy may not be terribly fractious, there are other spending decisions that may incite intense conflict. Who will do most of the childcare? Who will cook the meals? How will we use our household income? For instance, when education is not free, will both boys and girls go to school?

The view of the family as a harmonious group with common interests is dominant in mainstream economics. In this view, first popularized by economist Gary Becker, the male breadwinner–female caretaker gender division of labor within the family is nothing more than a particular case of specialization that has advantages for both women and men, as we discussed in the section above. Further, Becker posited, decision-making within the household around resource allocation, labor tasks, and consumption is undertaken by an altruistic head of household, considering the best interests of family members.[40]

While Becker's model sweeps questions of conflict power dynamics and inequality under the rug, other economic models of household decision-making focused on these issues have been developed by feminist economists such as Bina Agarwal and Notburga Ott.[41] These analyses acknowledge that family relationships have elements of both conflict and cooperation. Rather than positing an altruistic family decision-maker, allocations of resources and responsibilities within the household are viewed as the results of bargaining and negotiation between members. Such theories can explicitly acknowledge the different bargaining power of family members that accrues from access to income and/or social gender norms. Not surprisingly, having a good job or some other access to income is a major strength a person brings to the bargaining table.

Consequently, a woman's power in her family will be influenced by her labor market earnings, and these earnings are, in turn, influenced by her labor market status. Typically, women spend less time in unpaid homemaking activities when they switch from part-time to full-time paid employment.[42] However, the relationship between earnings and housework burdens is complicated. Researchers have discovered that women who earn more than their male partners end up doing more housework as their incomes rise. One explanation for this is that they are making up for challenging the gender norm that men should earn more than their female partners.[43] This research was reported in 2003. Have things changed much today? According to research done by feminist sociologist Aliya Hamid Rao, probably not much. While Rao does not look specifically at that question, she does report that the more economically dependent men are on their wives, the less housework they do. In addition, women with unemployed husbands spend considerably more time on household chores than their spouses.[44]

Feminist economists have also produced analyses of conflict and cooperation in same-sex couple families. M. V. Lee Badgett points out that most models of household decision-making, even feminist ones, assume a different-sex couple with heteronormative arrangements. Simply grafting these models onto same-sex families perpetuates heterosexist assumptions about "normal" family forms. She questions the assumption that same-sex and different-sex couples make decisions in ways that are fundamentally the same. Her research supports the view that the different legal, political, and cultural status of same-sex relationships lead gay and lesbian families to develop alternative family dynamics.[45] Further research into this question has shown that while the greatest predictor of a division of labor in the household for different-sex couples was gender, for same-sex couples the determining factors were ethnicity, education, age, and income. Those who are white, more highly educated, older, and/or higher paid will tend to do more paid work and less unpaid work. Another key factor determining the division of labor in same-sex households was access to marriage. For those who had legal recognition of their relationship and the protections that come with it, it was more likely that the lower earning member of the couple would spend more time in housework and care work and less time in the paid labor market.[46]

Conclusion

While the male breadwinner–female caretaker model of the family is often presented as a universal and natural arrangement, this chapter has demonstrated that it is a highly contested and contingent way of organizing family economic life. The ideology of female domesticity that props up this model is in fact an artifact of the industrial revolution. Yet that ideology holds the imagination of many, including mainstream economists and policymakers, even as it has increasingly been challenged by changing gender roles and a growing diversity of family forms. Challenging this ideology, and the inequalities that go along with it, is crucial work for feminist economics. Doing so makes the power dynamics of household decision-making visible. It highlights the negative influence of traditional gender hierarchies and offers ways to challenge those hierarchies and improve lives and livelihoods. It also revalues and makes visible the enormous amount of unpaid caring labor that takes place in households, work that is essential to human well-being. It is to this topic, the importance of caring labor to the functioning of the economy, that we turn to in the next chapter.

3 | Love's Labors—Care's Costs

How often have you heard the expression "a labor of love" to describe work done for the benefit of family and friends? Labors of love, such as the unpaid labor of cooking, cleaning, and childcare performed in households, do not fit neatly into economists' category of work, which revolves around wage labor. Unpaid care work is also excluded from calculations of national output such as gross domestic product (GDP). Yet it is not only caring labor's unpaid status that places it at odds with economists' definitions of work. The emotional aspect of care work also sets it apart. Nurturing feelings are not something we usually look for from the person who repairs our computer. But when we employ a paid childcare worker, we do hope that person will be concerned with our child's well-being, and not only motivated to care for our child as a means to a weekly paycheck. Does paying for care reduce the crucial emotional component of "caring about" our child? As a labor of love, this and other forms of care work are something that women have historically been expected to do, or something that comes naturally to them in their feminine role. Thus in terms of societal values, the motivation for doing caring labor should not be monetary. Such a perspective, however, contributes to the undervaluing of care work when it is performed as wage labor, even if such work is crucial to the economic and social well-being. These issues around the visibility and value of caring labor lie at the heart of research in feminist economics. Care work is central to what is now referred to as social reproduction, the many quotidian activities—cooking, cleaning, childcare, eldercare, and care for the community and the environment—that provide the necessary foundation for any economic system.

The Devaluation of Domestic Labor

In the last chapter, we traced the historical development of the sexual division of labor through which unpaid care activities became women's work, and women's work was increasingly not viewed as work at all. Through much of the nineteenth and twentieth centuries, wage labor was recognized as the only form of productive work in economics and the other social sciences, and unpaid household production counted for nothing. For example, it is not included in calculations of national income such as GDP, which are used as a measure of a national economy's level of development and well-being. GDP only measures market-produced goods and services, and this leads to some peculiar results. For instance, GDP falls when people cook meals at home rather than dining in restaurants, even though the service of producing a meal benefits households and contributes to overall national economic well-being. The same is true when people substitute vegetables from their home gardens for the ones they used to buy at the supermarket. GDP does not capture the vital contribution of these and other activities. This is not a small issue. It is estimated that approximately one-third of all economic activity in the world takes place outside the paid labor market.[1]

There have been a number of challenges to the invisibility and marginalization of women's unpaid household work over the past century. Hazel Kyrk, one of the first women to receive a PhD in economics (in 1920), was a pioneering researcher on the family, attentive to the contribution that the goods and services produced in households made to human well-being. Margaret Reid, Kyrk's PhD student, build on Kyrk's research to find ways to include the economic value of household production in economic measures of output. Reid's book, *Economics of Household Production*, published in 1934, defines what counts as work in the home and suggests ways that it could be measured. In order to exclude leisure, Reid defined household production as only those activities that could be farmed out to a hired worker or replaced by market goods. This "third party" criterion is still in use today and Reid's work on measurement remains foundational in statistical estimates of the value of household production.[2] However, in the years after World War II, when systems of national accounts were standardized, mainstream economists largely refused to include considerations of household production in their writing and teaching.[3] Throughout most of the century, these issues, if taken up at all, were relegated to the field of home economics.

In the late twentieth century, when a specifically feminist economics emerged, the work of Kyrk, Reid, and others was rediscovered as economists once again began to turn their attention to the economic significance of women's unpaid work. Scholars such as Marilyn Waring and Lourdes Benería offered influential critiques of the failure to count unpaid domestic and care work in official statistics such as GDP.[4] Others emphasized the ways that the leaving of unpaid household labor out of the equation contributes to gender inequality in policy-making. While men do engage in unpaid domestic activities, statistically speaking the disproportionate share of two and a half times more of household care, domestic, and unpaid farming work is done by women.[5] Not acknowledging women's contribution in this realm, then, leads to biased economic policy initiatives.

For instance, the development economist Ester Boserup showed that agricultural policies aimed at decreasing hunger in places like Sub-Saharan Africa supported men's market-based farming, when it was in fact women who were providing most of the subsistence agriculture. These policies undercut women's production of food and often increased the very hunger they were trying to resolve.[6] In the realm of macroeconomics, feminist economists Diane Elson and Isabella Bakker documented ways that the invisibility of women's care work led to fiscal cuts in supports for childcare, health care, food subsidies, and the like that dramatically increased the unpaid care burdens of women in economies undergoing restructuring.[7]

Not all feminist economists are in favor of valuing unpaid care work in economic calculations and policies, however. Liberal feminist economists such as the late Barbara Bergman, who believe that the focus should be on moving women into the masculine public sphere of money and markets, worry that valuing unpaid labor will only reinforce women's subordinate status in households. She provided the clearest articulation of this position in her 1998 article, "The Only Ticket to Equality: Total Androgyny, Male Style."[8] Feminist philosopher Linda R. Hirshman echoed similar sentiments when she criticized the choices of women who drop out of the labor force to raise their families. She argued that although the tasks of family life are necessary, they allow fewer opportunities for human flourishing than the public spheres of the market or the government.[9] For liberal feminists such as Bergmann and Hirshman, the goal of feminist empowerment would be better achieved if unpaid domestic and care labor tasks were commodified and/or provided by the state so that women could succeed in the paid labor market.

Other feminist economists argue that the commodification solution to inequitable unpaid work burdens is not so simple. One vein of critique contends that there are forms of domestic and care labor that should not be commodified. Some types of domestic labor may not fit easily into the definition of work as it is commonly understood in a paid labor context: a purposeful activity that takes time and energy and is separable from the person doing it. Who vacuums the floor is irrelevant as long as the job is done well. But caring for children and the elderly is different. Care activities require emotional labor, making the relationship between those who give care and those who receive care an important component of its worth.[10] Feminist economist Susan Himmelweit has argued that because of this difference, care is something best produced outside of market norms because it is based on relationships, while market labor is characterized by detachment.[11] Others have drawn attention to another danger regarding care's commodification. Most paid care and domestic laborers are women working in exploitative conditions for low pay. Thus a strategy to liberate some women by hiring out work formerly done in the home relies on the exploitation of other women.[12] This is a topic we will discuss in more detail in the section on paid care and domestic work below.

A different sort of challenge to the invisibility of women's household labor was the "Wages for Housework Movement" that emerged in the 1970s, led by Maria Dalla Costa, Selma James, and Silvia Federici.[13] Posed as a critique of the gender biases of Marxian economic thought, this movement called for a recognition and revaluing of the unpaid domestic labor that was necessary for the cheap reproduction of the waged workforce. Essentially, their argument was that because domestic labor contributed to capitalist profits it should be compensated within the capitalist system. They brought attention to what should have been obvious: unpaid household labor transformed purchased commodities into cooked meals, laundered clothes, and clean houses for adult workers and provided the childcare that were necessary to reproduce a future generation of workers.[14] Sylvia Federici, one leading voice the movement, points out that the problem of housework is that rather than being seen as work, it is transformed into a natural attribute of women, "an internal need, an aspiration, supposedly coming from the depth of our female character."[15] Her call for paying wages for housework was never about the money per se. Rather it was about recognizing women as workers and resisting the notion that doing housework was a natural part of feminine identity. That housework is unwaged reinforces the idea that it is not work, thus reducing women's struggles against it to mere personal complaints. As Federici once put it, "we are seen as nagging bitches, not as worker in struggle."[16] Demanding wages for housework was the first step toward refusing it: refusing both the work itself and its associations with femininity.[17]

The Devaluation of Paid Care Work

Along with care and domestic work in the home, care and domestic work performed in the labor market is also undervalued. Empirical studies by labor economists have shown that working in a care field results in a wage penalty that is consistent across countries and even across genders. Even men working in caring occupations have lower wages than an individual with similar skills, experience, training, and so on in another field.[18] There are a number of overlapping reasons for this. The association of care work with "labors of love" provides an uneasy relationship with the monetary motivations of the market. Feminist economists Nancy Folbre and Julie Nelson address this issue in their discussion of the dual meaning of care. On the one hand, care means the activities of "caring for" such as changing diapers, which women are often simply expected to do in their role as women. On the other, it refers to "caring about," the emotional labor one puts into the work. These feelings of caring about, it is assumed, motivate care activities—we do it for love—and also is assumed to contribute to the quality of care received. In a similar vein, sociologist Evelyn Nakano Glenn argues there is a moral code that says a paid care worker should not be invested in the work for purely monetary reasons. This is, for instance, reflected in the praise of those who go "above and beyond" the requirements of jobs such as live-in nannies, an effort that demonstrates their emotional investments. While many believe that care is best undertaken in the household so it isn't sullied by market values, when this isn't possible and people must turn to the market, the alternative strategy has been to pay a wage low enough so that care workers could not possibly be thought to take the work for monetary reasons only.[19]

We do not believe that paying for caring labor necessarily negates the emotional content of this work. Consider all the work done by nurses, teachers, and social workers. There is an important emotional aspect to such labors. For instance, nursing done well includes caring about the well-being of the patient. Sometimes these jobs are paid well; other times they are not. But they are typically paid more than childcare workers. The importance of this work is generally acknowledged because of its stressful, emotionally draining nature. No one seriously argues that transforming this paid labor into voluntary, unpaid work would enhance societal well-being. Indeed, the very suggestion of making such work voluntary and unpaid seems odd. Yet when the caregiver and care receiver are family, and the work is performed inside the home, our cultural assumptions lead us to believe that the quality of care is enhanced precisely because it is not paid.

Differences by race and ethnicity come into significant play in the valuation of paid care work. Some women are stereotypically imagined as being more naturally caring than others.[20] Immigrant women and women of color in particular encounter assumptions that they are more nurturing and thus better suited to care work. These ideas influence labor market outcomes in ways that exacerbate inequalities.[21] Those in care fields get paid less because the work is considered to be its own reward, and because caring is assumed to be unskilled because women are naturally good at it. Further, jobs as domestics and caregivers are often unregulated and unprotected, making the work more exploitative and precarious. As Evelyn Nakano Glenn notes, the Fair Labor Standards Act of the 1930s exempted in-home paid care and domestic work from regulation, preventing minimum wage and working hour limits from being enforced by the US government. Even with recent revisions to that act, she points out, many forms of home-based care and domestic work remain exempt from regulations, further subordinating the status of these jobs.[22] This in turn creates low-status, low-paid jobs in care fields that women of color and immigrants, because they face multiple forms of discrimination, will find themselves clustered in because they have few alternatives. Indeed, as labor economist Bruce Pietrykowski demonstrates, the wage and occupational gap between white women and black women and Latinas has widened over the past few decades. Comparing the top ten occupations of the three groups, white women moved into professional and managerial jobs while the latter two groups' top occupations were in housekeeping, cleaning, childcare, and jobs with the word "assistant" or "aide" in the title.[23]

The devaluation of paid care and domestic labor market creates urgent problems in our economy that call for solutions. If the quality of care received by infants, young and school-age children, the ill, the disabled, and the elderly depends on the quality of the connection between givers and the receivers of care, then care work is constituted by a social relationship in which reciprocity, mutual respect, and dignity play meaningful roles. In the current system, most jobs in care fields are hardly characterized by respect and dignity, which therefore reduces the quality of care received. The work of caring for others is crucial to the well-being of individuals and society, and ensuring high-quality care to meet societal needs should be a priority in any well-functioning economic system.

Care Crises

Economic restructuring and social changes in gender relations since the late 1970s have led to a global rise in women's labor force participation. The decline of industrialism in the global North led to the stagnation of male wages in those regions, causing more working-class and poor different-sex partner families to rely on both men's and women's wages to make ends meet. Because of the emerging second-wave feminist movement, increasing numbers of middle- and upper-class women felt that they deserved rewarding careers outside the home, and the independence that came with earning, no matter what their marital status. Poor women, of course, had historically taken paid labor out of necessity, but increasing numbers of these women joined the labor force during this time as well.

The rise of the service sector economy, including many feminine-coded jobs, increased the demand for women workers. The passage of legislation against discriminatory gender hiring and pay practices opened more opportunities to women. More people were delaying or opting out of marriage, living in single-person or single-parent households, and had to fend for themselves. These changes have rearranged the ways that households meet their care needs. While there has been a dramatic increase in women's full-time paid employment since the 1970s, particularly in different-sex married couple households with children, men have not picked up the slack. Thus many women work a second shift of care work after a full day in the labor market. But often families have to look to the market to provide some of these needs as well. No longer do we assume that families can resolve all of their care requirements through unpaid household labor. Rather, these requirements are met both inside and outside the household using a combination of family members, paid domestic workers, take-out meals, and so forth. The tensions of relying on a mix of unpaid care work and marketized goods and services to meet care and domestic needs are pronounced in many households. As prices of market-produced care goods and services such as prepared food, childcare, elder-care, and the like go up, it is women in households that often provide unpaid substitutes, resulting in what feminist economist Diane Elson has referred to as an "exhaustion solution" to the problem.[24]

The erosion of state supports for families such as aid for dependent children, subsidized food and education, health care, and the like since the 1980s has only exacerbated this crisis of care, in some cases leading to a depletion of care as market goods such as food and health care become more expensive but there is less unpaid women's labor available to produce nonmarket substitutes. This depletion of care creates negative out-comes for all of society in terms of declining health, nutrition, and educational attainment, as well as having negative effects on women's lives.[25]

Thus feminist economists are focused on developing social policies that will ensure an adequate supply of care. One approach for attaining a sufficient supply of caring labor advocated by Guy Standing at the International Labour Organization (ILO) is to make sure that care work is paid well, that there are adequate regulatory guidelines that ensure skill in care delivery, and that regulatory standards are enforced. This suggests that governments have a significant role to play vis-à-vis care work. Ironically, care work is both poorly paid and extremely expensive for many households. So to ensure that quality care is available to those who need it, the government also has a role to play in providing subsidies and income transfers to people who need care but who do not have sufficient income to pay for it. Families also have significant roles to play in care provision, and policies can be adopted that enable families to do that work, such as parental leave policies. As Standing argues, while formal, paid caregiving provides an important social service, we know that "most of us do not or would not want to rely either wholly or partially on formal care providers if we could avoid it."[26]

The Social Responsibility for Childcare

In the industrialized nations, there are two approaches to childcare. Many nations recognize a social responsibility for childcare and provide substantial public funding supporting parental leaves and subsidized childcare staffed by well-trained, well-paid workers. In other nations—the United States for instance–there is less emphasis on social responsibility. The economic and labor burden of children continues to rest on families, even as the benefits of well-cared-for children accrue to the larger society. National policies toward childcare begin with parental leave policies. Table 3.1 displays parental leave policies for ten industrialized countries.

There are several interesting things to note about this table. We generally expect all the Nordic countries to have the most generous parental leave policies. However, in fact, Latvia and Germany have more generous policies. The interesting thing about this is that Latvia was a part of the Soviet Union, which had quite high rates of female labor force participation and public supports for childcare. Another striking fact about this table is that the United States is the only country with zero weeks of paid parental leave. However, the Family Medical Leave Act (FMLA) does require firms to grant unpaid parental leaves of up to twelve weeks; but because the FMLA only applies to firms with fifty or more employees, and most women work in firms with less than fifty employees, there is a large gap in coverage. Also the FMLA does not replace the parent's income during parental leaves.

Likewise, quality, affordable childcare is in very short supply in the United States. Consequently, many families cannot afford full-time care and education for their children in accredited childcare centers. In many communities, fully certified childcare centers have long waiting lists even though the full-time tuition at these centers often exceeds the cost of a year at the local state university. It is important to realize that there are rarely any licensing requirements for these childcare centers. Only a few states and localities require annual safety inspections and set standards for fire safety. State health inspectors are not required to check centers for other hazards. When a home-based center offers an age appropriate curriculum, a high ratio of staff to children, and large and well-equipped play areas, these amenities are purely voluntary. Many less affluent families with young children place the children in childcare centers that meet minimal safety and staffing requirements. Even these centers are quite expensive. Elementary schools seem to hold out the promise of a solution to the cost of childcare. Elementary schools as day-care centers, however, pose another set of problems. One need not be an expert on workplace policies to know that even the most liberated companies do not yet synchronize the working day with school schedules.

Financially well-off families have other options. Women in these

TABLE 3.1. Paid Parental Leave Benefits for Ten Selected OECD Countries

	Parental leave (weeks)	Average payment rate (%)
Finland	161.0	25.5
Latvia	94.0	54.9
Germany	58.0	73.4
Japan	58.0	61.6
Sweden	55.7	62.1
Poland	52.0	80
France	42.0	42.9
Canada	51.0	52.1
United Kingdom	39.0	30.1
United States	0	0

Source: Data from OECD Family Database, Table PF2.1.A summary of paid leave entitlements available to mothers, 2018.

households may decide to put off reentering the workforce until their children enter elementary school. Or the family could hire someone to care for the children in their home rather than sending them to a day-care center. The globalization of the labor force has made this an easier and cheaper option for those families who can afford to bring in such help. Poor women from the global South are increasingly migrating to the global North to take work as nannies and maids in such households. Because even low wages from a global North perspective are higher than the incomes they could earn back home, the labor of these migrant workers is relatively cheap to the families who hire them. We provide an in-depth discussion of the globalization of care in chapter 7.

The Social Responsibility for Eldercare

Eldercare presents a similar set of issues, but with one important difference. Not only is care work devalued but the elderly are themselves devalued. Rather than being depositories of collective memory, experience, and wisdom, the elderly are seen as a financial burden on the younger generation. Individuals may dearly love and treasure their elderly relatives, but judged in terms of the social supports for the elderly, society as a whole does not. Women are having fewer children and people are living longer. Politicians and economists portray the pensions and other types of social security as "an economic time-bomb and a heavy mortgage of the future of the young."[27] Women constitute both the largest proportion of eldercare workers and the largest proportion of people needing care.[28] Moreover, there is little in the way of support programs, formal or informal, to assist eldercare providers. Liz O'Donnell, writing for *The Atlantic,* reports that working daughters may find the need to switch to a less demanding job, take time off, or stop working altogether in order to take care of elderly parents. The responsibility for eldercare generally hits women when they are in their mid-forties, and the impact on their careers and lifetime earning is substantial. The lifetime monetary value of the loss in benefits such as health insurance, retirement savings, and social security benefits has been calculated to be an average of $324,044.[29]

Feminist economist Agneta Stark points out that the income lost due to the unpaid care they provide for their aging parents, husbands, and other relatives may decrease the amount or quality of care that women can expect in their old age.[30] Moreover, as the population ages, the need for unpaid caregivers will increase. The United States alone will need between

5.7 and 6.6 million eldercare givers to meet that demand. The cost to business to replace women caregivers who quit their job is estimated at \$3.3 billion.[31] Stark looks at this issue from an international perspective and organizes the relatively affluent countries into three categories depending on their provisions for eldercare. They are: (1) countries in which a large public sector organizes care; (2) countries in which family care is supported by public general insurance; (3) countries in which families are left to care for the elderly with almost no outside support.

Sweden is an example of the first. Eldercare policy in the Nordic countries is based on the principle that the care of older people is a public responsibility, and that care should be provided by trained and qualified professionals.[32] Women constitute the majority of paid care workers and a majority of jobs are in paid care work. Germany is an example of the second. There the state supports families to undertake eldercare work through universal care insurance that provides monthly payments or material help to elderly people and their families. Home care is common and more than 80 percent of the caretakers are wives, daughters, and daughters-in law. The problem with this model is that it puts pressure on women to stay home, preserving old gender patterns, and the low remuneration of relatives who provide care. Spain is an example of the third. Its care regime is based entirely on families and there is no state support for caretakers. As in Germany and Sweden, care is provided mainly by female family members. Spain faces a care crisis because it has one of the lowest birth rates in the world and women's participation in paid work is increasing. Regardless of which of the three ways of organizing eldercare, the present feminized way that care is organized is not sustainable for the future. Consequently, Stark calls for a "new world order of care."[33]

The United States in many ways resembles the case of Spain: caring for the elderly is considered the responsibility of the family rather than the state. Medicare is available for citizens sixty-five and older, but it only covers hospitalization and short stays in nursing homes. Extremely poor people may receive Medicaid.[34] It pays the bare minimum for institutional long-term care. The quality of paid care a person receives, whether at home with a paid caregiver, in an assisted living facility, or a nursing home, depends entirely on their ability to pay. Formal eldercare fosters social inequality by splitting the elderly between "private payers" and the poor. Eldercare for the poor, the majority of whom are women, is not pleasant. They are consigned to nursing homes that are, in the words of Silvia Federici, "more like prisons than hostels for the old," and conditions range from bad to horrific.[35]

We do need a new world order of eldercare, but unfortunately it is even further away today than when Agneta Stark wrote those words in 2005. In this brave new world of neoliberal austerity, commitments to public spending for the social good are nearly a thing of the past. Many countries are severely cutting back on public support for health care, childcare, eldercare, and education. Among the OECD nations, the Nordic welfare states remain at the top of the care pyramid, although this may change under pressure from immigration. Greece is clearly at the bottom and provides the most extreme example of the consequences of neoliberal policies of all the industrialized economies. There life expectancy has fallen, enrollment in primary education has contracted, and women's workloads have increased dramatically.

The Economic Costs of Motherhood

Liberals and conservatives, feminists and antifeminists, all recognize that motherhood has pronounced negative consequences for women's labor market earnings. The effect of childbearing on earnings is so significant that journalist Ann Crittenden has dubbed it "the mommy tax."[36] The mommy tax is the income women don't earn because they've become mothers. Economists call this an "opportunity cost." Feminist sociologists Michelle Budig and Paula England argue that there is a 5 percent to 7 percent wage penalty for motherhood.[37] After children are born, women often lose job experience, which translates into lower lifetime incomes. In addition, mothers may trade off higher wages for "family friendly" jobs, or they may work part-time. A recent study of married couples in the United States provides an insight into this problem. Overall women earn $12,600 less than men before their children are born and $25,100 less afterward. This study also found that when women have their first child between the age of twenty-five and thirty-five, their pay, relative to their husbands, never recovers. But if they have their first child either before twenty-five or after thirty-five, they eventually close the pay gap with their husbands. The years between twenty-five and thirty-five are the times when most women have children, and they are also the prime career-building years.[38]

Working mothers who have the primary responsibility for childcare may find part-time work an attractive option, especially when high-quality, affordable childcare is unavailable. Choosing part-time work over full-time work contributes to mothers' lower lifetime earnings because part-time work almost always pays less per hour, it rarely has the benefits that come with full-time employment, and fewer total hours are worked (either weekly, monthly, or annually). Budig and England point out, however, that even after controlling for the differences between full- and part-time work and other objective measures related to higher pay (experience, seniority, and so forth), they still find that mothers earn less.

The assumption that women have primary responsibility for children, coupled with the absence of adequate social support for childcare, creates serious problems for women's careers. Research by law professor Joan Williams found that only "ideal workers" have much chance for career advancement because the best jobs for blue-collar or professional/executive-level workers are organized around the unencumbered "ideal of a worker who works full time and overtime and takes little or no time off for childbearing or child rearing."[39] Consequently, career advancement depends on the ability to work in the evening, travel on short notice, or go to the office on weekends. The problem is that children, especially those under age twelve, need adult supervision. It is both unsafe and illegal to leave young children unattended for any length of time. What is a working parent supposed to do if an important meeting is scheduled for 7:00 p.m. and the childcare center closes at 6:00 p.m.? Thus many women choose what has become known as the "mommy track," a less prestigious and less demanding career path.

An examination of the top tiers of the high-prestige, high-salary positions within law, science, engineering, accounting, medicine, and government service reveals a disturbing pattern: it is almost impossible to combine career advancement with raising children and/or caring for elderly relatives. As professors Randy Albelda and Chris Tilly famously quip, there are jobs for wives and jobs for people with wives.[40] Their point is that the "normal" expectations for career advancement assume the existence of a caretaker who is available 24/7 in the event of unplanned changes in work schedules. Absent such a caretaker, it is virtually impossible to fill employer demands for mandatory overtime, travel, or weekend work, since meeting such demands conflicts directly with parental responsibility. One study found that only 49 percent of women who have earned an MBA degree and who are within three tiers of the CEO position have children. In contrast, 84 percent of men with MBA degrees and within three tiers of the CEO position have children.[41] These figures underscore the fact that high-powered jobs are still "jobs for people with wives." Having a house husband who adopts the role of a traditional, stay-at-home spouse would certainly help the careers of many women. As feminists, however, we continue to find this problematic. More than forty years ago Betty

Friedan pointed out that "the problem that has no name" is the result of confining women to the home and denying their quest for meaningful work and self-fulfillment.[42] We do not believe that turning the tables and creating another caste of wives is an improvement.

Bridging the Work-Family Divide through Workplace Policies

Conflicts between work and family obligations have led to the creation of "family friendly" policies such as job sharing, family and medical leaves, and flexible work schedules. The stated goal of these policies is to help working families balance responsibilities to employers and families. Sweden has been a leader in adopting family friendly approaches, and its policies are often seen as a model. It has implemented policies designed to promote the participation of fathers and mothers (regardless of marital status) in child-rearing, paid work, and homemaking. Both parents are eligible for extensive, well-paid leaves upon the birth or adoption of a child, and Swedish law requires both parents to take time off during a child's infancy. Parents are further allowed to shorten their daily work hours (with a reduction in pay) after these leaves, while their children are young. Paid medical leave is likewise available to care for sick children and other family members. There is, in addition, a professionalized system of early childhood education and care available at very low cost to all workers. Thus in Sweden we see an explicit national effort to enable women to combine career advancement with motherhood, as well as to get parents to share child-raising and care tasks.

Nevertheless, the Swedish solution is not perfect and does not achieve all of its goals. In a study published in 2000, feminist economists Ellen Mutari and Deborah Figart demonstrated that despite the gender-neutral wording of the laws concerning parental leave, and efforts to encourage men to take advantage of it, only 6 percent of leave-takers were men.[43] A similar result has been reported from California's implementation of paid leave. While available to all parents regardless of gender, it was women, not men, who took advantage of the leave. The policy consequently widened the "mommy gap" in pay and employment.[44] However, shifts in attitudes toward childcare and gender—in part inspired by public policies that identify and support men as well as women as potential caregivers–may move parental responsibility-sharing closer toward equity in the long run. In Sweden, men currently make up one-quarter of parental leave-takers, a significant rise in their participation since Figart and Mutari's report from just two decades ago.[45] Still, statistically speaking, the responsibility for "balancing" work and family obligations remains with mothers. Case studies across a range of countries find that no paid leave, a short paid leave, and a very long paid leave all result in women dropping out of the paid labor force.[46] These findings seem to support Barbara Bergmann's argument that, given current gender role expectations that lock women and men into a gender division of labor at home, paid leave policies continue to allow women to reap the disadvantages of having primary responsibility for child-rearing and housework.[47]

When women's earnings are considerably less than the earnings of men, it makes sense for the woman, not the man, to drop out of the labor force when children enter the picture. Absent strong policies to create wage equity, women will continue to do the lionesses' share of unpaid, largely invisible work. But as women's wages near parity with men's, this advantage evaporates, leaving considerable space for discussions of ways to make parenting a more equally shared venture. Recognizing this, feminists support the deliberate pairing of policies that promote universal caregiver parity with policies that promote pay equity. Feminists have long advocated pay equity programs. These are relevant with respect to care work because reducing female-male income disparities reduces the rationale for women to drop out of the workforce to take care of their kids. Caregiver parity policies will encourage employers to treat male parents as equal partners with equal responsibility for raising a family. This requires a huge attitudinal shift, we know, but we still believe it is possible.

"Commoning" for Care

The responsibilities for providing care still largely rest with individual households who provide unpaid care work and/or have responsibility for addressing their care needs in the marketplace. Workplace and government policies aimed at supporting the care needs of families largely take that privatized model of care as given. However, care and social reproduction can also be produced at a larger scale than the household, by making it the responsibility of the community and/or society in which we live. The privatization of care work into households and families, and its gender and spatial division of labor, is, after all, a historically recent development in human history, as we discussed in chapter 2. One transformative alternative to our current arrangements is what Silvia Federici has referred to as "commoning reproduction." This entails collectively pooling resources to provide the childcare, eldercare, and other care needs of the community. Federici argues that such a shift toward commoning and away from privatized care has revolutionary potential for society. It would lead to a revaluing of caring labor as a central goal of the economy. It would also liberate women from their responsibility for housework and foster values of cooperation among those working together to provide care.[48]

There are myriad examples of historical and actually existing strategies of commoning for social reproduction. These include nineteenth-century experiments in the United States with housewives cooperatives, community-run day-care centers, new types of buildings meant to foster community care such as kitchen-less homes, and other ways of organizing care work outside the private realm of the household and family.[49] More recent examples include the Free Breakfast for School Children program launched by the Black Panthers in the 1970s and still active today, the Community Gardens movements in Detroit and Milwaukee, and cohousing arrangements that communally address care needs in the United Kingdom and the Netherlands.[50] There are also a range of different commoning communities that have formed to address environmental degradation. Care for the environment is another form of care that is deeply connected to human well-being and social reproduction.[51]

Conclusion

Feminists recognize that the best interests of society will be served when all people—fathers and mothers, poor and rich—have the time and economic resources needed for childcare, eldercare, invalid care, and self-care. Creating effective policies to address these issues requires an open discussion about the importance of this work, the obvious inequities of continuing to assume that caring labor is women's work, and the need to make this work well paid and well respected. There is simply no way around the fact that care is time-consuming and labor-intensive. No amount of technical change will alter this. We need social policies to ensure that all people have access to the resources necessary to create and maintain healthy families. As things stand right now, in most of the world, women do virtually all this work with little assistance from either men or the wider society. The costs remain private in the form of women's lower earnings, the exploitation of poor women as caregivers, and the psychic burdens on families. The benefits, in contrast, are social.

4 | Gender, Work, and Policy in the United States

In nearly every country in the world, men are more likely than women to engage in paid labor. But in the past few decades, gender differences in labor force participation have narrowed significantly. Globally, women now make up 40 percent of the workforce, and in the United States, Canada, and the European Union nations, that figure is closer to 47 percent, or nearly half of the working population.[1] However, women do not participate on an equal footing with men. On average, women across the world get paid 63 percent of what men make.[2] They are also tracked into different kinds of work. In the United States, before the passage of Title VII of the Civil Rights Act of 1964, which prohibits employment discrimination based on race, color, religion, sex, or national origin, it was commonplace for jobs to be explicitly advertised as "Help Wanted Male" and "Help Wanted Female." The jobs advertised for men were typically higher paid than those for women and often included opportunities for advancement, compared to the dead-end jobs in the "Help wanted Female" column.[3] Today, such blatant discrimination is rare, but gendered patterns of employment stubbornly persist. Men are clustered in higher-level positions and occupations coded "masculine" and women are disproportionately employed in subordinate and "feminine" ones. There is further segregation in occupation by race. For example, while women make up 90 percent of all housekeepers in the United States, nearly half of workers in this field are Latinas, even though they make up only 17 percent of the total US population.[4] Mainstream economists argue that these outcomes are justified, as they reflect the personal occupational preferences of different demographic groups, alongside personal attributes and choices that lead to different levels of skill, education, and work experience. Feminist economists disagree. Instead they demonstrate that such patterns of employment reflect deeply entrenched social hierarchies based on gender, race, ethnicity, and class. In this chapter, we discuss these employment patterns with a focus on the labor market of the United States.

Labor Force Participation

One of the most remarkable changes in the late twentieth century was the feminization of labor, or the steady increase in the number of women participating in the paid labor force. While beginning at different times in different locations, nearly all of the countries in the world have seen a dramatic rise in women's labor market participation since the 1960s. Of course, women have long worked for pay outside the home. In the late nineteenth century in the United States, for instance, poor, single women—typically women of color and recent immigrants—were employed in factories and as maids or day-laborers in other peoples' homes or farms. By the late nineteenth and early twentieth centuries, they were joined by women with enough access to education to qualify them for jobs in teaching or clerical positions. Most of these women workers were single and likely to exit the workplace upon marriage. Many employers, in fact, banned married women from working. During this period, women made up a small percentage of the total workforce. Paid work was generally considered the prerogative of men.[5]

This didn't mean women failed to contribute to the market economy during the late nineteenth and early twentieth centuries. Enslaved women produced an enormous amount of goods and services that were sold on the market, enriching others while living and working in unfree and brutal conditions. Women worked in family plots producing crops for sale, took in boarders, made food and handicrafts for market, and engaged in numerous other income-generating activities that fell outside the official definitions of paid labor. And of course, women were primarily responsible for the enormous amount of uncompensated social reproductive labor that provided current and future workers with sustenance.

Women started entering the US labor force in slightly more significant numbers by the 1920s and 1930s. In part this was due to growth of the modern corporation generating a need for scores of clerical workers to file, type, answer telephones, and keep records. As women's employment opportunities outside the home increased, simultaneously the type of work in the home changed. Instead of home production, the goods and services necessary for everyday life were increasingly being mass-produced and sold in retail stores. These stores in turn began hiring women workers to sell goods. Shopping, rather than making goods at home, became a much more central part of women's responsibility in the household, and with it the need for income to buy the increasing array of consumer goods. It should be remembered that, due to legacies of racial discrimination, these new employment opportunities in offices and retail spaces were generally opportunities for white women. It would take decades of struggle before women of color would have wider access to these kinds of jobs.[6]

From the 1930s to the 1950s, women's labor force participation increased as married women started entering the workplace in significant numbers.[7] World War II had a considerable influence on this shift, and on women's social and economic positions. The shortage of men due to the war, and the substitution of women for factory jobs, directly exposed the pretense that women could not do male jobs. In the United States, the image of "Rosie the Riveter" was the icon for working women. In Europe and other theaters of action, women's paid labor was even more important. Even in Nazi Germany, where party policy extolled the virtues of the good Aryan wife and mother, the demands of war forced the state to employ women in factories.[8]

Today, the feminization of labor is commonplace. The female labor force participation rate, or ratio of adult women who are either employed (full-time or part-time) or looking for paid employment divided by the total population of women, has risen since the 1960s. The increase in women's labor force participation rate is illustrated by table 4.1, which shows the rates of women and men in the United States from 1900 to 2015. Women's labor force participation rates have risen steadily over this period until about 2000, when the participation rates for both women and men decrease slightly. The table also shows the increasing share of women in the labor force.[9] Women constituted only about 18 percent of the labor force in 1900. In 2015 they made up just under half of the labor force.

An important factor explaining this upward trend is the change in female labor force participation over women's life cycles, particularly the sustained labor force participation of women during their childbearing years. During the 1950s it was commonplace for women to drop out of the labor force to raise children. Thus women's labor force participation rates for women in the twenty-five to thirty-four age group exhibited a marked decline. However, by the 1980s this began to change as fewer and fewer women left the labor force for sustained periods of time to raise children.[10] In 1980, 42 percent of women with children under the age of three worked full-time or part-time; by 1998, 62 percent did so.[11] This pattern has not changed much since then. In 2017 the labor force participation rate for married women with children under the age of three was 60 percent, and 68 percent for mothers with another marital status.[12]

This phenomenon is not unique to the United States. Consider, as an example, male and female labor force participation rates in ten different industrialized countries (table 4.2). In all ten countries, women's labor force participation has steadily risen. There are, of course, variations among the countries. For example, in 2016, about 55 percent of Italian women were in the labor force compared with 80 percent of Swedish women. These variations can be explained by differences in attitudes toward gender equality and women's paid employment, as well as a government that supports women as both mothers and workers. In a comparative study of nineteen countries, Pettit and Hook show that parental leave and public provision of childcare, especially during early childhood, significantly affect the sustained labor force participation of women during their childbearing years.[13] These issues are explored further in chapter 5.

How can we explain the increase through the decades in women's labor force participation over the course of their lives? Feminist economist Barbara Bergmann notes that as women's labor force participation rose, wages

TABLE 4.1. US Civilian Labor Force Participation by Sex

	Participation (%)		
	Male	Female	% Female
1900	85.7	20.0	18.1
1920	84.6	22.7	20.4
1930	82.1	23.6	21.9
1940	82.5	27.9	25.2
1950	86.4	33.9	29.6
1960	83.3	37.7	33.4
1970	79.7	43.3	38.1
1980	77.4	51.5	42.5
1990	76.4	57.5	45.2
2000	77.0	60.8	46.5
2005	75.5	60.3	46.4
2010	74.1	60.6	46.7
2015	71.9	58.4	46.8

Source: Data from US Department of Commerce, Bureau of the Census, *Historical Statistics of the United States, Colonial Times to 1970*, bicentennial ed., part 1 (1975), 131–32; US Bureau of Labor Statistics data, 1950–1990 annual averages, not seasonally adjusted, 2000–2015 from US Bureau of Labor Statistics, Civilian Labor Force Participation Rate, seasonally adjusted. United States Department of Labor: Women's Bureau.

Note: Figures for 1950 and after include persons sixteen years old and over; for prior years, those fourteen years old and over are included.

and salaries for women were also rising.[14] Thus women's retreat from full-time homemaking was at least in part a response to changes in the costs and benefits of full-time domesticity. As the benefits from working at a paid job rose, the benefits of staying at home declined since women had fewer children. Between 1890 and 1984, the real wage quadrupled—increasing the benefits of working outside the home. During the same period, women were marrying at later ages and having fewer children. Bergmann argues that one reason for the fall of the birthrate is that raising children has become progressively less economically rewarding. In agrarian societies children's labor was necessary to family enterprises. In modern, industrialized societies, on the other hand, children often remain economic dependents until they are in their early twenties.

Another factor leading to declining birthrates is that after the 1960s effective, legal, and relatively inexpensive methods of birth control were widely available. The economist Claudia Goldin has argued that birth control allowed women to respond rationally to economic signals and act in their own self-interest.[15] As women limited the size of their families, this further reduced the benefits of staying at home and reinforced the pull of the market. In addition to the decrease in fertility, another significant demographic trend that has affected women's labor force participation is the increase in female-headed households. This is due to divorce, to an increase in the number of unmarried women having children, and, in the developing world, to patterns of migration that led to the breakup of families.[16]

TABLE 4.2. Civilian Labor Force Participation Rate by Sex for Ten OECD Countries (%)

	1965		1985		2001		2016	
	Male	Female	Male	Female	Male	Female	Male	Female
Australia	85.1	34.8	76.5	47.0	71.9	55.1	70.6	59.3
Canada	79.9	33.8	77.4	54.7	72.3	59.8	70.3	61.3
France	79.2	38.2	68.4	46.4	61.8	48.3	60.7	51.7
Germany	80.9	40.0	70.1	41.1	66.3	49.3	66.5	55.6
Italy	77.5	27.8	65.3	30.7	62.0	36.4	59.3	40.5
Japan	81.1	48.8	77.9	47.6	75.7	49.2	70.4	50.4
Netherlands	—	—	73.8	37.9	72.4	53.8	69.6	58.7
Sweden	82.2	46.6	72.5	61.5	74.3	68.2	74.4	69.6
United Kingdom	85.4	41.7	76.1	50.0	70.6	55.0	69.2	58.0
United States	80.7	39.3	76.3	54.5	74.4	59.8	69.2	56.8

Note: OECD = Organization for Economic Cooperation and Development
Source: Data for 1965 and 1985 from Department of Labor, Bureau of Labor Statistics, "Comparative Civilian Labor Force Statistics," 10 Countries. Data for 2001 and 2016 from OECD Stat.

Another major factor that made paid work more attractive to increasing numbers of women was legislation aimed at outlawing discrimination against them at work, which we will discuss in more detail later in the chapter. For example, in the United States, an Equal Pay Act was passed in 1963, making paying different wages for the same work on the basis of gender or race illegal. As mentioned above, a year later, Title VII legislation outlawed discrimination by sex, race, religion, and nationality in hiring and promotion. No longer could employers legally search for only a man or woman for a particular job unless gender was a bona fide occupational qualification, such as when a maker of men's clothing is hiring male models for their advertising campaign. In the late 1970s, it became illegal to fire a woman just because she became pregnant, something that was a commonplace in the earlier part of the twentieth century. These and other acts of legislation barring discrimination improved women's earning potential and conditions of work in ways that made paid work a more attractive option.

Finally, we point to an important cultural change in the perception and valuation of full-time domesticity. As documented by Betty Friedan in *The Feminine Mystique,* the life of a housewife can be alienating, isolating, and frustrating.[17] She describes the pervasive dissatisfaction of white, suburban, college-educated women with the life of a housewife as "the problem that has no name." The women's movement was another significant catalyst for married women's entry into the paid labor force.

The Gender Wage Gap

Women, on average, make less money than men. A statistic called the gender wage gap tells us the value of female wages as a percentage of male wages. Around the world, the gender wage gap is calculated comparing the median or average weekly or hourly earnings of full-time workers by gender. If the gender wage gap is seventy-five percent, that means that on average for every dollar a man makes, a woman makes $0.75.[18] Table 4.3 shows the gender wage gap for ten selected OECD countries in 2001 and 2016.

In 2001 the gender wage gap in the United States, which like many countries compares only full-time, year-round workers by gender, was 76.4 percent, and in 2016 it was nearly 82 percent. The gender wage gap in the United States has slowly closed over time. Unfortunately, *slowly* is the operative word. And this does not mean that everyone is getting richer. According to feminist economist Deborah Figart, over half the narrowing of the gender wage gap in the 1980s was due to a decline in men's real wages.[19] The Institute for Women's Policy Research estimates that if the pace of change continues at the same rate as it has since 1960, it will take another forty-three years to achieve gender parity in the United States.[20] Women's part-time work, combined with their lower wages, is another source of their economic disadvantage relative to men, and one that is not captured in wage gap statistics. For example, on average for the OECD countries, 26 percent of employed women work part-time, while only 9 percent of men do.[21]

The gender wage gap differs depending on the racial and ethnic characteristics of the groups being compared. In the United States, for example, if we examine African American women and Latina women as separate groups, their wage gaps, with respect to all men, are 70 percent and 64 percent, respectively, and 53 percent of what white men are paid.[22] Moreover, white workers of both sexes earn more than did their African American or Hispanic counterparts. The wage gap for black women to white women is 83 percent; the gap for Hispanic women to white women is 76 percent.[23] In other words, white women earn, on average, more than black women and Hispanic women. Examining different ethnic groups in other countries yields similar results. Salaries, wages, and working conditions reflect nearly perfectly the social and cultural standing of different ethnic groups.

Age is also relevant to the size of the gender wage gap. In the United States, in 2018, the wage gap for young women between sixteen and twenty-four years was 91 percent, for women between thirty-five and forty-four years, it was 80 percent, and for women between forty-five and fifty-four it

TABLE 4.3. Gender Wage Gap for Ten OECD Countries, 2001 and 2016

Country	2001	2016
Australia	85.7	85.7
Canada	75.7	81.8
France	n.d.	n.d.
Germany	80.9	84.5
Italy	n.d.	94.4
Japan	66.1	75.4
Netherlands	n/d.	n.d.
Sweden	83.4	n.d.
United Kingdom	74.4	83.2
United States	76.4	81.9

Note: OECD = Organization for Economic Cooperation and Development. Expressed as the ratio of women's to men's median wages for full-time workers.
Source: Data OECD Data

was 77 percent.[24] A large part of the explanation for this widening of the wage gap is that as women enter their thirties, they are more likely to have responsibility for children than are younger women. As we discuss in chapter 3, gendered childcare responsibilities negatively impact women's labor market earnings, and this disadvantage persists over the rest of their lives. Many people dismiss the gender wage gap, then, as not so much the reflection of an unfair labor market as the choices women make to prioritize family over career, or to take on paid care work tasks rather than to go into the higher-paid science, technology, engineering, and math (STEM) fields. Of course, how much of this is a "choice" is something we covered in earlier chapters regarding women's disproportionate care work expectations and responsibilities in households. What should also be noted here is that even women who have just graduated college and have no family responsibilities earn less than their male peers. Even when controlling for field, the number of hours worked, and economic sector (corporate versus government/non-profit), full-time male workers were paid more than full-time women workers one year out of college.[25]

Occupational Segregation

The largest factor determining the gender wage gap, accounting for more than half of the difference, is occupational segregation, or the different jobs that women and men typically hold.[26] Occupational segregation is divided into two categories, vertical and horizontal segregation. Vertical segregation refers to the gendered hierarchies of work, in which men hold the higher status positions within a specific field. The fact that 95 percent of CEOs of the Fortune 500 companies are men is an example of vertical segregation.[27] Vertical segregation is so common among the ranks of senior executives and managers that it has a name, the glass ceiling, which refers to the invisible barriers that stop women from reaching the upper echelons of large corporations. This phenomenon has been studied extensively, and the overwhelming conclusion is that the most pervasive barrier to women's advancement to the senior ranks is prejudice.[28] Women's abilities are stereotyped and devalued; they are excluded from informal networks of communication and are not mentored. Women do not reach the top of the corporation because they are not allowed to start up the path.

Vertical segregation also captures the ways that men and women are clustered in different specialties within a particular occupation. In law, women are more likely to be practicing lower-paid family and criminal law, while corporate law remains the province of men. We find a similar situation in medicine. Women physicians are found mainly in five major and lower-paid specialties: primary care, pediatrics, psychiatry, internal medicine, and OB-GYN.[29] They are less likely to be working in higher-paid specialties such as surgery. In 2015, the Association of American Medical Colleges reported that 19 percent of general surgeons in the United States are women, and the UK Royal College of Surgeons reports that 1 percent of consultant surgeons in England are women.[30] Moreover, regardless of whether it is a male- or female-dominated occupation, women are paid less. Consider secondary school teacher as an example of a predominantly female occupation. With women constituting 78 percent of the workers, the wage gap is still 87 percent. On the other hand, consider civil engineering, a profession that is 84 percent male, the wage gap is 88 percent.[31]

The other kind of occupational segregation, known as horizontal segregation, is the clustering of women and men into different fields entirely. Women are more likely to be employed in "pink collar" service fields such as nurses, childcare workers, dental hygienists, elementary schoolteachers, clerical workers, secretaries, and receptionists. Doctors, dentists, construction workers, police officers, firefighters, and electricians are, in contrast, male-dominated fields. Horizontal segregation in part reflects social stereotypes about women's and men's roles and abilities. It is assumed that women are more caring and nurturing, that they are followers rather than leaders, that they have less physical strength than men, and that they are not as good at math and science. These stereotypes have an influence on employers' hiring decisions and also frame the expectations of workers themselves, often from a young age. Of course, such stereotypes and their application to different jobs vary according to historical and cultural differences and, hence, differences in occupational segregation. At the turn of the twentieth century in Europe and North America it was men, not women, who were considered the ideal secretaries. In Soviet Russia, to offer another example, it was assumed that women were better suited at medicine and the majority of doctors in the country during the Soviet era were women.

While there is still significant gender clustering in occupations, things have improved somewhat over the past half century, and we are no longer surprised to meet a female doctor or lawyer, or a male elementary school teacher. One thing that has remained constant, however, is that fields with more men in them tend to be higher paid. The "craft" occupations, which include plumbers, electricians, and skilled construction workers, are relatively high paid occupations for people without four-year college degrees, and the percentage of women who are in these occupations is quite low. In 2018, although the gender wage gap is 97 percent, only 3 percent of workers in these occupations were women.[32] That the fastest growing fields that employ high percentages of women, such as health aides, childcare workers, office assistants, personal services, and housecleaners are also some of the lowest-paid ones is also a reason to pay close attention to the impacts of occupational segregation on women's lives.[33]

Labor markets are segregated by race and ethnicity as well as by gender, reflecting the social and cultural status of the groups in question. In the United States, the lower wages and status of work done by poor women of color reflect historical patterns of racism combined with sexism. Until the 1960s the majority of African American women were employed as domestic workers, a condition that was reinforced by Jim Crow segregation laws in the American South and exclusionary practices of labor unions in the North.[34] Around the world, women from lower-status ethnic groups experience larger wage gaps than do higher-status women. The feminist economist Mary King has shown that in Great Britain relatively higher-status native-born black women are employed mainly in clerical jobs, while black immigrant women are employed in the relatively less prestigious service sector.[35] Similarly, ethnic Malay women in Singapore are concentrated in low-income occupations,[36] while on the Arabian Peninsula poor women from the Philippines or Pakistan can only find employment as domestic workers.[37]

The Human Capital Approach

The fact that much, although not all, of the gender wage gap is explained by occupational segregation raises two related questions. First, why do female-dominated occupations pay less than male-dominated occupations, and second, why are women clustered in these lower-paying occupations? For mainstream economists, the answer to this question lies in tracing out differences in human capital investments and innate ability by gender. According to human capital theory, pay is a direct result of a worker's productivity, which in turn reflects their human capital, or the value of the skills, education, and experience they bring to the job. Proponents of human capital theory advance several explanations for why women earn less than men. One is that women and men have different initial endowments of human capital, or innate abilities. These can include differences in language ability, mathematical knowledge, physical strength, ability to nurture, motivational drive, athletic prowess, and the like. A common argument regarding why men go into engineering fields at a higher rate than women, for instance, is that men have a supposedly greater inherent skill at mathematics. Similarly, women make better childcare workers given their supposedly innate talent for nurturing. Given these differently gendered abilities, then, men and women simply choose the educational and occupational paths that gives them the best return. Masculine fields, it turns out, tend to pay more. But human capital theory would remind us that this is because they are higher productivity fields. Another related explanation is that women may be more likely to invest in human capital that has a higher nonmarket return than men do. In other words, women may invest in human capital that is targeted toward nonmarket activities such as child-rearing, rather than focusing on market activities.

According to the mainstream approach, women's investments in human capital are the result of rational, cost-benefit calculations. Women, so the theory goes, expect to interrupt paid work to care for children. Since they expect to spend fewer years in the workforce due to time off for child-rearing, they have fewer years to reap the rewards from their investment in educational human capital and also fewer years of work experience to further build their human capital. That their human capital depreciates means that when they reenter the workforce they are even further disadvantaged.[38]

Seemingly, then, women choose occupations that fit their initial gendered endowments and are compatible with family responsibilities. These occupations pay less because of their lower human capital requirements. At least that's how the story goes. Feminist economists argue with both the presumption of choice and the presumption that the low pay of female-dominated occupations is due to their lower skill requirements. First, the argument about differences in women's and men's given abilities rests more on stereotypes and gender socialization than on any innate differences. The gender gap in math, for instance, has been shown to be more cultural than natural. In the countries where girls now have access to the same educational opportunities with math as boys, the gender gap in math performance has shrunken and in many cases disappeared.[39] Second, human capital theory can only view differences in human capital investment as a result of individual decisions, which doesn't capture outcomes that are the result of gender discrimination. For example, human capital may be acquired through on-the-job skill development or apprenticeships, both of which depend on the decisions of the employer, which may be colored by bias. For instance, in one study it was shown that employers were more likely to hire someone with a white-sounding name than a black-sounding one, even though both candidates had identical credentials.[40]

Economists have done empirical studies to analyze how much of the wage gap is due to human capital differences and how much is due to discrimination. These studies account for years of education, years of experience, interruptions in labor force participation, and differences between full-time and part-time work. In general, these studies show that human capital differences explain only 30–50 percent of the wage gap.[41] Such studies underscore the inadequacy of the human capital approach for explaining either the wage gap or occupational segregation.

Human capital theory has likewise been used to explain occupational segregation and wage inequality by race and ethnicity. Feminist, antiracist economists Rhonda Williams and William Spriggs have argued that explaining present-day racial economic inequality by human capital theory serves to justify such inequality by making it seem both normal and inevitable.[42] Human capital explanations of racial income inequality deny the presence of discrimination, fly in the face of the evidence, and serve to perpetuate labor market inequalities.

Another prominent feminist economist, Jane Humphries, has argued that an even bigger problem with the human capital theory is that it is an exercise in circular reasoning. According to the theory, women invest less in human capital or choose a less demanding job because they anticipate spending less time in the labor force than will their spouses. They anticipate spending less time in the labor force because their potential earnings are lower.[43] In other words, women earn less because they invest in less human capital, and they invest in less human capital because they are paid less.

Occupational Segregation and the Wage Gap Revisited: A Feminist Perspective

Are there explanations for the wage gap and occupational segregation that are consistent with feminist economics? One early approach is the "crowding" hypothesis advanced by Barbara Bergmann. She argued that there are fewer female-dominated occupations than male-dominated occupations, and thus women are "crowded" into them. The surplus of workers, relative to the demand for their labor, helps to keep their wages low and male wages high. She argues that, like other systems of dominance and privilege, occupational segregation perpetuates itself through the self-interest of its beneficiaries.[44] Of course, elaborate rationales are constructed to explain why such discrimination and privilege serve the common good. But the bottom line is that occupational segregation based on gender preserves male privilege just as occupational segregation based on race or ethnicity preserves the privilege of the high-status group.

Other feminist economists have argued that the very definition of human capital, and what is considered skilled, is itself deeply gendered. Work that is performed by women is considered unskilled not because it requires less training and ability but because it is done by women, and like women's work in the home, it is seen as emanating from natural abilities rather than acquired skills. For instance, when care for others is defined as an important skill in male-dominated fields such as firefighters or psychiatrists it earns a wage premium, which is not true of female-dominated fields where such characteristics are needed. The skilled work of caring and assisting others is thus valued differently when performed in differently gendered occupations.[45] Similarly, the "nimble fingers" associated with female production workers in the developing world, for example, are considered a natural attribute of women. On the other hand, the "nimble fingers" of dentists and surgeons are conceptualized quite differently. This is not to argue that production line workers should perform brain surgery! Rather, it is meant to draw attention to the different ways we represent male and female skills.

Feminists point out the affinities between occupations that are female-dominated and gender stereotypes about women's appropriate roles and responsibilities. One feminist approach to wages, pioneered by feminist economists Deborah Figart, Ellen Mutari, and Marilyn Power, is to consider wage setting as social practice that reflects, reproduces, and transforms social norms concerning gender and race.[46] In this view, stereotypes about the worth of women's work and their identification as housewives rather than as workers keep women's wages low. Consider banking: in the 1940s when most bank tellers were men, it was a path to becoming a bank manager or even president. Now nearly all bank tellers are women with little chance for advancement. Have the requirements for the position changed? Or has the gender composition of the workforce changed?[47]

Along similar lines, feminist economists and sociologists have forwarded a gender devaluation thesis to explain the link between occupational segregation and gender wage differentials. Research shows that occupations with a higher percentage of women in them pay less than those with a lower percentage, controlling for education and skill.[48] Thus the low pay of "feminine" occupations has less to do with skills than the fact that women are the ones doing the work and that traits and skills associated with women are less valued, and with men are more valued. One example of the devaluation process—in reverse—is the case of computer software development. Originally, software design was viewed as a feminine task, contrasted with computer hardware development which was considered more masculine. But the gendered character of software development changed in the 1970s for a variety of reasons, and it became coded as the masculine field it is today, even though the skill set needed to succeed did not change. Further, while a relatively high-paid job for women, it became even more lucrative when it became more closely associated with male characteristics.[49]

We also need to consider gendered patterns of socialization and their impact on labor market outcomes. Economist and living wage advocate Richard Anker argues that the patriarchal ordering of society explains why girls are less likely to pursue fields of study that are highly valued in labor markets, such as science or industrial crafts.[50] Expectations about women's appropriate gender roles lead to the perception that girls have a lesser need for such skills. For example, gender norms about appropriate activities for boys and girls discourage girls from acquiring the skills that would enable them to become skilled production and craft workers.

These occupations require fairly small investments in human capital but nevertheless pay relatively well. As the performance of many productive, skilled women has shown, women can and do learn these trades.[51] Nonetheless, when women try to enter such male-dominated occupations, they are often subject to subtle and not so subtle hints that their presence is unwelcome. Sexual harassment, lack of mentoring, and inadequate training and resources are common. Acquiring human capital, especially gendered human capital, is not just a matter of personal choice. It is also conditioned by institutional constraints and old-fashioned sexism.

Firefighting is an excellent example of an occupation that is well paid, has very good benefits, and is dominated by white men. Ninety-six percent of firefighters are men and 82 percent are white.[52] It has also been highly resistant to the hiring of women and minorities who do apply for the job. Consider the case of Julie Tossey and Kathleen O'Connor, two women who aspired to become professional firefighters in St. Paul, Minnesota. Both of the women were already working as dispatchers in the department and would have entered the force with considerable seniority.

The two women went through a yearlong vetting process that included medical and psychological evaluations as well as a grueling physical fitness test. They both passed and became recruits. The story does not, however, have a happy ending.

Tossey and O'Connor tell a story of intimidation, lack of mentoring, and arbitrary rule changes regarding the ongoing physical training for firefighters. In the end, they lost their jobs. Failure to pass later physical fitness tests was the official reason given for their termination. They maintain, however, that they were subject to a concerted effort to wash them out of the academy because their time as dispatchers would count toward seniority and put them ahead of many male firefighters.

A few of the firefighters in the St. Paul Fire Department are women. Probably some of them agree that Tossey and O'Connor were not physically fit. The question must be asked, however, to what extent these physical fitness tests are used to screen out women in order to preserve firefighting as a bastion of white male privilege, and to what extent they are legitimate requirements for the position. Note that the St. Paul department has also faced discrimination suits on behalf of African American males. Being a firefighter does require both strength and endurance. But is that all it requires? No. It requires a variety of technical and mental skills as well. The ability to respond well to others and to keep one's head in dangerous and chaotic situations is also fundamental. As one woman put it, when you go to a fire you are seeing people on the worst day of their lives. Skills to cope with situations like this are not gender or race specific.[53]

National Policies

Most industrialized countries have a variety of national policies explicitly designed to combat discrimination in the labor market. In the United States this began in 1963 with the passage of the Equal Pay Act. That act mandated equal pay for equal work. The notion of equal pay reflects the neoclassical economic notion that wages are the price of labor.[54] When women and men do equal work, they should receive equal rewards. This argument is absolutely correct, as far as it goes. The problem is that it doesn't go far enough in redressing the class and race dimensions of wage inequality among women, given the ongoing occupational segregation that characterizes certain segments of the labor force. As college-educated, mostly white women have moved into professional and managerial careers, equal pay for equal work promotes gender equality for them. Meanwhile, the gap between white women, black women, and Latinas has widened as the latter two groups of women remain clustered in poorly paid, female-dominated occupations.[55] Equal pay for equal work does less to promote the interests of those latter groups.

Opening up better-paid blue-collar occupations to women is another important strategy in combating discrimination in labor markets. Title VII of the 1964 Civil Rights Act was an important step in this direction. Title VII prohibits discrimination on the basis of race, color, sex, religion, or national origin. Prior to its passage, women were often kept out of high-paying blue-collar jobs by the protective labor legislation passed around the turn of the century. Title VII effectively eliminated these barriers to women's full and equal participation.

The US Supreme Court case *United Auto Workers v. Johnson Controls* provides a good example of the way that Title VII works to ensure that women have the right to participate in the labor market on an equal footing with men.[56] Johnson Controls, a battery manufacturer, instituted a fetal protection policy in 1982. This policy prevented all women who were capable of bearing children (regardless of whether they were, or ever intended to become, pregnant) from working in its battery-manufacturing division because they would be exposed to relatively high levels of lead, which could harm a developing fetus. The company knew that lead exposure could damage male and female reproductive organs, but nevertheless the ban applied only to women. The company was sued, the charge being that its policy constituted sex discrimination. Among the plaintiffs were two women who suffered economic damages and one man who was denied a leave of absence in order to lower his levels of lead before he became a father.

The Supreme Court agreed with the women, ruling that the policy violated the equal rights guarantee of Title VII. The court held that the policy was discriminatory because it did not apply to the reproductive capacity of male employees in the same way that it applied to the reproductive capacity of female employees. It also held that decisions about the future welfare of children should be left to the child's parents rather than the parents' employers. The court concluded that it is up to women to decide whether their reproductive roles are more important to them and their families than their economic roles. Clearly, this was an important decision in protecting women's rights and combating gender-based occupational segregation. In the 1980s, the courts also extended the provisions of Title IV to include sexual harassment, ruling that the harassment of a subordinate by their supervisor constitutes discrimination on the basis of sex.

However, Title VII has limitations in addressing discrimination beyond discrete categories of sex and race, leaving out the unique experiences of those who face discrimination by both sex *and* race. The critical legal scholar Kimberlé Crenshaw coined the now widely used term "intersectionality" to capture the failure of Title VII legal protections as well as the unique experiences of discrimination that black women and other women of color face at the intersections of race and sex. Crenshaw used the example of a Title VII lawsuit filed by five black women against General Motors, which argued that a recent set of layoffs had disadvantaged black women, who no longer held positions at the plant. But the court found against the plaintiffs, arguing that the layoffs had not discriminated by race or sex because black (men) and (white) women were still employed at the plant. The court also argued that combining the claims of race and sex discrimination to capture the unique experiences of women of color was outside Title VII's scope.[57] Crenshaw's call for the courts to recognize the intersectional nature of discrimination has met with mixed results, which means that many who face discrimination are still not afforded the legal protection they deserve.

Another limitation of Title VII is its failure to provide protections to lesbian, gay, bisexual, and transgender (LGBT) workers. While there are some state-specific laws preventing discrimination against these groups, most states have no bans on discriminating against or even firing someone for their sexual orientation or gender identity. Many millions of LGBT workers in the United States remain unprotected under US antidiscrimination law. Advocates for LGBT worker rights are making efforts to change this situation.

To address the wage gap that results from occupational segregation, feminists have advocated policies that are known as pay equity or comparable worth policies. Pay equity relies on comparable worth job evaluation systems designed to ensure that female-dominated jobs deemed equivalent to male-dominated jobs are paid the same. These policies go beyond the equal pay for equal work principle enshrined in current law. Pay equity policies require employers to come up with a way of evaluating and comparing different jobs. These sorts of job evaluations are already done in many large corporations and government offices as a way of setting guidelines for personnel managers. Jobs are assigned points that reflect the jobs' required level of education, skills, effort, working conditions, and responsibility. They are then ranked according to the number of points. What distinguishes pay equity policies from ordinary employee compensation guidelines is their commitment to an explicit comparison of predominantly male jobs and predominantly female jobs. As Barbara Bergmann points out, employee compensation guidelines often avoid this comparison by subdividing jobs into clusters that reflect similar market wages and job duties. So, secretaries and maintenance workers will be in different job clusters that reflect both the wage gap and gender discrimination. In contrast, pay equity policies explicitly address gender segregation and the wage gap by ranking all jobs by the same criteria. Implementing pay equity requires that jobs with the same score receive the same pay.[58]

The state of Minnesota legislated pay equity for local government in 1984. They found that maintenance workers (mostly men) and secretaries (mostly women) both received the same job evaluation ratings. But maintenance workers were paid $1,900 per month, while secretaries were paid $1,630. Similarly, a comparison of receptionists and custodians revealed that although receptionists have higher job evaluation ratings, they were paid less.[59] Minnesota's pay equity legislation corrected for these inequalities. It is important to note that in Minnesota pay inequalities must be eliminated by raising the wages of the disadvantaged group, not by lowering the wages of the other.

Although most large companies in the United States use some form of job evaluation programs to set pay for different jobs, very few have adopted explicit pay equity policies. Three states—Minnesota, Washington, and Maine—have mandated pay equity, but only Minnesota and Washington have made the subsequent wage adjustments. Canada is doing somewhat better. Both Quebec and Ontario have passed legislation that mandates pay equity as a principle for both the private and public sectors. The principle of pay equity has been endorsed by the ILO and the European Union as well as Australia and New Zealand. Its implementation, however, remains painfully slow.

The pay equity movement exists side by side with living wage campaigns, such as the Fight for Fifteen campaign. This movement started in 2012 in the United States and resulted in higher wages in dozens of cities and states by the end of the decade.[60] Because women and people of color are highly concentrated in fields such as food service, retail, child care, and hotel work that pay poverty-level wages, raising the minimum wage to fifteen dollars helps to close pay gaps by gender and race. Making this change at the national level would improve the pay of over half of all women workers and African American workers, and 60 percent of all Latinx workers.[61] Advocates of the living wage movement are concerned not only with gender and racial equity but also with the failure of the minimum wage to keep pace with inflation, the growing inequality between the rich and poor, the dismantling of welfare, the growth of low-paying service sector jobs, and the weakening of labor unions.[62] The movement explicitly recognizes that full-time workers should be able to make ends meet, and that wages and wage regulations should reflect social norms about appropriate living standards. Equality discourse demands that basic living standards should not differ according to gender, race, or ethnicity.[63]

Conclusion

Gender equity in labor markets is absolutely essential for any economic system that aspires to be fair, to improve the quality of life of its members, to provide economic security, and to use human resources wisely. Gender equity is, however, a necessary but not sufficient requirement for fairness. Sufficiency requires that labor markets also achieve equitable outcomes by race and ethnicity, sexual orientation, national origin, religion, and gender identity. Work, for many of us, is not just a job; meaningful and productive work is an integral part of life. Such work should not be reserved only for the privileged few. If it is, the economic system is not doing its job well.

Unfortunately, labor markets are not moving toward these goals. As the progressive labor economist Guy Standing persuasively argues, what we are seeing today is the emergence of a new class—the precariat.[64] The precariat is characterized by chronic insecurity, low incomes, lack of benefits, and precarious employment. For them work is simply a job—necessary to survive but not something that gives meaning to their lives or creates a sense of identity and purpose. Packing shelves, serving drinks, sweeping floors, or washing dishes are not routes to happiness or satisfaction. Nor are these jobs a route to economic security, something that is becoming an increasingly elusive goal for a growing number of workers in the United States and around the world.

Finally, equity in the labor market is necessary for an economic system to use its human resources to their fullest potential. If any group is disadvantaged in their access to acquiring the skills and technological expertise called for in this new century, then the economy is severely underutilizing its human resources. Besides being unfair, it is a waste of human resources and impairs the ability of the economy to meet human needs. And perhaps most importantly, a disadvantaged position in the labor market translates into higher poverty throughout a person's life. We turn our attention to this subject—poverty—in the next chapter.

5 | Women's Poverty in the Global North

Women face a disproportionate risk of poverty due to the interaction of several factors, including the gender wage gap, the gender segregation of labor markets, and their clustering into precarious, low-wage jobs without benefits such as medical insurance and pensions. Due to their duties as caregivers in families, women—particularly those with young children—are also less likely to work and more likely to seek part-time work when they enter the labor market. The poverty risk of women, especially those heading single-parent households, is compounded by the lack of adequate employment supports such as subsidized childcare. This often puts their participation in paid work at odds with attending to the health and safety of their children, placing them in a no-win situation. Soaring housing costs, medical costs, and rising debt burdens have put additional strain on poor households in the past few decades. During this same period, a war has been waged on antipoverty programs, particular those aimed at helping single women with children. All of these factors contribute to the *feminization of poverty*, a term sociologist Diana Pearce coined in 1978 to capture the factors at work making women more likely to be poor than men.[1] The extent of women's poverty means that even in some of the world's richest nations, such as the United States, the United Kingdom, and Italy, significant numbers of children live in families so lacking in resources that their normal health and growth are at risk.[2]

Meanwhile, the myths associated with poverty have kept many societies from adequately addressing its root causes. Many blame poverty on individual pathology and/or lack of individual effort, rather than examining the structural inequalities and dislocations that cause widespread economic insecurity. Contemporary characterizations of poverty and the poor are misleading and often play into racist, sexist, xenophobic, and other prejudices. The situation in the United States is illustrative. The myths we have been fed over the past few decades include the "welfare queen" who cheats the system, the promiscuous unwed mother, the undocumented migrant looking for a handout, and the lazy, drug-addicted rural "hillbilly," among others.[3] If the dysfunctional behaviors of the poor cause their poverty, then there is no social responsibility for reducing poverty. But these misconceptions and demeaning stereotypes about the poor have impeded understanding about the true causes of poverty, such as stagnating wages and lack of supports for working parents. They also divert our attention from the widespread and diverse experience of poverty in the United States.

In this chapter we trace the relationship between gender, poverty, and antipoverty programs in the global North, with attention to how gender intersects with class, race, sexuality, ability, and other dimensions of power. We address the issue of gender, poverty, and policy in the global South context in later chapters of this book.

Gender and Poverty: Concepts and Measures

Despite the overall economic growth that global North countries have experienced over the past few decades, an increasing number of people are facing economic insecurity and deprivation. As the income gap between rich and poor has widened, more people at the bottom have found themselves struggling to meet their basic needs. These deprivations are not distributed randomly. Gender, class, race and ethnicity, age, ability, migration status, and other markers of difference are key determinants of poverty. Women are, on average, more likely to be poor than men. In the United States, for example, 13 percent of women were poor compared to 11 percent of men in 2018, according to official poverty measures.[4] The poverty rate of black people was twice that of white people—approximately 20 and 10 percent, respectively.[5] Native American and black women were poorer still, each group experiencing a 28 percent poverty rate.[6] Single-parent households were more likely to be poor than married couple families with children, with 40 percent of female and 22 percent of male-headed households falling below the poverty line. Women over sixty-five years of age were nearly twice as likely as men in their age group to face poverty, owing to their lower lifetime income and less access to benefits such as pensions during their working years. LGBTQ seniors were also more likely to experience economic insecurity than their straight counterparts. More than a quarter of those with a disability in the United States lived in poverty.[7]

The data also show that children who are born poor are also likely to stay poor. As the economist Raj Chetty and his colleagues have argued, the chance of being born in the bottom 20 percent and making it into the top 20 percent of income earners during one's lifetime is less than 15 percent on average across the global North, with the United States having the lowest mobility of these countries at 7.5 percent. Further, while lack of class mobility in the United States means that most who are born into low-income families are likely to inherit their parent's income status, the chances of staying poor throughout one's lifetime are higher for blacks and Hispanics than for whites.[8] And where someone grows up plays a role as well. Among persons born into families with the same income level, those who are clustered in areas of concentrated poverty—with poor schools and health-care systems, high rates of incarceration, and the like—are far less likely to experience class mobility than their counterparts.[9]

In addressing women's poverty, then, it is essential to acknowledge the interplay between gender and the other factors that structure economic insecurity. A white woman born into a low-income household will have a much greater chance of being poor in her lifetime than a middle-class white woman. Race and gender intersect to uniquely structure black women's labor market experiences, their vulnerability to housing discrimination, and the inaccurate stereotypes about black women—particularly black mothers—that disadvantage them in educational, medical, and other institutional settings. LGBT persons in the United States have higher rates of poverty, but those in rural settings are even more likely to be poor, and the poverty rate of transgender persons is much higher than that of gay men, lesbian women, or the rest of the population at large.[10] Policies that aim to pull all women out of poverty must therefore address multiple systems of power and privilege in order to be successful.

So far, this discussion of the US context has drawn on information and definitions of poverty derived from the official poverty measure (OPM). This measure classifies as poor all of those households falling below the minimum threshold of before-tax income required to meet its basic needs. This threshold is set at three times a subsistence food budget relative to family size, annually adjusted for inflation. Created in 1961, it was based on consumption patterns at the time, when the average family spent one-third of its income on food. It has come under significant criticism, however, for not adequately capturing the true rate of poverty for a few reasons. First, the relative price of basic food has fallen during that period while the cost of other basic needs such as housing and transportation has risen. Thus the measure understates the true cost of basic needs. Second, it does not consider nonincome transfers like food stamps, Medicare, housing subsidies, and so forth. Third, standard measures only consider before-tax income and hence ignore the need to pay taxes as well as tax adjustments such as the earned income tax credit.[11] Finally, the OPM doesn't take location into account. While the OPM is still used in the United States to determine who qualifies for support, since 2010 an alternative called the supplemental poverty measure (SPM) has also been calculated by the Census Bureau. It addresses all of the above criticisms by calculating basic needs for consumption differently than the old food shares model, addresses standard of living differences by region, subtracts taxes and certain out-of-pocket expenses such as medical costs, and adds transfers and tax credits. The SPM is now being used by the government to more accurately capture poverty thresholds.[12] It is higher than the OPM for some locations and populations (such as the elderly who have high out-of-pocket medical expenses) and lower than the OPM for others. Still, the SPM does not adequately capture the true extent of poverty in the United States or the differential experience of poverty by gender.

Over the years, a number of economists have worked to come up with better poverty threshold measures. Feminist economists Barbara Bergmann and Trudi Renwick developed a basic needs approach to poverty in 1993 that anticipated many of the innovations of the SPM but also calculated the poverty threshold income much higher than the SPM.[13] Bergmann and Renwick began by identifying the actual expenses a household must pay for necessities such as housing, utilities, food, transportation, childcare, health-care insurance, and taxes. Household costs for these items will vary by household size, the age of household members, their labor force status, and their location. A great advantage of the basic needs budget approach to measuring poverty is that it establishes the income a household needs to live at a level widely accepted as "decent." There is, of course, room for debate over the meaning of decent, but most people would agree that in the richest nations of the world even low-income households should have safe housing with functioning utilities, healthy food, reliable transportation to and from work, basic medical care, and quality childcare.[14] Basic needs budgets cover these costs while accounting for the value of noncash benefits received by households as well as the taxes they need to pay. Building on these ideas, economists at the Economic Policy Institute (EPI) constructed a basic family budget model to capture the income below which a household would face deprivation.[15] This model accounts for every major budget item, including local costs of housing, childcare, health care, food, transportation, and taxes, and provides a more accurate picture of the income needed to achieve economic security. The EPI model yields a poverty threshold that is two to four times greater than that of the OPM, depending on location. Basic needs budgets like these present a far more accurate picture of poverty, as well as the cash assistance and subsidized services needed to relieve it, than do traditional measures.[16] They also make clear that official poverty statistics seriously undercount poverty in the United States.

All of the measures described above capture poverty via a purely material approach, where income or consumption are used to measure the well-being of households. While a useful tool for capturing trends in poverty across time and across nations, and for identifying which groups might be at higher risk of poverty, the material approach provides limited explanation for the deprivation of women and other groups.[17] Some feminist economists and policy experts have therefore called for a reconceptualization of poverty along multidimensional lines that consider both economic and social factors to capture the gender gaps in well-being. The most influential of these alternative framings of poverty measurement is the capabilities approach, developed by feminist economist Amartya Sen.[18] The capabilities approach to understanding poverty is complicated, but a basic explanation is that it focuses on the constraints that are placed on a person's ability to achieve basic levels of well-being. These constraints include income, of course. But they also include other elements such as differential access to food, education, and medical care based on one's social location; differential treatment from sexism, racism, homophobia, ageism, and the like; other forms of social marginalization and social exclusion such as incarceration; physical, legal, and housing insecurity; lack of ability to participate in decision-making and have an influence on factors that affect one's life; exposure to environmental harms; and other related factors.

An illustrative example would be the social norms in many parts of the world that have historically favored boys' education over girls. Globally, boys' disproportionate access to school enhances their capabilities to achieve financial and other forms of security that improve their well-being, while girls' continued lack of access constrains them. Another example would be that boys who are born into low-income families in poor cities in the United States do not have access to the educational, care, community support, or other resources needed to achieve a decent level of well-being. As a consequence of these capabilities deprivations, they make far less than the national average for their gender and also have lives that are much more insecure.[19] This deprivation is especially acute for young

African American and Latino men. The capabilities approach is captured in key international indicators of poverty and inequality, such as the United Nations' Human Development Index and the Sustainable Development Goals.

The capabilities approach has helped feminist scholars explain why official, income-based household-level poverty data doesn't capture inequitable gender distributions of food, medical care, education, and other resources that put women and girls at greater risk of poverty. Women and girls' abilities to access these resources is determined not only by overall household income but also by their agency in household decision-making, the ideas that families and societies have about their worth, their access to and control over income or income-producing assets, vulnerability to violence, legal rights within the family, and/or other noneconomic factors.[20] These insights, and attention to the economic vulnerability of women and girls in traditional patriarchal households, are lost when understandings of poverty are based on official, material, household-level measures rather than multidimensional approaches.

Lack of attention to these issues also creates misunderstandings about the poverty of single mothers. Since much of the literature has focused on the crisis of poverty for this group, clearing up these misunderstandings is crucial if we aim to improve their well-being. While being without a male partner (and their earnings) can certainly exacerbate poverty for female heads, they could actually gain in other ways. Households headed by women may, for instance, have more control over the income that does come into the household, have less vulnerability to erratic support from their male partners, and/or enjoy a greater degree of well-being because they have less conflict or violence in their lives.[21] Policies aiming to reduce the poverty of women heading households through marriage promotion strategies, such as the United States has implemented since the 1990s, may therefore fail on their own terms. Some of these women could very well face more economic insecurity in coupled arrangements than otherwise. Moreover, such policies may provide an incentive for women to stay in abusive situations because of economic necessity, sometimes with tragic consequences.

Yet despite these valid criticisms of the material approach to understanding policy coming out of feminist economics, most of the existing research on poverty in the global North continues to use it. Therefore, in the discussion of antipoverty policies below, we will largely draw on such measures but will take a more multidimensional approach where possible.

Causes of Women's Poverty in the Global North

The reasons that women find themselves at greater risk of falling into poverty are interconnected. Many of these revolve around women's experiences in labor markets. The fact that working women earn less than men, as we discussed in the previous chapter, is part of the story. Occupational segregation by gender, also discussed in the previous chapter, plays a role as well. Women are concentrated in lower-paying occupations that are also less likely to come with benefits such as retirement plans, health insurance, or other job-related supports, which places women at higher risks of poverty now and in their retirement future. These jobs are also more likely to be precarious, part-time, and temporary than those in so-called masculine occupations, although since the 2008 global economic crisis, men and women alike have increasingly found themselves in the kind of insecure positions that make them vulnerable to poverty.

The difficulty that those on the bottom of the job ladder have finding full-time and reliable employment, coupled with stagnating wages in these fields, has placed many workers into the ranks of the working poor who earn less than the official poverty threshold, which already drastically understates actual poverty. Among those who are officially defined as poor in the United States and are not children, the elderly, or disabled (meaning those who are part of the working population), 52 percent were working. Women are more likely to be among the working poor in the United States than men, with over 7 percent of women and 5.5 percent of men in the labor force falling below the poverty line. Migrant workers were also more likely to be among the working poor than other groups, as are black and Hispanic women.[22] In the European Union, women and men were as likely to be among the working poor, but for somewhat different reasons. For men, being a migrant worker, a sole father, the primary source of income in a dual partner household, or disabled creates a higher risk of being among the working poor. For women, citizenship status is also a large factor, but so is working part-time—which for many women workers is not their choice—along with old age, sole motherhood, and especially primary responsibility for unpaid care work at home.[23]

Changes in the economy over the past few decades, related to globalization and restructuring, have in many ways influenced these labor-related aspects of poverty. Since the 1980s, the view that unregulated "free" markets are the best way to promote economic growth has gained credence. Many have been negatively affected by economic policies, enacted in the name of economic growth, that have led to deteriorating conditions of employment. Of course, a handful of those at the top have benefited enormously as well. Evidence of this can be seen in the relative decline of the wage share of national income, the stagnation of wages and other employee compensation relative to profits and executive pay, and the secular trend toward higher rates of underemployment and unemployment across the global North.[24] The related shifts of transnational corporations seeking out the cheapest workers, the decline of unionization, the dismantling of national protections for workers, the erosion of social supports, and waves of economic crisis have contributed to stagnating wages, particularly in the English-speaking countries of the United States, the United Kingdom, and Australia. These shifts have also pushed more people into precarious working conditions. More recently, automation, the "gig" economy, and new technologies such as algorithmic scheduling of workers have trapped many workers in situations where their incomes are unpredictable.

Another key factor that contributes to women's disproportionate rates of poverty is age. Elderly women are at greater risk of poverty because of the income inequality they experienced over the course of their lives. They are therefore likely to have fewer savings and other assets compared to men. Further, many national pension and social security benefits are based on earlier earnings. These issues are compounded by the fact that women tend to live longer than men. Feminist scholars have pointed to programs that provide universal supports to the elderly regardless of work history, such as those in Finland and the Netherlands, as a more equitable alternative, alongside policies to address the labor market inequities that create the gender income gap that places elderly women at a higher risk of poverty than men in the first place.[25]

Women's disproportionate responsibility for care work is a key reason they are more likely to face poverty. The burden of these responsibilities either reduces the hours they can work, limits the range of occupations available to them, or keeps them out of the labor force entirely. For single parents of all genders and races, these tensions between care responsibility and income-earning place them at risk of poverty. But single parents who are in groups that already face discrimination in the labor market have the highest likelihood of poverty. In the United States, more than one-third of all female-headed households are in poverty, a statistic that has remained more or less constant for a couple of decades. Rates in the United Kingdom are about the same, and in Germany, France, and southern European nations they are a bit lower. In contrast, Nordic country rates of poverty among single mothers are on average below 10 percent.[26] What explains these differences? In the Nordic countries, single mothers have higher employment rates because of strong policy supports such as paid parental leave and subsidized childcare. Their wage is also higher compared to other nations. The United States in particular is a country where poverty-wage jobs, not low employment rates, play a role in structuring single mothers' poverty. Compared to other countries, US single mothers who work full-time are less likely to work in jobs that pay wages above the poverty line than their counterparts in other global North countries.[27] Another major factor in explaining different national outcomes in the poverty of female-headed households is the variance in antipoverty programs between countries in the global North, a topic we turn to in the next section of the chapter.

Gender and Welfare Regimes

As we have already touched upon, the poverty alleviation policies of different countries have a large effect on women's poverty risk, as well as on the poverty rate of the population in general. These policies are also deeply gendered. Generally speaking, the nations with the highest level of assistance have the least poverty, while the nations with low levels of support have the most poverty. Comparing poverty rates among the Western nations that are at similar levels of economic development, we find that the United States has the highest incidence of poverty despite being one of the wealthiest countries in terms of per capital income. During the 1990s, 16.9 percent of the US population lived in poverty. In 2016 that number rose to 17.8 percent. Poverty in the European nations is far lower, but it too has risen since the 1990s. In that decade the poverty rate for the Netherlands and France was 8.1 percent; by 2016 it rose to 8.31 percent. The German rate during the same period rose from 7.5 percent to 10 percent, Sweden from 6.6 percent to 9.3 percent, and Finland from 5.1 percent to 6.3 percent. The reasons for these differences have a lot to do with the different antipoverty policies these countries adopted. Those differences, in turn, have to do with the variety of ways that national regimes imagine how economies can deliver a decent standard of living, different national attitudes about inequality and social justice, and different gender ideologies that guide policy frameworks.

The history of modern antipoverty policy in the global North emerged in the wake of the worldwide economic downturn of the 1930s, when the persistence of widespread poverty led many to share the view that all citizens were entitled to protection from the economy's worst effects. Consequently, by the mid-twentieth century, most countries in the global North put social welfare policies into place. However, there were significant differences in how such programs were designed and implemented, and over time there have been additional shifts in policy.

The classification of welfare-state programs developed by Gøsta Esping-Andersen provides insight into these differences. Looking at the global North, he divided welfare states into three categories: liberal, corporatist, or universalist.[28] A liberal welfare state is one that is based on the idea that free markets are the best way to resolve income distribution and poverty. Policies in countries that take this approach tend to do little to alter the market distribution of income and offer meager assistance to the poor. Assistance is itself means-tested—in order to be eligible a person needs to prove they are poor—and those who receive support are often stigmatized. Poverty tends to be blamed on individual failure in the liberal schema, but some accommodations may be made for children, the disabled, and the elderly. The United States today, the United Kingdom, Australia, and Canada are examples of liberal welfare states.

Corporatist regimes, in the Esping-Andersen schema, are premised on the notion that the state has a significant responsibility to alleviate the inequities resulting from markets. Although corporatist state policies are relatively more generous than liberal ones, class status and gender hierarchies are reinforced because benefits are differentiated according to occupation and status. Germany and France are good examples of corporatist welfare-state regimes.

Universalist regimes, in contrast, are premised on the notion that all citizens are entitled to a decent standard of living. These regimes provide widely available, generous income subsidies to the poor, universal access to health care, subsidized or free childcare and eldercare, inexpensive public transportation, and/or significant housing subsidies. The Scandinavian countries and the Netherlands have adopted this approach with the positive result that in these countries poverty rates, including those for women and children, are the lowest in the world.

Esping-Andersen's classification, however, does not take gender ideology into account, and consequently only gives us part of the picture. To better understand the interconnected causes of women's poverty we discussed earlier in the chapter, feminist scholars consider the ways in which welfare-state regimes either transform or reproduce gender relations.[29] To this end, Diane Sainsbury proposes a typology that classifies welfare regimes based on how well they help women form autonomous, nonpoor households absent marriage to a male or living with other related adults.[30] The male breadwinner regime is one premised on traditional gender ideology. It assumes that men should participate in the paid labor force and women should remain economically dependent in the home, responsible for housework and child-rearing, but not income earning. Here marriage is a privileged institution, supported and encouraged by the structures of tax and benefit policies. Women's benefits are tied to their marital status, and married women's labor force participation is discouraged. Since traditional marriage is the preferred norm, single women and divorced women are at a relative disadvantage. The US welfare state regime, while it has undergone some changes, continues to fall into this category.

Sainsbury's individual earner-carer regime, in contrast, is based on an ideology of equal rights for women and men based on their shared roles and obligations. Both women and men are entitled to benefits. Policies are structured to encourage men to become caregivers as well as workers, and likewise for women to become workers as well as caregivers. Social rights and tax obligations accrue to individuals rather than to families. Shared parenting, female labor force participation, and gender equality are all features of these sorts of regimes. Moreover, the costs of children and other dependents are shared through the public provision of services and childcare allowances. These are the policies that have been pursued in the Nordic countries.

Sainsbury's work helps us understand the persistent and disproportionate poverty of lone mothers, especially in the English-speaking world. It also helps us to understand why more than three times the percentage of single mothers are poor in the United States and United Kingdom when compared to the Nordic countries, as we discussed in the section above. Despite ongoing conservative rhetoric to the contrary, this poverty is not the result of the pathological behavior of single mothers. It is instead the result of the gendered structures of our current policy regimes. Tax policies, transfer payments, parental leave, and the provision of generous public services including childcare can dramatically reduce the poverty of female-headed households. Thus, if the object of social and economic policy is to improve the well-being of families, then policymakers can and should enact welfare-state regimes that couple employment supports with generous subsidies. If, in contrast, the object of social and economic policy is to punish the poor by making lone-mother families scapegoats for social problems, then policymakers will enact welfare-state regimes that compel low-skill workers to choose between caring for their children or working at jobs that do not pay living wages. In this latter case, lone mothers and their dependents suffer even greater deprivation as material poverty interacts with increasing social isolation, demeaning regulations, and public humiliation. Unfortunately, recent changes in US economic and social policy seem far more concerned with scapegoating the poor, especially poor mothers, and transferring the burdens of care at least partially on to the backs of poor women from the global South, than with actually alleviating economic hardships.

A Brief History of US Antipoverty Policies

The history of the United States' contemporary antipoverty policy can be traced back to the Great Depression of the 1930s. During that period, almost one-quarter of the workforce was unemployed, the nation's output fell by a third, severe drought combined with falling agricultural prices led to massive waves of farm foreclosures, and hundreds of thousands of businesses and banks went bankrupt. These ruptures in the economy and society challenged the reigning ideas of the time that free markets were the path to the widest prosperity for all. It was in this environment that political leaders gained support for the social legislation of the New Deal such as unemployment compensation, publicly funded retirement pensions, workers' compensation, and other supports aimed at providing some measure of economic security for workers and their dependents.

Of the many policies and agencies comprising the New Deal, the most important was the 1935 Social Security Act which created a system of benefits including Supplemental Security Income, social security pensions, widow's pensions, and income for the disabled. Everyone was, in theory, eligible for these benefits. Further, they were not means-tested. But access to these programs was not, at the outset, available to all citizens. Pressure from conservatives, especially those in the segregated Jim Crow South, led to policy guidelines that excluded agricultural and domestic workers. As a result, African Americans and other ethnic minorities who were largely employed on farms and as household help were not covered by these programs. In addition, eligibility standards were not enacted at the federal level, leaving state and local authorities (especially in segregated rural areas) free to discriminate at will.

Even more important for our understanding of the gender politics of these programs, both social security and unemployment compensation were premised on a traditional male breadwinner–female caretaker model of the family.[31] It is important to note here that African American women and working-class white and migrant women, who had a long history of working for pay, were effectively excluded from these benefits because they were structured around a male-breadwinner household model. Male breadwinners and their dependents were seen as deserving because the hardships they faced—loss of income due to retirement, disability, or unemployment for men, or widowhood for women—were due to circumstances beyond their individual control.[32] Thus programs that benefited men and their traditional families were considered entitlements and were relatively secure. Such was not the case for programs aimed at women with children who were not connected by marriage to a male earner. They were cast in a negative light. Since women were supposed to be economically dependent on men, those women who were not dependent—because they had never been married, they had been deserted, or they were divorced—were seen as morally deficient. Thus a moral code separated the deserving from the undeserving poor, a way of thinking about anti-poverty programs that continues to this day.

The one program designed specifically to help poor mothers who were neither married nor widowed was Aid to Dependent Children (ADC), which later became Aid to Families with Dependent Children (AFDC). AFDC was not an entitlement but rather a publicly funded charity. It provided low levels of means-tested support for mothers who were divorced, abandoned, or never married. In addition, program provisions required that persons receiving these benefits have their lives closely scrutinized by caseworkers who had enormous power to increase or decrease benefit levels, to provide or withhold access to noncash benefits, and even to break up families by declaring a woman "unfit" for motherhood.

In the early 1960s, President Johnson's War on Poverty programs expanded US welfare-state policies. Civil rights groups, women's groups, welfare rights organizations, and other activists worked with the Johnson administration to create a host of new programs and policies. In this period there was an increase in the minimum wage to lift the working poor out of poverty, Medicaid and Medicare were enacted, food stamp programs were expanded, and new public housing projects were constructed. In addition, other subsidies and services to expand opportunities for low-income Americans were enacted. Civil rights activists were able to get obstacles to African American participation in many entitlement programs removed so that African Americans too could receive benefits for which they were eligible. Other notable gains for African Americans were won in Congress and at the state level, and for the first time an African American served on a president's cabinet. These policy changes were an important positive step toward the expansion of opportunity, greater economic equality—especially for Americans of color—and the reduction of poverty.

But despite their progressive intent, these Great Society programs were, like the New Deal policies of the 1930s, built on a male breadwinner–female caretaker model of the family that disadvantaged many women, particularly the increasing numbers of single mothers. AFDC, the primary program for poor women, was premised on the idea that mothers with young children ought not be in the labor force. As a result, this program contained many strong disincentives for mothers' participation in the paid labor force. AFDC recipients, for example, faced an effective tax of 100 percent on all earned income since for every dollar they earned they lost a dollar of benefits. Another disincentive included the treatment of assets. Even when a woman's only asset was her house, the value of the asset could be used to disqualify her from receiving benefits despite her level of need. A third disincentive was the lack of affordable childcare. This left single mothers with no real choices about how to organize their lives. Lacking access to the income of a man, they could either try to take care of their families by stretching the miserly benefits paid by state welfare agencies, or they could take low-wage jobs that by and large did not offer benefits (medical, paid vacations, or contributions to retirement account) and pay for childcare out of pocket. This policy combination did indeed create a trap for lone mothers.

In addition, as the feminist historian Linda Gordon points out, the AFDC program was stigmatized from the very beginning. Under the prevailing male-breadwinner gender ideology, women and children were seen as male dependents. Needing government support due to the absence of a male head of household was seen as evidence of deep moral failure. This attitude allowed conservatives to cast income transfers to lone mothers as undeserved handouts that lead to dependency, promiscuity, and other social pathologies. Even though many other income support programs are analytically indistinguishable from what Americans have come to call "welfare," the beneficiaries of those programs—veteran's benefits, social security, Medicaid, and unemployment compensation—were far less likely to be stigmatized in this way.

In the 1980s, the rhetoric in the media and in political speech about poverty became increasingly racialized. This was not something new. The race coding of America's poverty problem certainly helped conservative politicians mobilize support for the dismantling of the progressive policies of the 1960s. But in the 1980s, then-president Ronald Reagan escalated things with constant references to epidemic welfare fraud, personified in a black "Welfare Queen" whose cheating of the system enabled her to drive a Cadillac and otherwise live in luxury. The Welfare Queen eventually became a symbol of all black women who received welfare, and this symbol influenced the public's views of assistance to the poor. Even today most Americans wrongly think that the majority of recipients of public benefits are black. At that time other myths about welfare recipients, including the idea that mothers on welfare have additional children only to qualify for greater benefits, as well as the idea that welfare spending had skyrocketed and was a burden on the taxpayers, began to circulate widely. In fact, no reputable research has ever shown a positive correlation between benefit levels and the number of children of welfare recipients, nor was AFDC (as a share of federal spending) particularly large. Nevertheless, this inflammatory rhetoric shaped a political climate favorable to the virtual elimination of any federal guarantee to a decent standard of living for lone mothers and their children.

In 1996, during President Bill Clinton's first term, AFDC—welfare as we know it—was eliminated and replaced by a block grant called Temporary Assistance to Needy Families (TANF). While the old regime of anti-poverty programs for lone mothers were aimed at replacing the wage of the male breadwinner, the new regime celebrated the "dignity of work" and required these mothers to ultimately get off of public support by getting a job. One provision of TANF, for instance, is that recipients whose youngest child is over a year old and have received benefits for two years must get a job or lose their benefits entirely. Benefits under TANF are time-limited, with a lifetime maximum of five years and with no provisions for exceptions. Not surprisingly, in the boom economic conditions of the mid-to-late 1990s, coupled with the aggressiveness with which recipients were denied benefits, there was a reduction in the number of people receiving welfare. There was also an increase in the number of single mothers in the labor force. Prior to the passage of TANF, 63.5 percent of single mothers were employed, and fifteen years later that number rose to 67.8 percent.[33] Poverty rates among single mothers during this same period fell initially from approximately 36 percent in 1996 to 29 percent in 2000, but then rose during the first decade of this century to reach 34 percent. This suggests there was not a significant impact on poverty in the long run.[34] In fact, more than 1.5 million households in the United States are living on less than $2 a day as a direct consequence of the rollout of TANF.

Why is that? The jobs of former TANF recipients are almost all low-paid, service sector jobs with irregular work hours, lacking in benefits such as paid sick days, and little chance for advancement. In fact, over three-fourths of former TANF recipients are concentrated in four low-wage occupations: service, clerical, laborers, and sales.[35] Because the increase in social spending for childcare, housing, public transportation, education, and skills development has been minimal, these policies failed to reduce poverty among lone mothers and their families.

Consequently, many low-income lone mothers have been forced into what feminist economist and poverty expert Randy Albelda calls a match made in hell.[36] That is, their lives are characterized by low-paid work with few benefits that keeps them poor, plus very few public supports for childcare or other needs, which makes it difficult for them to both work and make sure their children's health and safety are assured. Although there is some money allocated for childcare subsidies by the federal government, it is in the form of a block grants, and the states have a great deal of flexibility to set the rules governing eligibility and the amount of funding provided. Consequently, childcare subsidy programs vary greatly across states. Moreover, the funding is inadequate as it can only serve about 15 percent of eligible families.[37] Families living at or below the poverty line face childcare costs that are nearly 20 percent of family income, and the high cost of childcare is one of the greatest threats to a poor family's economic security. Almost all families, of course, struggle with childcare, but in contrast to the poorest families, the average family devotes about 10 percent of their income to childcare.[38] This is in contrast to the European countries, where families enjoy relatively generous support and subsidies for early childhood care. Thus many poor women struggle to balance meeting their children's needs with the need to work as required by TANF. The link between women's poverty and the well-being of children could hardly be clearer.

The situation for poor black mothers and their children is compounded because of the intersection of gender, race, and class in structuring their experiences of poverty. Black women in poverty are even more likely to find themselves in low-wage and precarious work than their white counterparts. Their unemployment rates are higher also. Consequently, their households are twice as likely to be poor as households headed by white women.[39] They also continue to be subject to the stereotypes and biases associated with the Welfare Queen trope and are more often than other groups punished by society as dysfunctional "bad mothers." The case of Debra Harrell, a black single mother, is illustrative of this point. Unable to afford childcare on her McDonald's wages, she let her daughter play under the supervision of other adults in a local park one day when she had to work, giving her a cell phone so that she could call in case of emergency. But then a person walking by the park asked the daughter where her mother was and discovered she was not in the park with her child but at work. Consequently, the passerby called the police to report child neglect. This led to Harrell's arrest and the removal of her daughter and placement into foster care. Harrell's is not an isolated case of criminalization of a poor black mother because of the impossibility of juggling both work and care in the absence of childcare supports. Shanesha Taylor, a homeless black mother, left her children in a car while going to a job interview that she believed would turn her family's fortune around. But a person saw Taylor's son crying in the car and called the police. Taylor was arrested and her children placed into foster care. While the mothers were initially stigmatized in both of these cases, they also eventually gained significant social support, as many could relate to the desperate situation they were in.[40] One can only imagine the many similar cases that never attracted attention in the media. Moreover, the initial shaming and criminalization the mothers faced is at least in part related to the way that stereotypes about the failings of the poor, particularly poor women of color, continue to be highlighted in US political discourse. These stereotypes distract attention from the structural inequalities, such as a lack of good jobs and lack of supports for those responsible for unpaid care work, that are the primary cause of poverty. They also distract attention from the fact that many in United States are themselves just one step away from poverty, with 40 percent of Americans unable to come up with $400 in an emergency situation.[41]

Gender and Alternative Poverty Alleviation Policies

Given the failures of current antipoverty policies to address deep and persistent hardship in the United States, poverty researchers and activists have offered a range of alternative policy proposals. Some of these tackle the work side of poverty, both in terms of unemployment and the high proportion of the poor that are in low-wage and precarious jobs. Some proposals aim to improve the education and training of low-wage workers so that they can get better jobs. One innovative proposal is a national community college program that provides low- or no-cost tuition plus additional supports to improve employment prospects for low-wage workers.[42] Other proposals aim to help families address their lack of resources in other ways. Various proposals for addressing the lack of resources in poor families include a transfer for poor families with children, a renters tax credit for poor families to address the high cost of housing, and a minimum guaranteed benefit through Social Security for elderly people who do not have an extensive work history.[43]

Among the most widely discussed and innovative antipoverty strategies is the federal jobs guarantee, in which the government would provide voluntary job opportunities at a living wage and a basic benefits package for anyone who wants them. While the idea of a jobs guarantee has been in discussion for a while, in recent years it has gained significant traction among economists and progressive politicians. One element of the Green New Deal being discussed widely in the United States, for instance, is the jobs guarantee program to provide employment for those who have been displaced from work because of natural disasters, economic restructuring, recessions, and the like into employment in the emerging green economy.[44] The jobs guarantee addresses a failing of TANF, namely its assumption that getting poor mothers into the labor force would end their poverty. In too many cases the jobs that were available to many of these mothers did not enable them to provide an acceptable, basic standard of living for their families.[45] The reason is quite simple: these jobs did not pay a living wage. The jobs guarantee as a poverty alleviation strategy, in contrast, can help eliminate working poverty, reduce the high rates of unemployment that plague some communities in America, and alleviate the economic insecurity that low-wage workers experience in a volatile economy.[46] Experiments in national jobs guarantee antipoverty policies include Argentina, which spent 1 percent of its annual GDP on a works program that provided half-time work to poor people. This program enrolled approximately two million people, or 5 percent of the population. Approximately two-thirds of the participants were women, and the program was successful in lifting them out of poverty.[47]

Universal basic income (UBI) is another poverty-alleviation strategy idea that has gained significant traction in the past few years. UBI is a cash transfer program in which the government provides individuals with enough to meet their basic needs regardless of their work status. Ideas about basic income have been around for decades, but lately concerns about income inequality and poverty, precarious work, and the expansion of labor-replacing technologies have renewed interest in this policy idea. While UBI is often associated with one of its conservative proponents, Milton Friedman (who advocated it largely as a bureaucracy-reduction strategy),[48] it also has more radical, and feminist, roots. For instance, in the 1960s the National Welfare Rights Organization, a coalition of poor black mothers, called for basic income to support the important but unrecognized unpaid care work of low-income women. UBI has been implemented on a trial basis in a number of the Nordic countries, forms the spine of antipoverty policy in South Africa, and has been rolled out in selective provinces of Canada. A growing number of economists and politicians are recommending it as an effective poverty-alleviation program for the US context. While critics argue that a universal basic income will result in a strong disincentive to work and thus decline in overall economic productivity, evidence from some experiments with the idea show that most people do not stop working, with the exception of women previously in low-wage work, who used the stipend to stay out of the workforce and care for their children.[49] Feminist theorist Kathi Weeks strongly advocates for the implementation of UBI to challenge women's historical dependence on wages or marriage to support themselves and their families. Weeks, who believes that changes in technology and labor processes are ushering in a "post-work" world, also supports basic income because the economic system is currently not providing an adequate number of quality employment opportunities. She contends, and we agree, that guaranteed income can provide people with the increased time and freedom they desire, while altering the rules of the game in terms of what kinds of productive contributions are valued by society.[50]

Conclusion

Contemporary poverty research recognizes not only the material but also the personal and social costs of poverty. Poverty is more than just a lack of income. Poverty creates multidimensional hardships when people and communities confront unemployment, low income, family breakdown, inadequate housing, bad schools, high crime, and poor health. Since poverty is multidimensional, solutions to it require multidimensional responses. Unfortunately, in many countries power has accrued to politicians who advance the view that the private costs of market intervention are greater than the social benefits of reduced poverty, deprivation, and misery. Further, and contrary to a growing body of evidence on the subject, these politicians argue that hard work and effort alone allow people to lift themselves out of poverty. Anyone who is poor, then, is seen as lazy or otherwise pathological. These characterizations often fall hardest on poor women, who are portrayed as "bad mothers" in addition to all of the other negative stereotypes, and fall harder still on poor women of color who continue to be haunted by the trope of the Welfare Queen. It sometimes seems as if there is an unbridgeable gulf between an explanation of poverty that rests on a negative characterization of the poor and another that roots it in the structure of the economy. And yet as different experiments with pro-market solutions to poverty show, all too tragically, the cracks in such logic, and alternative regimes that address structural factors yield better results, the conversation seems to be turning toward more effective solutions to gendered poverty and inequality.

6 | Globalization Is a Feminist Issue

Globalization, as we know it today, is made possible by digital technologies that make global communications instantaneous; by improvements in transportation that decrease costs; and by neoliberal policies that deregulate flows of people, financial capital, and goods and services. It is a process of integrating countries, peoples, economies, and cultures into a larger whole through politics, commerce, and trade. It has its roots in the 1960s and 1970s, when technological improvements enabled profound structural changes in the global economy. Global financial markets were able to operate around the clock on a global scale. Multinational corporations from the global North were able to outsource manufacturing to plants in the global South, where wages were a fraction of what they were in the North, and consumers, whose incomes allowed it, were able to buy commodities from all over the world. However, globalization's long history stretches back to the Venetian traders of the late thirteenth century. Trading then entailed long, arduous journeys along what came to be known as the Silk Road and, later, perilous sea voyages that led to the "discovery" and ensuing colonization of the Americas and, subsequently, Africa, India, and Southeast Asia. The legacy of colonization, including the enslavement of African people during the mid-seventeenth century, and the resulting hierarchies of gender, race, and nations that it created, continues to haunt the global economy.

Legacies of Colonialism

In its early years, globalization was a story of increased wealth for Europeans and one of colonization, exploitation, and enslavement for the peoples of the conquered continents. Consider the living conditions in Europe before the fifteenth century. Peasants and nobles alike subsisted on an ordinary and meager diet that consisted mainly of bread, barley, and other grains (of course, the nobles had more). Other foods such as meat, dairy, vegetables, and fruit were subsidiary to grains.[1] Their clothing was made from wool or animal skins, warm in the winter but hot and itchy in the summer (although the wealthier classes had access to linen as well). Perhaps it is no wonder that they would relish the silks and spices brought back to Europe by Venetian traders. We have all heard of Marco Polo and his account of his travels along the Silk Road. Less well-known, however, is the role that women played in this story. Silk production in China was women's work. The skills and knowledge necessary for silk production were firmly in the hands of Chinese women. The meticulous production process involved raising silkworms and then carefully unraveling the cocoons to creates long threads, which were then spun together and woven to make silk. It was women's work, skills, and knowledge that lay behind the thriving economy of China and the global connections forged by the Silk Road.[2]

The desire for silk and other commodities from Asia, such as tea and spices, posed a problem for the Europeans. As the economic anthropologist David Graeber puts it, the Asians were not interested in much of anything that the Europeans produced. So, Europeans had to pay in gold and silver, and to do this they needed to find new sources for these minerals. In 1492, Christopher Columbus landed in the Americas and came upon vast reserves of gold and silver. The Spanish and Portuguese saw these riches as theirs for the taking. Since the weapons possessed by the indigenous people were no match for the Spaniards' guns, swords, and armor, it was easy to brutally and viciously exploit their labor in order to extract the precious metals.[3]

The period between the fifteenth century and the late seventeenth century is called the Age of Exploration. During this time, European nations embarked on sea journeys to seek out new lands and new riches in the Americas, Africa, and South Asia. The colonies of England, France, Holland, Spain, Portugal, Germany, and Russia provided the raw minerals, precious metals, and cash crops that were essential to the emergence of capitalism and consumer society.[4] A trade triangle emerged as ships traveled from Europe to West Africa carrying manufactured goods; Africans were enslaved and transported to the Americas to work on plantations growing sugar, cotton, and tobacco, which were then transported back to Europe, where they fueled the industrial revolution and enriched the living standards of the Europeans. As Eric Hobsbawm's *Industry and Empire* makes clear, Western economic development depended on colonial exploitation.[5]

From the fifteenth through the twentieth centuries, the imperialist nations of Europe relied on a combination of bribery, force, and persuasion to impose political, cultural, and economic systems on the institutions and customs of indigenous peoples. When indigenous kinship structures, economic relations, or patterns of land use interfered with colonial interests, they were undermined or destroyed. Consider the transformation of indigenous family life. European colonizers brought with them a model of the Western, patriarchal family, with all its rigidities regarding the sexual division of labor and appropriate spheres for women and men. When this gender ideology was grafted onto existing traditional, patriarchal social norms, gender inequalities in colonial societies were exacerbated, worsening women's social and economic status. In some cases, the colonizers created inequitable societies where women once had significant power. The historian Carolyn Ross Johnston's 2013 book, *Voices of Cherokee Women*, documents the ways that settler-colonial policies in the United States eroded Cherokee women's political and economic power within the tribe during the nineteenth century by, for instance, refusing to trade or make political treaties with women. Women did not regain their power until the American Indian Movement of the 1960s and 1970s.

Limiting women to the domestic sphere, classifying domestic labor as unskilled, and denying customary land rights damaged both women and their communities. In many African and Asian countries, women, not men, had primary responsibility for agricultural work, and land was held and farmed communally. When the Europeans changed the laws of land ownership and the patterns of land use to mirror those of the West, women lost their customary rights to farm the land. As women were squeezed out of agriculture and pushed into economic dependency in the household, their social and economic status declined, and with it the well-being of their communities.[6]

Western gender ideology was also an intrinsic part of the concept of colonialism as a civilizing mission. In the Victorian era, the treatment of women was considered the measuring rod of civilization, and freeing women from the oppression of their own cultures was part of the moral justification for the colonial enterprise. These words by Thomas Jefferson are a telling example,

The [American Indian] women are subjected to unjust drudgery. This I believe is the case with every barbarous people. With such, force is law. The stronger sex imposes on the weaker. It is civilization alone which replaces women in the enjoyment of their natural equality.[7]

No doubt there were some who truly believed in this civilizing mission of gender equality. We cannot know. What we do know is that the laws and policies that were forthcoming undermined women's autonomy and destroyed indigenous ways of life. Although Jefferson is talking specifically about American Indians, similar sentiments were expressed about the peoples of India and sub-Saharan Africa. The feminist political scientist Cynthia Enloe points to the hypocrisy of the British in India who banned traditional practices such as sati, while at the same time enacted laws that imposed a system of prostitution that provided Indian women to sexually service British soldiers stationed in India. The actual purpose of these contradictory policies was not to end male domination of women, but rather to establish European male rule over the men in the colonies.[8]

The period of colonial expansion came to an end in the decades following World War II. The European colonial empires in Asia and Africa were overthrown, and newly independent nation-states were formed.[9] The new nations came into existence in the context of an international order shaped by the Cold War between the United States and the Soviet Union, which created serious challenges for creating cohesive national identities and sovereign political institutions.[10] Many were extremely poor. Their industrial infrastructure—roads, factories, and communication networks—had been built to meet the needs of the colonial powers rather than their own. Moreover, their economic, social, and political structures and institutions had been severely disrupted. These problems were exacerbated by the Cold War because these new countries had become the terrain on which the ideological battles between the United States and the Soviet Union were played out. This created a fertile ground for an international economic order that overwhelmingly favored the interests of the industrialized North while pushing the new nation-states of the Third World deeper into poverty and militarism.[11]

The institutions for regulating international economic relations—the International Monetary Fund (IMF), the International Bank for Reconstruction and Development (now called the World Bank), and the General Agreement on Tariffs and Trade (GATT)—were created after the end of World War II to manage this new world order. Regulating international finance was the job of the IMF, providing long-term development loans the function of the World Bank, and setting the rules for international trade the province of the GATT (which is no longer in existence, having evolved into the World Trade Organization, or WTO). All of these institutions were dominated by policymakers and academics trained in Western Europe and the United States. They believed that the solution to the extreme poverty and immiseration of the Third World was Western-style economic development. Economists and policymakers endorsed a simple recipe: Third World development required rural, subsistence-agricultural economies to transform themselves in the image of the West and become modern, industrialized, high-consumption market systems. The stages through which economies passed in their development from traditional to modern could be speeded up through large-scale, government-directed investments in infrastructure like dams, factories, roads, and energy generation.

Global Poverty

In the first edition of this book, we argued that globalization had increased poverty and exacerbated inequality, both within countries and among countries. We reported that half of the world's population, 2.8 billion people at that time, lived in poverty on less than $2 per day, and that 1.2 billion lived in extreme poverty on $1 per day or less. According to the World Bank's calculations for 2015, this has improved. To account for changes in the purchasing power of money, the World Bank's poverty thresholds have changed to $1.90 per day for extreme poverty and $3.20 per day for poverty. In 2015, 1.94 billion people live below the poverty threshold of $3.20 per day and 737 million live below the threshold for extreme poverty of $1.90 per day.[12]

On the face of it, this seems to bolster the argument that globalization and neoliberalism bring prosperity to the impoverished people of the world through free markets and Western-style economic growth. Jason Hickel, an economic anthropologist, calls this the "good news narrative," and argues that it serves as a potent political tool. It implies that sticking with the status quo is the best way to end poverty and that we are "living through the golden age of poverty reduction."[13] However, there are many problems with this story. The poverty threshold is extraordinarily low. Hickel suggests that a minimum of $7.40 would be necessary for basic nutrition and normal life expectancy. Using that poverty threshold, he estimates that the number of people living under $7.40 per day has not fallen, indeed it has risen—from 3.19 billion in 1981 to 4.16 billion in 2013, or 58 percent of the world's population.[14]

While we do not have precise statistics for the number of women and children living in poverty, we do know that women are far more likely than men to live in poverty. The reasons are simple. First, consider the wage gap. Across the world women earn 24 percent less than men, and 700 million fewer women than men are in paid work. Second, there is a lack of decent work. Seventy-five percent of women in the developing world work in the informal economy with little social rights or protections. Third, they do the vast majority of unpaid care work, and this is on top of their paid work. Fourth, they work longer hours than men, especially when paid and unpaid work are both included.[15] Fifth, the distribution of goods within households has been shown by researchers to be inequitable and often disadvantages women and girls.[16]

Income, wealth, health, and education are concentrated into fewer hands, while an ever-larger share of the world's population is consigned to poverty, disease, and illiteracy. The evidence supports this contention. In 1997, the economist Lant Pritchett published an article titled "Divergence Big Time."[17] He argued that between 1870 and 1990 incomes in the developing countries had fallen behind those in the developed countries both proportionately and absolutely. In 1870, the per capita gross domestic product (GDP) of the United States was 8.7 percent greater than that of the poorest country. By 1990, it was 45.2 percent higher. The per capita income gap increased from $1,286 in 1870 to $12,662 in 1990, an increase of 985 percent.[18] Pritchett's findings were borne out by additional research by the United Nations Development Programme (UNDP). Increasing income inequality and a lack of convergence of the rich have become accepted facts of global life. That this contradicts the good news narrative seems to have escaped notice.

This narrative changed recently in part due to the work of economist Branko Milanovic. To explain Milanovic's findings we must first explain another way that income inequality is measured: the Gini coefficient, which is a statistical measure of the distribution of income. In a place in which everyone earned the same income, the Gini coefficient would be zero. If one person earned all the income while everyone else earned nothing, the Gini coefficient would be one, or 100 if expressed as a percentage. Branco Milanovic, an acknowledged expert in measuring inequality, used the Gini coefficient to measure inequality on a global scale.[19] He found that the Gini coefficient decreased from 72.2 in 1988 to 70.5 in 2008, and 67.0 in 2011. He attributes this to the fact that although the top 1 percent grew much richer between 1998 and 2008, which would add to income inequality, inequality was reduced by the strong economic growth among people living in the areas in the middle of the global income distribution, mainly China and Southeast Asia.

These people were, in Milanovic's estimation, the clear winners from globalization because they experienced the highest rates of growth, although they remain poor relative to the developed countries. He calls them the emerging global middle class. However, the middle classes in the richer countries, Western Europe, the United States, and Japan, were the losers under globalization because their growth rates were stagnant. The richest people in the world, whom he calls the global plutocrats, were the biggest winners both in terms of income growth and absolute incomes.[20] The World Bank was happy to spread this joyous story (with far less emphasis on the winners at the top), publishing a report entitled, *Taking on Inequality: Poverty and Shared Prosperity.*[21]

But, as Jason Hickel points out, there are political and ethical implications within this story.[22] First, as noted earlier, it leads to the moral justification of the Washington-led project of globalization and the current state of the global economy. If growth in China is taken out of Milanovic's calculations, then the Gini coefficient increases rather than decreases, a fact acknowledged by Milanovic but treated as a footnote to the larger story. In addition, by examining inequality among the world's peoples as if they were one big country, and between countries as individual units, the Milanovic/World Bank story obscures the divergence between the global North and the global South. Most importantly, it understands global inequality as having nothing to do with politics or North/South power imbalances. This fits nicely with the Bank's approach to the South, which sees continuing poverty as the result of faulty institutions and misguided policies, while income growth is the result of market liberalization.

This is a misleading story. Growth in China and other countries in Southeast Asia was not due to market liberalization but rather to state-led development policies. Moreover, these development policies depended on the availability of a cheap labor force consisting mainly of young women. Gender norms encouraging young women to take care of their elderly parents, as well as pressures created by international debt regimes, provided the necessary incentives. Market liberalization policies in sub-Saharan Africa, Southeast Asia, and parts of the Caribbean and Latin America have had the opposite outcome. The gap between the richest and poorest countries is not closing. As Jason Hickel puts it,

> [a]s long as a few rich countries have the power to set the rules to their own advantage, inequality will continue to worsen. The debt system, structural adjustment, free trade agreements, tax evasion, and power asymmetries in the World Bank, the IMF, and the WTO are all major reasons that inequality is getting worse instead of better.[23]

Climate Change

The discussion thus far has centered on well-being as measured by national income, but as feminist economists we know that this is a faulty metric. The failures of using official income to measure the quality of life are generally acknowledged even by mainstream economists such as Joseph Stiglitz, who, in recent years, has called for alternative measures. But feminist economists have been at the forefront of rethinking GDP as a measure of well-being. They have called attention to its failure to account for the value of unpaid domestic labor and care work, as well as for environmental harms. As the feminist economist Marilyn Waring pointed out many years ago, because national income counts only money spent, disasters such as hurricanes or oil spills can actually increase its value.[24] National income is not adjusted for the costs of pollution and climate change, issues related to well-being that have become of increasing concern. When we first wrote this book, climate change was on the horizon but still far enough in the future that humans could take steps to deal with it.

Today, that future is here, and we have yet to act. Hurricanes, tornadoes, flooding, and drought are increasing in their intensity and likely to get worse. Huge portions of the world, particularly in Southeast Asia and sub-Saharan Africa, are becoming nearly uninhabitable. Neither the consequences of climate change nor the efforts to stop it are gender-neutral. The United Nations narrative about gender and climate change is that it has greater impact on people who are reliant on natural resources for their livelihoods and have the least capacity to respond to natural disasters. Women in poverty are the most vulnerable, and the majority of the world's poor are women. Despite the fact that gender inequalities prevent them from contributing equally to making and implementing policies, these women play a critical role in the response to climate change because of their local knowledge and their leadership in sustainable practices.[25]

Women in the United Nations story are both vulnerable and virtuous. There is truth to part of their narrative: poor women are more vulnerable to climate change, and women all over the world are more likely than men to experience poverty. According to the Women's Environment and Development Organization (WEDO), poor women are more likely to die or become injured in climate change disasters such as hurricanes and floods. In much of the global South they are responsible for providing food, fuel, and water for their families, and they are the ones who care for the children and the elderly. As access to shelter, food, fertile land, water, and fuel becomes more difficult their workload increases. Girls drop out of school to help their mothers gather wood and fetch water. Shortages of resources amplifies existing gender inequalities, and the relocation of people disrupts social support networks and family ties.[26]

The problem with the narrative of vulnerability and virtuousness is that it draws attention away from the complex intersections of gender, race, ethnicity, and poverty. Moreover, it obscures the role of power inequalities in the design and implementation of environmental policies.[27] While gender norms and gender inequality are the reasons why women are disproportionally burdened by climate change and climate disasters, power imbalances in environmental decision-making are less a matter of gender inequality than of inequalities in wealth and political influence. Consider recent changes in environmental policy in the United States. Despite the overwhelming scientific evidence that climate change is caused by the burning of fossil fuels like coal and oil, a small but extremely wealthy minority have gained control of environmental policy. They have enacted policies that favor the fossil fuel industry and hampered initiatives in sustainable energy sources such as solar and wind power.[28]

That the countries in the global South will bear the worst consequences from climate change while the global North is by far the most responsible for its causes is indisputable.[29] This is not to say the global North is immune to the effects of climate change. Severe flooding in Texas and Louisiana, wildfires on the Pacific coast of the United States, and unprecedented summer temperatures in Europe are evidence of the global nature of the crisis. Climate change is not as yet a threat to the actual survival of the people in the global North (although it certainly is in the Arctic, where rising sea levels and warming ocean currents threaten the survival of the Inuit people).[30] It is a matter of degree. A global feminist analysis of climate change needs to understand how gendered power imbalances in global governance allows the comforts and status quo in the North to take precedence over the survival of the residents of the South. The rise of neoliberalism in the West is an important factor here, and that story begins with the end of World War II.

From the Golden Age of Capitalism to Neoliberal Globalization

The period between the end of World War II until about 1975 has been called the Golden Age of Capitalism. Countries in the global North experienced strong economic growth, rising wages, and stable jobs. The economy was characterized by the mass production of standardized goods, unionized workers, and mass consumption. The implicit social contract between labor and capital ensured rising wages and stable employment, at least for white men. National governments were able to provide social welfare systems and to intervene in their economies to maintain full employment.[31] It was, however, sort of a Faustian bargain. Women were expected to fulfill their duties by happily accepting their roles as housewives and mothers. However, as we have stressed elsewhere, this never applied to all women. In the United States, people of color were excluded. Women were relegated to domestic service and men to menial jobs; both sexes worked as sharecroppers.[32]

By the late 1960s, the Faustian bargain began to unravel for reasons that were both political and economic. On the political side, mass movements for civil rights, an end to the Vietnam War, and calls for women's liberation were challenging the status quo. On the economic side, oil prices skyrocketed in 1973 after an oil embargo was imposed by OPEC on nations that supported Israel during the Yom Kippur War. Unemployment and inflation surged and ushered in a global phase of "stagflation" (little economic growth and high inflation) that lasted through the rest of the decade.[33] The economic policies that had previously seemed so successful no longer worked. Although we think that other choices could have been made, for example, a deeper market socialism that was not based on racialized and gendered labor markets, this is not what happened. Instead neoliberal ideology and policy emerged triumphant.

Neoliberalism is a school of political economy associated with Milton Friedman and Friederich von Hayek. It holds that people's well-being can best be served by "liberating entrepreneurial freedoms and skills within an institutional framework characterized by strong private property rights, free markets, and free trade."[34] Ironically, despite neoliberalism's rhetoric of freedom and choice, its first national implementation was in Chile, quite literally at gunpoint. In 1973, a coup deposed the democratically elected president, Salvador Allende, and replaced him with a military junta led by Augusto Pinochet. The University of Chicago economist, Milton Friedman, best known for selling the idea that markets and "freedom" should be one and the same, and "the Chicago Boys," a group of economists who had trained at the University of Chicago, served as consultants to Pinochet. Following their recommendations, his government instituted a series of neoliberal reforms designed to contain inflation and liberalize the economy, which meant rewriting regulations to favor business and lessen government supervision, lower taxes, and privatize state-owned companies.

There was no question that Chile's economy faced serious economic problems, including hyperinflation. But were neoliberal economic policies the right answer? Were they popular among anyone but the Chilean business elite and their allies in the United States? No, according to David Harvey, a distinguished Marxist scholar. He argues, and we agree, that putting these policies into practice required the violent repression of all social movements and political organizations of the left, including the murder and torture of activists opposed to the dictatorship. It also included the dismantling of popular organizations such as community health centers, the privatization of social security, and the "freeing" of labor markets from regulations and unions. The economic experiments carried out by the "Chicago Boys" in Chile, touted as pure economics, were in fact profoundly political, unethical, and undemocratic. Although in the short run economic growth did increase somewhat from the earlier period and inflation declined, the Pinochet period as a whole was characterized by instability, rising unemployment, and a dramatic increase in the poverty rate.[35] Although Chile was a dictatorship, and the United States is not, the brutal experiment carried out in the global South became a blueprint for economic policy in the United States and Britain as well.

Neoliberalism in the United States and Britain gained ascendancy during the 1980s through the policy decisions of President Reagan in the United States and Prime Minister Margaret Thatcher in Britain. Once again, the rhetoric of free markets trumped all other arguments. Deregulation allowed manufacturers to subcontract their labor-intensive production processes to factories in the global South, the power of the unions was neutralized, and "hot money" circulated internationally.[36]

The days of national economies organized around large, primarily national corporations employing a stable, unionized work force were gone. Flexibility became the new corporate mantra. Flexible accumulation refers to the strategies that corporations use to accumulate profits in a globalized economy. These include moving capital-intensive production to places where labor is cheapest, taxes are lowest, and workers are unprotected by government regulations.[37] As the feminist political scientist V. Spike Peterson argues, flexibilization changes the conditions of employment and identities of workers. At the top end are the workers valued for their technical, informational, and knowledge-based skills. At the bottom are the semi- or unskilled workers, who although valuable to their employers are devalorized by their location in feminized jobs. Flexibilization feminizes the labor force by increasing the proportion of jobs that require few skills, and the workers in most demand are those perceived to be docile, reliable, available for part-time and temporary work, and willing to work for low wages.[38]

The Third World Debt Crisis

Debt is another significant feature of the global economy, and the story begins with the Third World debt crisis. In the 1960s and 1970s, development agencies like the World Bank financed massive, large-scale industrial projects encouraging global South countries to borrow funds to finance building high-technology factories, introduce large-scale mechanized farming, and build huge hydroelectric systems to provide energy to growing urban centers. While this was partially an imperialist strategy to ensure that the global North retained access to the resources of the global South, it was also in line with the developmentalist policies of the global South that we discuss in chapter 8.

We cannot know what might have happened were it not for the steep rise in the price of oil that took place in 1973 and 1979, which fattened the bank accounts of the oil-exporting nations and contributed to recessions in the industrialized countries. The infusion of this cash, or petrodollars, in international banks allowed bankers to go on a lending spree, ignoring virtually all known principles of sound lending policy.[39] Simply put, in the 1970s international financial markets were flush with cash, demand for loans in the industrialized economies was weak, and real interest rates were extremely low. Governments and entrepreneurs in what was then called the Third World sought financing for ambitious development projects and, presumably, personal enrichment. The international financial community was happy to oblige.[40]

In the 1980s, the economic climate changed with serious repercussions for the international balance sheets of the export dependent Third World nations. The industrialized economies were in yet another recession, the prices of basic commodities (grains, coffee, sugar, and the like) were falling, and real interest rates were rising. The interest on Third World nations' debts rose at the same time that their foreign export earnings fell. As if these problems were not serious enough, double-digit inflation and badly managed, often corrupt, governments further undermined their economies. In this situation, many Third World countries were simply unable to meet the payments on their international loans.

The crisis came to a head in 1982, when Mexico announced that it was close to defaulting on its $800 million foreign debt. Other countries soon followed suit. These countries faced a difficult choice. They could defy the international financial community and default on their debts, which would mean that they would lose the opportunity to borrow in the future. Or they could accept the funds from the International Monetary Fund (IMF), which would enable them to service their debts and remain a part of the international financial system. However, this "help" to the indebted countries was only available if they agreed to conditions that resulted in the imposition of neoliberal structural adjustment policies (SAPs). Countries were required to impose austerity measures by decreasing government spending on education, health, and income supports, eliminating price controls and subsidies, and devaluing their currencies. They were also required to deregulate (liberalize) their economies by opening their markets to foreign competition, curbing environmental and labor protections, and privatizing state-owned industries.

On paper, at least, SAPs were intended to restore investor confidence and create the economic conditions that would enable the Third World nations to repay their debts. They were a miserable failure on both counts. Instead of growth and prosperity, they resulted in stagnation and poverty. In the face of all evidence, the belief that government planning (with help from development experts) was good for economic development was soundly rejected. Whereas in the old view, tradition was seen as the principal impediment to economic development and growth, in the new, neoliberal view, government intervention in markets was seen as the main problem. While this new faith in markets did not help the global South economies, it did do one thing very well. It protected the financial interests of the banks. We discuss this in greater detail, with focused attention on the gender implications of these policies, in chapters 8 and 9.

Privatization

In addition to being a major part of SAPs, the privatization of industries and services, which had historically been provided by the government, remains a key component of neoliberal globalization all over the world. Health, education, and water services are all targets of transnational corporations who view them as profit-making opportunities rather than as services that states are obligated to provide for their citizens. Reducing public spending on water, health, and education creates opportunities for private, for-profit companies to come in and sell these services as commodities. As a result, many people who lack the income to purchase these basic services must make do without them.

Similarly, the assumption is that the costs of socially necessary reproductive activities that occur in public institutions, such as hospitals, schools, nursing homes, and day-care centers, should be the responsibility of private individuals rather than the government. Predictably, as state support declines so does the availability of services, and more and more the provision of these socially necessary activities falls disproportionately on the shoulders of women. As shown time and time again, women are generally responsible for providing health care, education, safe food, and clean water for their families, tasks that are made far more difficult by the privatization of social services.

The trend in water service is particularly troubling. Water, which is an absolute necessity for human life, is becoming increasingly scarce. In 2010, the United Nations Assembly recognized the right of every human being to have access to sufficient water for personal and domestic uses. Still, in 2017, according to United Nations estimates, 2.1 billion people do not have access to clean water and 4.5 billion do not have adequate sanitation and sewage.[41] Even in the face of this scarcity, water is becoming just another commodity to enhance corporate profitability. As a matter of fact, it is a page in the neoliberal playbook that privatization is the solution to water scarcity.

Water issues are women's issues. The privatization of water has come at the cost of an increase in women's unpaid labor.[42] Worldwide, women walk upward of four miles per day toting barrels of water on their heads, which when full weigh about forty pounds. The time spent collecting water is time that is not spent on education, income generating activities, or leisure.[43] Water issues are also race and class issues. In South Africa, 600,000 white farmers consume 60 percent of the water while 15 million black citizens lack access to any water at all.[44] Sadly, the lack of potable water is no longer a problem only for the global South.

As readers may remember, in 2014 the city of Flint, Michigan, was on the brink of bankruptcy and the governor appointed an emergency manager to oversee the city and cut costs. Switching the city's water supply from Lake Huron to the Flint River was one such cost-cutting measure. The results were tragic. The water was highly corrosive, and lead leached into the aging pipes of thousands of homes. Complaints from the mainly African American residents were ignored, and nearly 9,000 children drank lead-contaminated water for eighteen months. Although steps have been taken to ensure water safety now, the damage to these children may last a lifetime.[45]

This is just one type of privatization; there are many others: education, medical care, childcare and eldercare, even penal institutions. The negative consequences of privatization are always gendered. Consider the case of education: as quality education becomes costlier, boys are given priority over girls. Thus girls are less likely than boys to be enrolled in private schools, and lack of education is both a cause and a consequence of women's low status in the family and in the labor market.[46] Now consider a less obvious example, penal institutions. One of the ways that private prisons earn profits is by charging exorbitantly high prices for telephone calls, personal hygiene items, and various foodstuffs. It is through the generosity of the mothers, sisters, partners, and friends on the outside that inmates are able to have a decent quality of life.

Trade Agreements

Trade has always been at the center of globalization, and free trade is not a new idea. Indeed, it has been at the heart of mainstream economics for centuries. It comes from the idea that different countries have different natural resources, labor force talents and skills, and industrial capacities. Due to these differences, some countries can produce certain goods at relatively lower costs than others. Thus it is argued that every country will benefit if it specializes in the production of those goods and services where it has the largest relative cost advantage (i.e., faces the lowest relative production costs) and trades for the others.[47] This is the principle of comparative advantage, and it provides a theoretical and rhetorical justification for free trade.

Free trade is, however, somewhat of a misnomer. In practice, the statutes and regulations that govern international trade fill countless volumes and vast libraries. Trade agreements—the formal, negotiated rules and regulations guiding how and what nations can trade with each other—can be multilateral (like the WTO), regional (like the North American Free Trade Agreement, or NAFTA), or bilateral (between two countries). International trade in goods and services is a significant part of globalization, mostly under rules set by the World Trade Organization (WTO). Trade agreements do more than just eliminate tariffs on imported goods and services. They also require nations to eliminate what are called nontariff trade barriers, which are national regulations that prohibit imports that do not meet certain content standards, licensing requirements, or safety and environmental regulations. For example, the WTO has required

Europe to allow the importation of hormone-treated beef despite well-founded concerns about its health effects, and the United States has been forced to abandon its efforts to outlaw the sale of tuna caught with nets that endanger turtles and other fish.[48] When national standards about content, safety, and the environment are replaced by international standards (set by supranational organizations and negotiated in secret), trade "harmonization" allegedly occurs.

Indeed, the WTO is replacing democratically enacted laws and regulations on the national level with international edicts. The rights of sovereign governments to enact laws protecting public health, workers' rights, or the environment may be secondary to the "rights" of corporations to expand their markets and earn profits. The right of foreign investors to sue the governments of countries in which they invest for harming their profits is enshrined in what was, until recently, a relatively obscure legal doctrine known as investor-state dispute settlement (ISDS). Cases are decided by international tribunals that determine whether the investor is owed compensation. Multinational corporations are able to sue for lost profits as well as expected future profits. Moreover, domestic investors cannot sue, and no appeals system is yet in place. ISDS was originally intended to protect foreign investors from undue interference from host governments.[49] However, current thinking is that the scales have tilted too far in favor of transnational corporations. ISDS is profoundly undemocratic, and in an era that demands measures to combat climate change, it hamstrings efforts to enact health and environmental protections.

One of the earliest examples concerns Ethyl, a US chemical company. It sued the Canadian government over its ban of MMT, a toxic gasoline additive that is a known human neurotoxin. The case was ultimately settled for $13 million, and what is even worse, the settlement required Canada to lift the ban and post advertising saying that MMT was safe. More recently, in 2007, the Swedish energy corporation, Vattenfall, obtained a provisional permit to build a coal burning power plant near Hamburg, Germany. To protect the Elbe river from contamination by wastewater dumped by the plant, environmental regulations were added before final approval.[50] Then there are the people of Rosia Montana, a little town in the mountains of Romania, who recently banded together to stop the Canadian mining corporation, Gabriel Resources, from building an open-pit gold mine, because its use of toxic cyanide posed a serious environmental threat. The company fought back viciously by any means they could, both legal and illegal. Thus far the people opposing the mine have prevailed, and the government has withheld the necessary permits. However, the story does not end there. Factoring in the loss of expected profits, Gabriel sued the government for between $3.3 billion and $4.4 billion. This is the equivalent of 2 percent of Romania's GDP. As of this time, the case has not been decided.[51]

Finally, consider cigarettes. In 2012, Australia required that all tobacco products conform to plain packaging without any branding such as colors, images, mascots, and corporate logos. In addition, health warnings were required to be prominently displayed. In other words, Joe Camel would be banned. Other countries followed suit, including France, Ireland, and the United Kingdom. Not surprisingly the tobacco industry vehemently opposes this restriction on what they see as their right to advertise their brands, filing endless lawsuits. So far they have not won, but the costs to the governments, and ultimately to the taxpayers, are incredibly high. For example, Australia incurred $39 million in legal fees fighting the lawsuit brought by Phillip Morris. Even though they prevailed, Phillip Morris only paid half of that. The deterrent effect worked, and other small countries, such as Namibia, Togo, and New Zealand, have delayed enacting similar regulations.[52]

International trade agreements and ISDS provisions are designed to protect corporate profits at the expense of environmental protections, human rights, and democratic processes. Women are at the forefront of these fights on behalf of people rather than profits. No matter that the people in Rosia Montana do not want toxic cyanide released into their environment or that countries want to put the brakes on cigarette smoking. These are secondary to the almighty pursuit of corporate profits. Although advocates of trade agreements say that their aim is to reduce trade barriers and level the playing field for foreign investors by ensuring that they are not negatively impacted by national laws or regulations that preference locals, the facts tell a different story. In reality, trade agreements are designed to the advantage of large multinational corporations. They displace local businesses and use their economic clout to gain political advantages. As we have seen throughout this book, while women's lives are affected, they are mainly shut out of the decision-making processes.

Women, Class, and Differences on the Global Stage

Globalization has also affected the organization of domestic labor markets. As we discussed in previous chapters, although domestic labor largely remains "women's work," relatively affluent women have always been able to hire others to do it for them. Increasingly these others are poor, migrant women and racially stigmatized men. This is, of course, not a new story. Black women in the American South cleaned the houses of white women and cared for their children and the elderly. In Britain, Irish and lower-class British women performed the same functions. In India, lower-caste women served in the households of higher-caste Indians. Globalization changes the picture. Now this work is increasingly provided through transnational labor markets.

Sadly, the old goal of the women's liberation movement, sisterly solidarity, is even less possible than it was when Robin Morgan wrote *Sisterhood Is Global* in 1984, because transnational domestic labor markets exacerbate class divisions among women.[53] It is a depressing fact that women at the top of the income pyramid in every nation have benefited from changes in the global/gender division of labor at the expense of poor women of color in both the global North and the global South. What privileged women have in common is access to social, cultural, and economic resources. This is true regardless of whether they live in middle-class or wealthy neighborhoods in the global North, guarded compounds in the wealthy Gulf States, or elite enclaves in Latin America and Africa.[54] It is also not likely that poor women from the global South have shared class interests with poor women in the global North. The cheap clothes and food produced by poor women (and men) from the global South are extremely important to poor women across the world. Just visit any Dollar Store or Walmart in the United States and look at who the shoppers are. They are mainly poor people looking for the cheapest prices.[55]

Conclusion: Globalization's Rocky Path

History shows us that people have always been interested in what is over the horizon. Whether the earliest migrations across the Bering Strait, travels on the Silk Road, or sea voyages across the oceans, people are travelers. (Although not all migration was or is voluntary: slavery in the past, trafficking and refugees in the present.) Still it is somewhat ironic that while goods, services, money, and ideas can travel with relative ease across national borders, people cannot. They are constrained by border police and immigration regimes. The asymmetry of free-flowing commodities and capital, combined with complex barriers to legal migration, increases the power of transnational corporations to maximize profits and disregard human costs. The mobility of capital severely limits the ability of national governments to protect their citizens and undermines the power of workers to organize for better working conditions. All of this is aided and abetted by a neoliberal rhetoric that champions free markets and rationalizes the dismantling of progressive labor legislation, health and safety standards, environmental protections, and social welfare programs.

We have been critical overall of the effects of globalization on the lives and material well-being of the majority of the world's population, and we have stressed that women and girls are the ones who suffer the most. The rights of corporations to cross borders and earn profits are enshrined in law, while the rights of citizens to protect their health, their environment, and their economic futures are swept aside. Our critique does not, however, make us protectionists or isolationists. It is that we recognize that globalization is an uneven process; people are affected quite differently depending on complex intersections of gender, class, race, ethnicity, location, and citizenship status. Globalization creates winners and losers that are not easily defined by tried and true identity categories such as race and gender. We offer an analysis that recognizes this complexity. Finally, we are arguing against the unchecked power of elites to use people and natural resources without regard for the real social costs of their actions on social reproduction.

7 | Gender Matters in the Global Labor Market

In chapter 6, we showed that globalization is deeply gendered. In this chapter we more closely examine the intertwining of gender and globalization through its impact on labor markets and livelihoods, with a focus on women in the global South. Using examples such as global supply chain production, labor informalization, labor migration, and transnational sex work, we highlight the role that gender plays in determining the risks and opportunities created by global economic restructuring. Drawing on existing feminist scholarship, we also consider the complex interplay of gender with race, ethnicity, class, and location in determining women's labor market experiences.

From a mainstream economics perspective, the employment and livelihood effects of globalization on women in the global South are by definition positive. Mainstream economists often challenge concerns about the low wages and working conditions for women in global labor markets with the argument that the work is not exploitative because women workers have entered the exchange freely. Further, they argue that while wages may be below decent living standards initially, they will eventually rise as the industry expands. As Nobel prize-winning economist Paul Krugman once stated with regard to the growth of low-wage, global-export industrial jobs, "the overwhelming mainstream view among economists is that the growth of sweatshop employment is tremendous good news for the world's poor."[1]

However, the actual outcomes of globalizing labor markets on poverty, development, and well-being are more complicated. Not everyone who is drawn into globalized labor enters it freely. Sometimes workers are held captive, such as the migrant female garment workers who were found locked into the El Monte clothing factory outside Los Angeles a few years back, or the coerced, unpaid laborers who produce much of the shrimp that is exported from Thailand. Often they find themselves working in jobs or conditions that are far different than for what they were recruited, such as the women who migrated from villages to work in blue jean factories in Chinese cities under vastly different conditions than they were promised, as highlighted in the documentary film *China Blue*. But in most cases women do choose these jobs "freely," meaning only with the coercion of economic necessity and lack of other good options. What the "free exchange" model of mainstream economics obscures, however, are the power relations that structure these workers' choices—interlocking forms of global corporate power, class exploitation, caste, racism, religious exclusion, and gender—which have created a source of women workers to fill most of these low-wage jobs in the first place.

The bottom line is that, "choice" or not, women are heavily exploited in global labor markets. Factory jobs in female-dominated industries are often in export processing zones with few labor rights or safety protections. The mainstream economics argument that this will change through the inevitable growth in demand for workers in a particular country does not typically bear out either. And when conditions and wages do improve, men often take over these jobs from women, as happened in the Mexican and South Korean cases. In addition to factory work, globalization has led to more women doing informalized, unregulated, sometimes risky and precarious work. Women's transnational labor migration is often exploitative, especially since employers can take advantage of workers' often tenuous immigration status and lack of familiarity with, or protection by, local labor laws.

As we mentioned in chapter 6, the prevalence of women in transnational garment production, export manufacturing assembly, informal sector work, and migration to perform paid care work reflects a feminization of labor in which gender assumptions and power dynamics have cheapened certain kinds of labor.[2] Activities such as sewing, "light" manufacturing, and care are associated with femininity and thus devalued, resulting in low pay for those who do them. The feminization of labor is also closely related to processes of labor market informalization, where flexible production and work schedules are justified not only on profitability grounds but by widespread beliefs that women don't need stable or full-time employment. These include assumptions that women are only working temporarily until they marry or—if they are married—that their work is only a secondary contribution to their husband's wage. These is also the assumption that flexible and/or home-based work suits women well given their care responsibilities. Finally, the corporate assumption that global South workers are ideal workers because they are docile and won't organize for improved labor rights plays a role in making both relocation and a female labor force attractive. However, like the other assumptions that corporations make about global South women workers, this one is way off the mark.

In addition to the feminization of labor, another aspect of globalization that explains the prevalence of women in certain paid employment areas in the global South is the feminization of survival that was also discussed in chapter 6. With shifts in the global economy, households, communities, governments, and women themselves are increasingly reliant on women's paid labor for their survival. The concept of the feminization of survival was first coined by Saskia Sassen to explain why over the past few decades so many more women were migrating across national borders and sending home remittances to families who relied on those funds to live. The remittances, she noted, also benefitted the women's home governments by providing essential foreign exchange, and many governments have encouraged women to work abroad for this very reason.[3] While Sassen was not writing about factory workers, informal sector workers, or sex workers, we note that many women have sought out these jobs for the same reason—to meet their survival needs and those of their families, communities, and nations. While facing exploitation in many of their economic activities, they are not victims. They are actively seeking better lives and often organizing to improve their conditions.

Global Supply Chains and Gendered Labor

On April 24, 2013, the deadliest garment factory accident on record took place when the Rana Plaza factory complex in Bangladesh collapsed, killing more than 1,100 workers, most of them women. This was only one of many tragedies that had plagued the global garment industry in the first two decades of the twenty-first century. Consumer demand for cheap "fast fashion," global brands' drive for high profits, deregulated international trade, export-oriented development strategies, and national dependence on foreign exchange from garment exports have together fostered a remarkable expansion of the global factory for clothes. In Bangladesh, for instance, where the garment industry accounts for 80 percent of the country's foreign exchange,[4] there are five million workers in the industry, most of them women. Many mainstream economists and development institutions have advocated for the unbridled expansion of export apparel manufacturing on efficiency, growth, antipoverty, and even gender empowerment grounds.[5] They have argued against the regulation of these industries to improve labor standards since the World Trade Organization considered adopting a labor rights clause in the late 1990s and early 2000s.[6] But the Rana Plaza disaster, coming only a few months after the highly publicized Tazreen factory fire in Bangladesh, where 112 workers were killed and many hundreds injured, refocused international attention on addressing the dangerous and exploitative conditions in these global factories. Western brands who had subcontracted to firms producing in the Rana Plaza and Tazreen factory, such as Benetton, H&M, Walmart, Zara, and others, found themselves under fire and pledged to change their practices. Global institutions such as the International Labor Organization pushed for new regulations and agreements to ensure worker rights on the global stage. And Bangladeshi garment workers had an opening to renew their longstanding fight for improved working conditions and fair wages, mobilizing on the ground as well as forming alliances with international worker rights organizations.

In the middle of the twentieth century, most of the clothing worn in industrialized countries such as the United States was produced domestically and subject to hard-won national labor standards, occupational safety laws, and environmental regulations. But due to the processes of globalization that we described in chapter 6, most of the clothes we wear today are produced elsewhere, in global supply chains that can turn a new style around in six weeks to meet consumers' desires for fast, disposable fashions. Global garment companies, like many labor-intensive industries, have moved production to countries with lower labor costs, minimal regulations on workplace safety or pollution, and weak or nonexistent unions in order to enhance their profits. In some cases, they invest in factories elsewhere, which is called foreign direct investment (FDI), and make the product from beginning to end. But a far more common strategy is subcontracting out different aspects of production, particularly the manufacturing part, limiting transnational corporations' direct involvement to only the beginning and end of the product chain—the design and marketing/sale to customers. Typically the factories where the garments or shoes are produced are owned by local entrepreneurs who themselves subcontract out certain aspects of production to other factories or to home producers who produce for piece-work rates, in order to meet the tight deadlines for producing new styles to meet consumer demand.

The growth of global supply chains for many labor-intensive goods—not only garments and shoes but also electronics, toys, and even food processing—has been facilitated by the creation of specific geographic areas, variously called Free Trade Zones (FTZs), Export-Processing Zones

(EPZs), or Special Economic Zones (SPZs). These are areas within which firms import components for assembly and then export the finished, or nearly finished, products. The owners of the firms that assemble the products are not required to pay tariffs on the unassembled goods when they are imported or the assembled goods when they are exported. In addition to offering tariff-free imports and exports, governments attract foreign investors to their EPZs by subsidizing infrastructure support services such as water and electricity and exempting employers from labor laws and other regulations. In the words of the government of Bangladesh, "the primary objective of an EPZ is to provide special areas where potential investors would find a congenial investment climate, free from cumbersome procedures."[7]

Why have women been the majority of low-paid workers producing labor-intensive goods such as export apparel in these supply chains? The low pay and poor working conditions that women face are often presented as some sort of inevitability in mainstream economics, due to their lack of human capital and "laws" of supply and demand that are out of human hands. But feminist economists see nothing inevitable or natural about it. Instead they examine the processes that have created these outcomes. One of these is clearly related to corporate power and the drive for profitability, on the one hand, and the need for poorer nations to attract corporations and foreign exchange, on the other, as the reference to "congenial investment climate" in the Bangladesh government statement above attests. But that still doesn't explain why it is *women* who are drawn into this work.

Building on the notion of the feminization of labor that we described in the introduction to this chapter, the feminist politics scholar Cynthia Enloe has written about the "interlocking genderings" through which women's work is made cheap, and their low pay and lack of rights to decent working conditions are justified. These include the perception that they are a "naturally" better fit for light manufacture and garment production, rather than having learned skills. When a skill such as sewing, or doing detailed assembly work, or for that matter being a good caregiver is dismissed as natural rather than learned, it justifies lower pay. Another major factor that makes women's wages cheap is that managers often reserve their supposedly skilled jobs for men only. Women are slotted in as the unskilled sewers or assemblers of components in electronics, while men are assigned the specialist tasks and managerial roles that are higher paid.[8] This gender division of labor is by no means inevitable. Managers of export factories in Mexico explicitly organize the shop floor around a gender division as a mechanism of workplace control, not because of actual skill and ability differentials by gender.[9] While we don't have good data on gender divisions of labor in factories around the world for many reasons, it is safe to assume that these processes occur elsewhere. One report—using disaggregated numbers for three Asian countries, Malaysia, Vietnam, and Thailand—put the number of women in electronics factories between 60 and 90 percent. For their part, men rarely sit on the assembly lines and generally occupy higher and better paid positions.[10] In those cases such as Mexico and South Korea where export industry became more capital intensive, masculinization of the shop floor occurred as wages rose.[11]

Another factor that makes women's wages cheap is the assumption that they are being financially supported by a father or husband at home, and only earning secondary money. This is also a justification for not providing them with employment security, employee benefits, and social insurance to cover retirement, unemployment, or worker disability.[12] In reality, many women are the chief or even the sole income earners for their households.

A final reason that Enloe gives for why women's labor is made cheap is the assumption that women, particularly global South women, are docile, passive, and hence easily subject to the discipline of factory work and unlikely to complain about poor working conditions.[13] For example, feminist political economist Juanita Elias uncovered the government's attempt to create a gendered, racialized image of a docile and diligent factory girl in Malaysia, an image pushed on Malaysian factory women as a feminine ideal, and also sold to foreign investors as a reason to place factories in that country.[14] However, poor working women all over the world challenge this perception of their docility. At great personal cost, often risking their lives, they resist exploitative conditions through forms of creative resistance, strikes, organizing, developing coalitions with global and local NGOs, and other mechanisms to improve their work lives and force employers to provide more humane working conditions. However, there is often great risk associated with these challenges to the status quo, especially if these women are extra vulnerable due to their caste, class, or migrant status. Thus the extent to which women do not protest their conditions reflects their extremely limited options and power dynamics that constrain their ability to resist, rather than any essential gender traits.

Informalization and Feminization

When you step off a bus on vacation in the Caribbean you may see street vendors selling their wares and trying to get your attention. Street musicians serenade travelers waiting for the metro in Paris, Berlin, London, and Amsterdam. In the early morning, middle-class suburban joggers in Southern California run past Latinx persons hustling to their jobs as maids, nannies, and gardeners. College students sign up to be Uber drivers, shuttling their classmates to bars and restaurants on the weekend. All of this is informal work. But not all informal labor is so visible. Hidden in homes and small, subcontracted sweatshops around the world, poorly paid workers sew clothes, weave rugs, stitch soccer balls, and assemble electronics in unregulated, insecure conditions.

Alongside the development of global supply chains and export-oriented production, neoliberal globalization has resulted in an informalization of economic activities around the world. Work has increasingly become flexibilized, temporary, part-time, insecure. A growing percentage of paid work is unregulated, with no minimum wage, work-hour limits, or safety regulations. Rather than being supplied materials by the firm they work for, subcontracted informalized workers are often responsible for all of the capital expenditures, thus shifting risk, but rarely reward, onto the worker rather than the firm. Piece-rate workers sewing clothes, for instance, must advance cash for sewing machines and raw materials. Uber drivers are responsible for supplying their own cars, gas, tolls, and upkeep, making their wages quite low after all of that is covered. Street vendors only make what they can sell that day after expenses, making their livelihoods precarious. Small-scale enterprises, either individual or family-run, often involve risks such as borrowing that can result in loss of land or long-term indebtedness. The progressive labor economist Guy Standing calls these workers the global precariat, a new social class consisting of millions of people around the world without an anchor of stability whose lives are characterized by the precariousness of work and social protections.

Most mainstream discussions of informalization attempt to create a hard boundary between the formal and informal sector activities to create distinct categories of work. In contrast, we follow the approach taken by feminist political economist V. Spike Peterson in viewing informalization along a continuum of distinctions.[15] Informalization is a contested process of transforming work practices into flexibilized, devalued, labor conditions. Peterson highlights the blurring between informal and formal activities, between informal and unpaid social reproductive activities, and the increasingly precarious nature of all work in contemporary global capitalism. Many jobs have elements of both formal and informalized work, and workers often move between these different labor spheres and/or their activities are hard to fit into a particular category. For instance, the unpaid labor of women and children often enables the survival of families engaged in street vending, home-based piecework, and similar activities, making the distinction between unpaid labor and paid informal labor less clear.

Informalization is highly feminized, not only in terms of the increase in women's labor force participation but also in terms of the devaluing of informal work as feminized "secondary" work as we described in the section above. This devaluation is in effect no matter what gender is doing the work. It is also highly racialized. Historically, racialized occupations have been characterized by the absence of contracts, by instability, and by part-time, temporary, and low-paid conditions (Peterson 2003). While both men and women have been increasingly drawn into these informal sector activities over the past few decades, in the global South women are more likely to be represented in this sort of work than men are. Women's work, particularly in the fields that draw in poor women of color and migrant women, is also more likely to be vulnerable, such as day or seasonal temporary domestic help, home-based pieceworkers who have to pay for the materials of their work up front, independent sex workers, and unpaid contributing labor in a small family firm.[16] This work is poorly paid, unreliable, and, to use the ILO's own term, precarious.

The reasons for informalization are multiple and complex. They differ in both scale and form between the global North and global South. In this chapter, we focus on the latter. The earliest accounts recognized informality in the global South as an aspect of underdevelopment related to the survival economy and assumed it would be eliminated with economic growth.[17] But since the 1980s, GDP growth and informalization have gone hand in hand, causing researchers to rethink their earlier assumptions. The expansion of global export industries in developing countries has contributed to informalization. These industries rely heavily on subcontracted industrial outworkers producing at piece-rate from their homes or from small unregulated shops. Growing free trade and the importation of cheap substitutes for formerly domestically produced goods has also put local farmers and manufacturers out of business, with many seeking alternative livelihoods in the informal sector. Cuts in real wages due to economic restructuring have led people to seek out informal work to supplement their earnings and to maintain their livelihoods. Structural adjustment and budget cuts have reduced the number of formal jobs in education, health, and other areas of the economy, causing those workers to move into the unregulated and more precarious informal sector.

Employers in informal sector firms often seek out women workers because they can pay them less for all of the reasons we discussed in the previous section. And research has shown that women—because they carry the disproportionate share of care tasks—are often not able to take formal, full-time regulated work opportunities due to their need to balance household obligations with market work. This, coupled with a formal labor market organized around the "unencumbered worker model," providing no allowances for care work responsibilities, makes informal, part-time, and temporary work the only real option.[18]

Today many mainstream approaches celebrate the expansion of informalization—particularly in the rise of self-employed activities and small family firms—as good for growth and well-being. They view it as the unleashing of individual initiative outside cumbersome regulatory channels, unlocking the potential of the poor for growth and poverty reduction (e.g., de Soto 1989). However, there is little to recommend informal sector expansion for its impact on inequalities by income level and/or gender. Recent research has found that it widens income inequalities and increases the likelihood that peoples' livelihoods will be precarious.[19] The lack of labor rights protection and social benefits puts women in unsafe conditions, at greater risk for sexual harassment, and without a safety net, which has a long-term impact on women's well-being—hardly the conditions of empowerment.[20] As a response to these negative impacts of informalization on women, some have mobilized to secure better work conditions, most famously the Self-Employed Women's Association (SEWA), an Indian trade union and umbrella of cooperatives that has successfully organized more than 1.5 million poor, self-employed women. SEWA provides services such as affordable health care, childcare, and legal and other supports, including skills training and low-cost loans, for women experiencing gender-based violence.[21]

There are, however, some potential positives associated with informalized work, even among those who are not organized to improve its conditions. It may be the only option for the poor and stands between them and abject poverty. Further, informalized labor can provide low-cost goods and services to other poor households, which can mitigate poverty somewhat. Informal sector labor can also contribute to sustainable development. For instance, informal workers are engaged in the recycling and processing of waste in urban areas, and approximately fifteen to twenty million persons worldwide earn their living through these activities, which produce far fewer emissions than waste management companies and also recover more resources.[22] Street traders, because they are more likely to source locally than large corporations, are also environmentally friendly in comparison. However, we agree with the ILO and other organizations working on this topic when they argue that on balance informality is a major challenge for sustainable development because it widens inequality and precarity. The ILO continues to push for a global commitment to reversing processes of informalization and fostering labor markets that provide decent, regulated, fairly paid, protected work.

Transnational Caring Labor

While migration within and beyond national borders has been a central feature of global capitalism for a very long time, neoliberal globalization has created new forms of mobility and drawn different groups of people into the migrant labor force. Since the 1980s, one greatly expanding category of labor migration is transnational care, where workers, mostly women, leave global South countries to provide care services to households in wealthier countries. The movement of women taking on jobs such as nannies, maids, eldercare workers, and the like has contributed to the feminization of immigration, in which now half of the approximately 150 million immigrants worldwide are women. It has also contributed to the feminization of informalization, as many of these jobs are unregulated, unprotected, temporary, part-time, and/or insecure.

What has fostered this transnational reorganization of care? The demand for migrant help in wealthier nations has been fueled by a care crisis in the global North as more women move into the paid labor force, escalating the need for affordable paid care for children and aging populations. The crisis has been exacerbated by the public withdrawal of support for care, shifting the burden back onto households that were already overworked. For those that can afford it, relatively low-cost immigrant care workers appear to offer an attractive solution to their own personal, family care crises. On the supply side, the restructuring of developing economies, lack of decent and well-paid work, and consequent rise in poverty has caused women in the global South to seek higher-paying earning opportunities overseas. Some of the women seeking work as nannies and maids in other countries are leaving behind skilled jobs such as nursing and teaching. The growing gap between rich and poor countries that we described in chapter 6 means that skilled jobs in their home countries pay less than jobs that are considered menial in the global North. These dynamics highlight the importance of intersectional analysis. Women's increased labor force participation in the global North has created not only a new class of professional women but also new feminized jobs that are low-wage, temporary, part-time, insecure, and precarious for global South women.

The role of the state in facilitating care migration is often overlooked, yet the state plays a large role in structuring the macro and micro politics of gendered migrant care work. The governments of sending countries, often reeling from waves of global economic crisis and structural adjustment, are hoping to secure a steady stream of remittances, or flows of money that migrants send back to their communities of origin. The governments' encouragement of women in particular to migrate is in part due to the increased demand for female migrant workers in nations that have historically viewed paid care and domestic work as racialized, feminine labor. It is also fueled by stereotyped but unsubstantiated assumptions that women migrants, because they are more altruistic than men, will remit a higher percentage of their income. Maximizing remittances is a big deal for some poor countries. Officially recorded remittance flows are estimated to be more than $430 billion, providing foreign exchange to fund imports and pay off foreign debt and constituting up to 30 percent of some nations' GDPs.[23]

Policies toward migration in receiving countries also shape the experiences of migrant care workers and the differential power relationships that structure the employer/employee relationship. Some nations do not issue work permits for domestic workers, nannies, or other care workers, and as a result many workers may end up undocumented. Such policies make domestic work much more precarious, as workers are made vulnerable and insecure. It is harder for them to resist exploitative conditions at work lest their employers turn them into immigration authorities. Those who are documented are typically not allowed to bring their children or other dependents, which keeps down the public costs associated with education and care for those dependents, and also makes the worker available to her employer 24/7. In some countries legal migration is facilitated through a visa sponsorship system, such as in the United Arab Emirates (UAE). There a worker is tied to a particular employer for the entire term of their contract and can be arrested or fined for leaving early. This obviously shifts the balance of power in ways that make workers extra vulnerable to exploitation and abuse. A study by Human Rights Watch documented that migrant workers in the UAE put in on average sixteen to twenty-one hours per day with few days off, earning as little as fifteen cents an hour, and often sleeping under stairs or on living room floors and receiving a substandard diet. Some workers were also subjected to physical and sexual abuse.[24] In response, migrant worker rights' groups and international human rights NGOs have put pressure on the government of the UAE to pass labor laws to limit working hours, mandate days off, and offer minimum wage and decent working conditions for migrant domestic workers.

One influential feminist approach to making sense of the conditions of transnational care is the "global care chain," a term coined by feminist sociologist Arlie Hochschild. In her study of Filipina nannies working in the United States, Hochschild documented a chain of care that links the parent who needs paid help caring for her own child because of their work demands in the global North to the migrant nanny who does this care work, whose own children are then cared for by a lower-paid nanny back home, whose own children are subsequently cared for by her daughter because she is too poor to hire someone. These international chains of caretaking, for Hochschild, constitute a "new imperialism" in which the exploitative transfer of love and care from poor to wealthy countries results in the deprivation of children in the global South. Thus the global care chain represents a form of what scholar Shellee Colen has referred to as "stratified reproduction," or the relations that empower some people to nurture and reproduce their children while disempowering others.[25] While compelling, the global care chain approach has also come under some criticism. Scholars have challenged its assumption that migrant care workers are typically mothers migrating to support their own children back home. This relegates women's migration to the family even as many of them migrate independently. It also reproduces a heteronormative family model of care that ignores the variety of arrangements and roles in transnational families.[26]

It is also important to highlight the agency of migrant care workers, rather than treating them as victims caught up in the machine of global capitalist restructuring. These workers often engage in everyday forms of resistance to exploitation in the homes where they work. They form support and mutual aid networks with others from their home country. They often channel their remittances into local businesses that provide more stable work opportunities for people in their home communities. Further, performing care work abroad is potentially empowering when it allows a woman worker to sidestep gender expectations at home, or leave a bad marriage.[27] That said, much of this work is isolated and isolating, undervalued and low-paid, and the conditions of work are often precarious. Societal changes that might improve these worker's lives include a revaluing of care labor to recognize its essential contribution to human livelihoods, changes in state regulations and migration policies that improve the quality of work life for migrants, and addressing the global inequalities that have created the desperate situations that have caused many women to migrate in the first place. In addition, because migrant care workers provide a private solution to a public problem—the care crisis—policies that support work/life balance, changes in the division of labor within households, and growing public support for health care, childcare, eldercare, and the like should be pursued as well.

Sex Work in the Global Economy

In 2016, Amnesty International issued a report, *Sex Workers at Risk*, supporting the decriminalization of consensual commercial sex on human rights grounds.[28] The outcome of extensive case study research and a multiyear set of conversations with different stakeholders—including sex worker rights organizations—this report concluded that criminalization had decreased the rights of sex workers. It exposed them to violence, police harassment, extortion, discrimination, denial of health services, and other rights abuses. Of particular concern to Amnesty International were the life conditions and rights of transnational sex workers, especially poor women of color, whose migrations were forced into dangerous and precarious underground channels due to the illegality of their work. Amnesty International made clear that forced sexual labor, child exploitation in the sex trade, and trafficking—situations where power, threat, and deception is used to control someone for the purposes of exploitation—should be criminalized to the fullest extent. Recognizing that employment in sex work might be the result of significantly constrained choices, the statement also called for expanded educational and training opportunities for marginalized persons to provide livelihood options outside of sex work.

When a draft copy of this statement was circulated in 2015 for comment, a letter denouncing decriminalization was sent to Amnesty International Offices from the Coalition Against Trafficking in Women (CATW), a leading antiprostitution organization based in the United States. It included hundreds of signatures from a varied group of antiprostitution organization leaders, United Nations workers, academics, and celebrities such as Meryl Streep and Charlize Theron.[29] The letter called Amnesty's proposal "incomprehensible" and argued that it would lead to an explosion of sex exploitation against women. It should be noted that neither side of this controversy was calling for the arrest of the sex workers themselves. The argument was about whether eliminating or maintaining the criminalization and prosecution of those who broker or buy sex would improve or diminish the rights of those in the sex trade.

We open with this example to highlight the contested conversations that have taken place around sex work and economic rights on the global stage. For the CATW, commercial sex of any sort is viewed as harmful to women and a source of gender inequity. Buying and selling of bodies is never about free choice, the organization argues, and women who find themselves in the trade need the protection of criminalization to deter predators. Thus you will often hear people from this camp refer to all activities associated with commercial sex—adult and consensual, coerced adult, paid sex with children, and people in slave or slave-like conditions forced to perform sex work—lumped together as unfree trafficking in persons. In contrast, the assumption behind the Amnesty International report is that commercial sex is a form of work for those adults who consensually participate in it. It may be chosen out of a set of very unappealing alternatives or because the pay is higher than other options, but it is work nonetheless. The criminalization of sex work makes the work more dangerous and precarious than it could otherwise be. Amnesty also makes a hard distinction between consensual and coerced paid sex, recognizing that like other forms of transnational labor, some doing sex work are trafficked and others are not.

As feminist economists, our interest in this topic has less to do with a moral debate about the commercialization of sex and more to do with the material conditions of sex workers' labor. For this chapter, with its focus on global labor markets, we are particularly interested in the ways that globalization has structured the commercial sex industry and with the implications for the livelihoods of those who work in it. Like other forms of feminized labor, sex work has been affected by the forces of globalization. The economic hardships and dislocations that have accompanied globalization have created conditions where sex work is an increasingly viable option. For many young women, sex work is likely to be better paid, more flexible, and less time-consuming than factory work. Feminist sociologist Wendy Chapkis cautions us to remember that prostitution is often chosen from a desperately limited range of options.[30] Likewise, feminist economist Jean Pyle argues that deciding whether or not to engage in sex work is not made in isolation from broader economic conditions.[31] The sex industry is flourishing because the global liberalization of trade, migration, and finance has eased international travel for sex workers and sex customers. Moreover, debt obligations require countries to generate foreign exchange earnings, and sex tourism, by catering to men from the rich nations, is one way to do this. The country of Thailand is one leading sex tourism destination that fits this description. While prostitution is illegal there, the government tolerates it in large part because it brings in so much foreign exchange, which the Thai government uses to service foreign debt and fund imports. Sex tourism is a growing industry. And men are not the only ones who purchase sex. Jamaica's Negril beach is a popular destination for women from the global North to solicit young Caribbean men.

The global sex industry is characterized by a diversity of economic forms and practices. Some who work in commercial sex do so as independent contractors. Others work in bars, escort services, massage parlors, or brothels in consensual situations, where some have more control over their work conditions than others. Some involved in commercial sex are children, a highly immoral and unethical practice of trafficking for sexual exploitation. Some adults are trafficked into this work as well, forced through coercion, fraud, and even abduction to provide commercial sex. Working conditions vary widely along the lines of class, race, age, ethnicity, and nationality, as do the precarious life situations that bring many people into the trade in the first place. The feminist sociologist Kamala Kempadoo points out that in general white sex workers have safer, more comfortable, higher-paid work, while persons of mixed ancestry, Asians, and Latinas form a middle class, and Black and indigenous women are disproportionately the poorest sex workers in the most dangerous street environments.[32] This can be partly explained by the colonial ideology that eroticized women of color. One of the ways that the colonial system produced a racialized gender ideology was to link inferiority to heightened sexuality. Thus the inferiority of indigenous women was constructed, in part, by seeing them as more sexual than white European women. As "primitives," sex was "natural" to them.[33] As we have demonstrated repeatedly, that which is deemed natural is treated as deserving of less compensation and prestige than that which is not. Race, class, age, and ethnicity do not only influence the experiences of those in paid consensual sex. They are also factors in trafficking, as the poorest people with the fewest opportunities are more likely to be vulnerable to trafficking. According to the ILO, among the twenty-one million laborers who have been trafficked across borders globally, approximately 4.5 million are subject to forced sexual exploitation.

Widespread layoffs in manufacturing and services are likely to drive women into the sex industry as opportunities for paid employment decline. The net effect is an increase in the supply of sex workers. A recent example of this is Greece, where the country's economic crisis led to an increase in the number of women engaged in sex work. On the other hand, the demand for sexual services by men is not negatively affected by unemployment or the decline in national income. In fact in Greece the number of domestic clients for women's sexual services actually rose during the austerity period.[34] The total demand for sexual services may increase even more in the aftermath of economic crises if hard-hit nations devalue their currencies and make sex tourism even cheaper.[35]

This dynamic presents an important challenge to feminists interested in improving the working conditions in the sex industry and protecting the rights of sex workers. It goes back to the perennial problem in feminism, which is how to reconcile the often-conflicting interests of women who are in different social and economic locations in a way that will create a collective agenda for change. Today many women migrate due to economic hardship. Many of them end up as domestic workers. Many also end up as sex workers, and they are not always well received by their more fortunate colleagues who enjoy the status of citizenship. For example, in the Netherlands, where sex work is legal, Asian, African, and Eastern European women are prohibited from working in licensed brothels and are consigned to working in illegal establishments or streetwalking. The now defunct Dutch sex worker lobbying organization, Red Thread, did not allow illegal migrants to join. They viewed the migrants as a threat to the wages and benefits earned by and for Dutch sex workers.[36] Of course, the issues raised here in the context of the sex industry are much the same as debates about the influx of migrants on any other sort of labor market.

The Dutch case is also interesting because it sheds light on the debates between legalizing prostitution and decriminalizing it. Legalization generally entails regulating and taxing the industry. Such laws are often made to protect the health of the prostitutes' customers and increase state revenues. State regulation of prostitution is an old story. Wherever armies are sent, prostitution is tolerated, if not encouraged. Indeed, this is the origin of the term hookers, which refers to General Joseph Hooker's policy during the US Civil War (1861–65) of bringing prostitutes along with the troops. Regulations that required sex workers to undergo regular medical exams were supposed to safeguard the soldiers' health. These regulations put the responsibility for safe sex on the sex workers rather than on the customers. The regulations were often intrusive and humiliating, so feminists concerned with the rights of prostitutes argued for decriminalization rather than legalization. Feminists emphasize the importance of protecting the health of sex workers as well as their customers and point out that sex workers, like all workers, need protection from violence and coercion. From this perspective it is clear that the issues facing sex workers are not terribly different from the issues facing other workers in the informal economy.

Conclusion

When it comes to global labor markets, gender makes the world go around. Gender power dynamics, as they intersect with other forms of power, have shaped global supply chains for clothing, fostered the out-migration of care and sex work from one region of the world to another, and been a major factor in the rapid growth of the informal economy around the world. Women working on the global stage are often engaged in forms of labor that have been feminized, in that gender assumptions about the work has cheapened it. At the same time, changes in the global economy have contributed to the feminization of survival, where responsibility for livelihood at the personal, familial, national, and even global level rests increasingly on women's shoulders. The working conditions in these fields are often exploitative, the livelihoods often precarious, and the overall outcome is inequitable. Over the past few decades, many social and labor rights movements have recognized these inequities and mobilized for change. Labor movements have forced the payment of living wages in garment factories. Protests by college students have led to the monitoring of factories that make college logo clothing and improvements in working conditions. Growing numbers of consumers are realizing the human toll of "fast fashion" and changing their buying habits. Global feminist activists, highlighting the gender aspects of corporate abuse, have made headway toward the passage of a binding treaty on transnational corporations and human rights at the United Nations.[37] The organization of SEWA, described earlier in the chapter, has reduced the precarity of women workers in the informal sector. Amnesty International's proposal to decriminalize sex work is but one of many efforts to reduce the danger and precarity of that form of labor. These are but a few examples of the myriad forms of vibrant activism aimed at achieving the goals of decent work, fair wages, and security for women in global labor markets.

8 | Gender and Economic Development

Today you will find gender issues infused throughout contemporary economic development theory and policy. Gender equity is central to the 2030 Sustainable Development Goals adopted by all United Nations member countries. Every week, it seems, a new initiative on gender and development is launched by a global institution or corporate philanthropy. Yet just fifty years ago virtually no attention was paid to women or gender issues in development. In fact, as recently as the turn of the twenty-first century, there was minimal financial support for gender-equity initiatives in global development organizations. What happened to move concerns about gender out of the margins of economic development over the past few decades? What sorts of feminist economics issues and questions are included, and which are left out, in current gender and development initiatives? What implications does increased attention to gender have for achieving the criteria we have laid out in this book for a well-functioning economy such as improved quality of life, increased fairness, enhanced economic security, and sustainability? These are the main questions we will address in this chapter.

The Emergence of Development Economics after World War II

Development economics is a relatively new subfield of economics. The push to develop the nations of the global South did not begin until after World War II, with the liberation of formerly colonized nations. Prior to decolonization, the idea of developing these regions to promote poverty reduction and domestic income growth was far from the imagination of the ruling countries, which were more focused on exploiting their colonies' cheap natural resources, cheap labor, and ready markets for exported manufactured goods. The demise of colonialism in the mid-twentieth century and desire of the former colonies for self-determination, however, ushered in a change in thinking. The ascendancy of interventionist Keynesian economics after the Great Depression and World War II also contributed to the idea that management of national economies toward growth and poverty reduction was possible. The success of the Marshall Plan in rapidly rebuilding the economies of Europe and Japan after the war further made economists and policymakers optimistic that similar economic policy interventions could transform other parts of the world. Such optimism was captured in US President Truman's 1949 inaugural address, where he stated:

> More than half the people of the world are living in conditions approaching misery. Their food is inadequate. They are victims of disease. Their economic life is primitive and stagnant. Their poverty is a handicap and a threat both to them and to more prosperous areas. For the first time in history, humanity possesses the knowledge and skill to relieve the suffering of these people.[1]

There was more going on here than altruistic concern for those living in poverty, of course. This period marks the beginning of the Cold War, and the "threat . . . to more prosperous areas" Truman was referring to in this passage was the specter of communism. So, in addition to relieving poverty and suffering, one of the goals of development was to discourage nations not politically aligned with the "First World" of the capitalist industrialized countries or the "Second World" of the communist bloc from joining the latter. The best way to achieve this, Truman and others thought, was to foster economic development and modernization in those unaligned "Third World" countries.

What's in a Name?

Development economics, which focuses on addressing the causes of maldevelopment in the poorer nations, was initially heavily invested in the "First, Second, Third World" taxonomy we introduced above. Imagining all the nations of the non-Soviet world as moving through stages of growth culminating in the high mass production and mass consumption economy of the United States, development economic policy aimed to help those in the Third World catch up to the First World quickly. But this 1-2-3 classification, first developed in the early 1950s and still in use today, also reveals quite a bit about global hierarchy and privilege.[2] While the meaning of the term "Third World" has shifted since the Cold War, it has tended to refer to the majority of countries and peoples of the world as poor, backward, and in need of emulating the advanced nations of Western Europe and the United States. This dualistic framing of First World/Third World, rich/poor, modern/traditional, and advanced/backward contributes to flattening stereotypes of both regions and demeaning images of the Third World. It fails to capture the enormous economic, political, and other forms of diversity *among* countries that fall into one of the categories, as well as the diverse economic situations people face *within* each of the nations of the world. Today the 1-2-3 classification system, while still in use, is increasingly rejected as confusing, insulting, and completely out of date. For one thing, with the fall of the Soviet Union there is no more Second World. Further, it makes little sense to consider a wealthy country like Kuwait, neither communist nor North American/European, as part of the Third World.

What do we call the regions of the world studied by development economists then? Some scholars still use the term "Third World" but in ways that call attention to the power dynamics behind this term. For instance, feminist scholars such as Chandra Mohanty use the term "Third World women" to capture the disadvantages that non-Western women face in current imperial contexts and in resistance to dominant understandings of global politics. Another taxonomy, and one that you will find throughout this book, distinguishes between the global North and the global South. While not perfect, the term global South is now used by many to refer to the uneven power dynamics that disadvantage most of the nations that lie roughly below the United States and Europe (with the exception of Australia and New Zealand, of course). Others, such as Arlif Dirlik, understand this distinction as metaphorical rather than geographic, where the North refers to the pathways of capitalism and the South to the marginalized peoples of the world, regardless of geographical location. Mohanty likes the distinction between One-Third World and the Two-Thirds World, as first discussed by Gustavo Esteva and Madhu Suri Prakash, because it distinguishes between the quality of life experienced by social minorities, the "haves" in the North versus the social majorities, and the "have nots" in the global South.[3]

Yet another taxonomic approach is used by international organizations such as the World Bank and the International Monetary Fund. They classify nations by income or by their degree of development: as high, middle, or low income or as industrialized, developing, or less developed. These classifications require us to specify exactly what we mean by the term economic development. Is economic development a synonym for market-driven economic growth? Or is it a process that is directed at creating greater income equality, less poverty, cleaner and safer environments, better maternal health, reduced infant mortality, improved mass literacy, and greater longevity? The United Nations tacitly adopts the latter view of economic development in the Human Development Index (HDI), a way of ranking nations that goes beyond the simple metric of per capita income to address the degree of human development, which, as we described in chapter 1, is measured by life expectancy, education, and income.

Male Bias in Development

Early economic development theories and policies all but invisibilized women's material contributions and needs. Women were typically viewed as "unproductive" housewives despite the enormous role they played in agricultural production, urban manufacturing, social reproductive labor in the household, and more. In part this was because development economics made the same mistakes as twentieth-century mainstream economics in terms of leaving out the incredible amount of nonmarket labor that women—and to a lesser extent men—were doing in these economies. Early development theories were fixated on increasing the output of market goods and services, and to the extent they recognized nonmarket production, they viewed it as inferior. Further, economic development theories assumed that the sort of male breadwinner-female housewife ideal of the global North was also relevant in global South contexts. Thus they neglected the diversity of economic arrangements within households, not to mention the range of affective arrangements such as extended families, households in which women and men each controlled their own farm plots and income, female-headed households, and others.

By the 1970s, pioneering research on women's role in economic development highlighted some of the failures of this biased thinking. This, combined with pressures from the global feminist movement to take women's needs and contributions seriously, helped to put women's issues on the development map. The United Nations declared 1975 the Year of the Woman and marked this with a world conference on women in Mexico City, which essentially launched the field of gender and development as we now know it. Subsequently, 1976 to 1985 was designated by the United Nations as the Decade on Women, including two more conferences in

Copenhagen (1980) and Nairobi (1985) that further refined the gender-equity goals to be pursued in global South contexts. The final 1995 World Conference on Women in Beijing, which grew out of this initiative, continues to guide global gender-equity thinking to this day.

While the push for a new agenda through the Decade on Women was largely spearheaded by women in the global North, the role of women in developing countries in identifying biases, problems, and solutions was influential as well. For example, a network of women's organizations working through the Economic Commission for Africa brought critical attention to the unrecognized economic contributions of women on that continent in the 1960s.[4] However, many of the concerns raised by women in the global South, such as improved access to water and the need to address food security needs, were not always viewed as feminist in global North contexts, where the focus was on removing barriers to women's inclusion in markets and politics. Further, the issues that were likely to get a hearing in policy settings were those taken up by Northern women who had clout in institutional development organizations, an effect of global power dynamics that unfortunately haunts gender and development to this day. Thus the policies that emerged from the Decade on Women emphasized the integration of women into development through market participation, job training, and schooling. Dubbed the "women in development" (WID) framework, this approach stressed the complementarity between women's liberation and the economic goals of efficiency and growth.

The research of the Danish feminist economist Ester Boserup played a crucial role in the emergence of WID, particularly her 1970 book, *Women's Role in Economic Development*. For instance, the book was used to support a congressional bill in the United States that required the US Agency for International Development (USAID) to include women's issues in all of their development programs. Boserup was not a critic of the existing paradigm of market-led development as much as concerned that women were not able to benefit from it. She accepted the dominant view that development involves modernization and marketization, e.g., a change from subsistence family production to specialized market production. Her important insight was that as development takes place, the socioeconomic functions of the family change, transforming women's roles and status. Boserup particularly questioned the prevailing gender ideology embedded in development policy that saw men as farmers and women as housewives. On the contrary, in much of the developing world food was produced primarily by women. In these female farming systems, women's agricultural work was essential to familial and hence national well-being.

Nowhere was this better exemplified than sub-Saharan Africa, which Boserup deemed the region of female farming par excellence. Further, women's status in agricultural societies was determined by their contributions to food production. Thus the change from female to male farming systems entailed the loss of output as well as the status and freedom of women. The upshot of Boserup's analysis was that women's full integration into modernization schemes, land reform, jobs, and the like would offer a solution to both equity and efficiency concerns in development.[5]

From Women in Development to Gender and Development

Boserup's work, and indeed the entire WID framework, offered a progressive alternative to viewing women as nonproductive members of society. But it also fell short in some key ways, particularly its embrace of capitalist market solutions and instrumental, efficiency criteria for achieving gender equity. Because of this it came under increasing criticism by the late 1970s and early 1980s. Some who attended the first World Conference on Women in Mexico City in 1975, for instance, argued contra Boserup that women in the global South had long been drawn into the public sphere of paid work, but that this led to their impoverishment rather than their liberation. Critical feminist economists Lourdes Benería and Gita Sen pointed to the failure of the WID framework to address the impact of global political and economic structures on women's exploitation.[6] While WID saw the spread of capitalism as a liberating force through the expansion of wage labor and the commodification of goods and services formerly produced in the home to free women from drudgery and domestic subordination, Benería and Sen showed that even with marketization women had remained economically marginalized. Anthropologist Adele Mueller went one step further, decrying the increased visibility of women in development through WID as an attempt to further exploit them within the global capitalist system. She writes of a "contradiction between the emphasis of the women's movement on advancing women's right to speak, be heard and to take economic and political initiative for themselves, and . . . concerns and interests of a very different kind . . . the capitalist world order."[7] Other critics focused on the fact that WID paid insufficient attention to women's unpaid labor and the tensions between women's care work and their market activities. Another important critique of WID focused on its frequent portrayal of traditional patriarchy in global South countries as the primary force oppressing women. This reproduced a colonial script of locating women's oppression within patriarchal relations in "backward" countries while positioning Western women as the liberated saviors of women of the global South.[8]

Eventually, these critiques of WID, along with other concerns that the framework was not attentive to the range of social, cultural, economic, and political transformations needed to challenge gender inequity, gave rise to a new approach, labeled gender and development (GAD). GAD theories challenged the "add women to markets and stir" approaches of WID by examining the gendered power dynamics that worked to structure gender inequities in all spheres of social life. Viewing gender as a category of analysis allowed GAD theorists and practitioners to better understand how relations of power were embedded in development initiatives and how patriarchy, capitalist markets, and modernization might reinforce each other in assigning women inferior roles. For instance, many GAD theorists identified the continuation of neoimperialist relations of development itself as a major factor in ongoing gender relations of power, thus calling into question WID ideas that integrating women into global circuits of work and money would liberate them. Finally, GAD focused on broader social transformation as the key to women's liberation and empowerment.

One important feature of GAD was its emphasis on examining the gender implications of all development policies, rather than looking at "women's issues" in isolation. Whether agricultural policy or financial reform or antipoverty initiatives, all development projects had a potential impact on gender relations. Thus, in order to achieve gender equity, gender analysis had to be central to the design, implementation, and evaluation of development across the board. The GAD call to mainstream gender into development eventually became widespread and remains the primary way that institutions such as the World Bank and USAID operationalize their gender policy. Another important feature of GAD was the attention it gave to men and masculinity, and reforming some of the more pernicious aspects of masculine socialization and gender expectations to improve both men's and women's lives.

However, as GAD ideas were filtered through institutional practices of the major donor organizations, they were often appropriated toward the very systems and ideas that GAD theorists were trying to challenge. For instance, "gender" was, and still is, often a stand-in for "women" in policy contexts. Further, institutions often use the term "gender" as a way to talk about reified behaviors of women, such as all women being carers, rather than tracing out the complexities of socialization and power dynamics in different contexts. Another major concern with how GAD was rolled out in institutions was the tendency to represent women in the global South as victims of "local patriarchal culture" that needed saving, thus reproducing the colonial script of earlier WID approaches that many early GAD theorists had challenged.

Gender and Structural Adjustment

At the time when GAD ideas were just making their way into policy in the 1980s, however, a broader shift was taking place that had enormous implications for policies aimed at resolving gender inequity in development. This was the turn to neoliberal, market-centered policy in the context of the debt crisis in the global South, a crisis we discussed in detail in chapter 7. This policy shift was implemented by the IMF and the World Bank, which instituted Structural Adjustment Policies (SAPs) on cash-strapped nations, making loans conditional on privatizing national industries, devaluing currencies, encouraging exports, drastically reducing social spending, and removing price controls and state subsidies. The predictable results were reduced support for education, health, and social care; increases in the prices of basic commodities like food, milk, and electricity; and labor market dislocations. While policymakers acknowledged that these adjustments might be tough at first, they argued that their benefits would soon trickle down to the poor. In reality, the social dislocations were severe. In Latin America, SAPs ushered in a "lost decade" of development characterized by economic stagnation, widening inequality, and declines in health and education.

The negative impacts of structural adjustment fell particularly hard on poor women. Their responsibilities for care work were increased exponentially as the state reduced support for health care, day care, education, and more. Further, women often lost decent work in the government sector due to budget cuts and then found themselves in precarious export industry or informal sector work. The cost of imported necessities such as food rose, which was another burden on women trying to feed their families. Women often found themselves pursuing an "exhaustion solution" to these changes by increasing their care work at home while spending more time in the labor market. Yet little attention was paid to these gender effects by mainstream economists. Thus feminist economists set out to document these issues and challenge the policies that caused them.[9] Because structural adjustment was increasing unpaid domestic and subsistence activities of women without addressing the fallout, there was also increased attention by feminists to making women's unpaid work visible to policymakers. For instance, at this time there was a push by feminists to get unpaid labor counted in official statistics, which was partially victorious when the United Nations system began to include shadow accounts of the production of goods and services by unpaid workers in households in the 1990s.[10]

Another key area of feminist thinking and policy transformation during this time revolved around the impact of SAP-driven export promotion industrialization on women, discussed in chapter 7. These effects of export promotion on women, as we showed earlier, were highly uneven despite the promise that these jobs would bring liberation and prosperity to female workers. Instead these jobs were more likely to be characterized by unsafe working conditions, low pay, gender stratification, and job insecurity.

While the mainstream development organizations remained largely resistant to taking such concerns seriously, by the 1990s the negative gender impacts of SAPs were irrefutable—as were many of the other negative impacts of these policies on people in the global South—and could no longer be ignored. Mounting empirical evidence plus pressure from activist groups to address the negative effects of liberalization and debt repayment eventually led to an overall conceptual shift in policy that put questions of equity back on the map again.

Human Development and Inclusion

The emergence of an alternative human development approach at the United Nations, influenced by the work of economist Amartya Sen, was part of this shift. The human development approach measures the progress of nations not simply by looking at standard GDP growth but by also examining life expectancy, inequality, and educational attainment. It is based on Sen's idea that the goal of development should be the fostering of human capabilities to help people lead the lives they have reason to value. Human capabilities are fostered by access to economic opportunity, health, knowledge, and ability to make choices for oneself.[11] Ultimately, these new ways of thinking about development ushered in a move away from the strict growth and market efficiency policies of SAPs to an acknowledgment that the human impacts of policies mattered.

The United Nations published its first *Human Development Report* in

1990, which offered a way to measure the success of development not only in the standard terms of GDP growth but also in how well countries were doing at meeting human needs and reducing inequities. The United Nations soon followed the *Human Development Report* with the publication of a Gender Empowerment Measure in 1995, which has since transformed into the Gender Inequality Index, which measures maternal mortality, adolescent birth rates, education rates, political participation, and labor force participation of women to capture their position in different countries.

The World Bank's "Challenge of Inclusion" initiative in the mid-1990s also reframed development away from a strict growth and stabilization project to one that took inequalities and quality of life seriously. The World Bank had long been the most resistant to including gender in any meaningful way in its policies (the only major development institution more resistant, historically, has been the International Monetary Fund), and it showed a change of heart with the release of its first major Policy Research Report on gender launched under the "Challenge of Inclusion" banner. Titled *Engendering Development: Through Gender Equality in Rights, Resources and Voice* (World Bank 2001), the report called for addressing the social and cultural factors that influence women's inability to be included in the development process. It also focused on achieving social development goals such as education and health for women. This represents a far broader approach than the previous World Bank focus on market efficiency only. The report even acknowledged women's disproportionate burdens in care work, a major breakthrough for feminists who had long called for the Bank to acknowledge the social reproduction burdens of its previous structural adjustment policies.[12]

Another example of the expanded space for including women is the extension of ideas about gender budgeting into development policy. This policy framework emerged originally from feminist economists' concerns about the differential impact of structural adjustment on women and men and, combined with the focus on achieving women's human rights in the Beijing 1995 Platform for Action, argued that all budgets are not simply technocratic exercises but have an impact on the human rights of the most vulnerable. Gender budgets are used to account for gender biases and gaps in government tax and spending policy in at least forty-five developing economies around the globe. These gender budgets have been drawn on to support policies addressing women's unpaid care burdens, education for girls, and even gender-based violence. Feminist economists Diane Elson, Radhika Balakrishnan, and James Heintz have called for a further development of gender budgets that employ a rights-based approach to implementing and evaluating taxation and spending for its impact on the rights of poor people and women.[13] This idea has been taken up by UN Women, which is supporting gender budgeting initiatives in a growing number of countries.

Taking Unpaid Care Work Seriously

Attention to unpaid care work and social reproduction, based on lessons learned from the negative impact of SAPs on women's lives, also made its way into the mainstream of development policy in the late twentieth and early twenty-first centuries. Feminists pushed to get unpaid labor counted in official statistics, achieving a partial victory when the United Nations system of national accounts created satellite statistics that included the production of goods by unpaid workers in households. There was also a successful push to get gender-equity policy frameworks at the World Bank, United Nations Development Program, and other institutions to address women's unpaid social reproductive burdens. Some of these policies drew on the feminist economic theories we discussed in earlier chapters, but most of them did not value social reproduction on its own terms as much as considering its impact on women's ability to work outside the home. Realizing that the social reproductive burdens of women kept them out of the paid labor force, policies began to try to reduce these burdens. In some cases, this meant policies that encouraged the market production of care, which would allow women to purchase childcare, elder care, and cooked meals and other goods and services formerly produced in the home, while simultaneously creating paid employment for women. Other policy recommendations, including the UN Women's 2019–2020 Progress of the World's Women: Families in a Changing World, call for public support for care work to reduce women's unpaid labor exploitation and drudgery.[14] Other policy prescriptions called for transforming the way that work was divided in households itself, often tied to women's ability to earn income, which would give them more power to demand task sharing with their male partners at home.

An interesting companion policy to these strategies of providing women access to income to empower them at home has been the explicit encouragement of more egalitarian relations between heterosexual couples by development agencies. As political economist Kate Bedford discusses in her book *Developing Partnerships*, World Bank policies rolled out in Ecuador and elsewhere pursued a two-pronged approach of giving more resources to women through paid labor, which would empower them at home, plus training sessions for their male partners to be more responsible for care work at home. While the idea of using development policy to make heterosexual relationships more egalitarian is an appealing one, the actual policy did not help to resolve the care crisis for the many working women who had care responsibilities but were not in coupled partnerships.[15]

Microcredit and Microfinance

The idea of providing women with small loans to foster their economic well-being and empowerment also moved from the margins to the mainstream of development policy in the late twentieth and early twenty-first centuries. Giving women microcredit loans, that is, very small loans of less than $100 to start small-scale informal sector enterprises, is an idea that dates back to the early 1980s. At that time, Grameen Bank founder and CEO Muhammad Yunus pioneered the idea of providing subsidized credit to the "poorest of the poor" in Bangladesh, where lack of collateral was a barrier to borrowing otherwise. In order to be considered for a subsidized Grameen Bank loan, a woman had to be a member of a "loan circle." If one woman in the loan circle did not pay back her loan, then all other women in the circle would be ineligible for future lending or held responsible for repayment of her loan. In this way, the solidarity among women—being invested in each other's success—and the collective liability of the group served as a form of collateral.

Early recipients of Grameen Bank loans typically used their funds to start at-home businesses such as handicraft production, marketed foodstuffs, or piecework for local factories. Working at home allowed these women to earn money while meeting the domestic responsibilities that, as we discussed earlier, typically fall largely on women's shoulders. But because these enterprises were located in the highly competitive, low-paid, and insecure informal sector of the economy, the work and income stream were often precarious. Yet the Grameen Bank trumpeted its successes in achieving repayment rates of around 95 percent and empowering poor women to earn their own income so they are not dependent on handouts.

Microcredit was not initially embraced by mainstream development, but by the 1990s it was increasingly adopted as an innovative way to tackle global poverty by major development institutions, national governments in the global South, and NGOs. However, at this point, private sector loans by and large replaced the subsidized loans of the Grameen model, making such lending highly lucrative. Microcredit became a way to eradicate poverty through profits. For the past twenty years or so, there has been an expansion of profitable financial services to the poor, including savings accounts, insurance, and loans of all kinds (not just to foster new businesses provided and dispensed through loan circle lending). Increasingly, this range of services to the poor, dubbed microfinance, has been overtaken by commercial bank lending at relatively high rates of interest. The mission of such lending has moved further away from poverty alleviation and more about financial inclusion, of bringing the poor into the global credit system.

Research by Lamia Karim and Ha-Joon Chang and Milford Bateman has shown that the impact of microcredit and microfinance has not been as positive as its champions have claimed. While some women have benefited, microcredit and microfinance have not been a way out of poverty for most. It has increased insecurity for some groups, especially poor farming families who struggle to pay back loans and who have to sell off family assets or divert income to loan repayment. Microcredit fosters the growth of the informal sector, which rarely generates decent working conditions and pay for its participants. Finally, it increasingly enriches the holders of capital in the name of development.[16] However, in many circles microcredit is still viewed as a "magic bullet" for achieving women's empowerment and poverty alleviation. The idea of microcredit taps into a popular discourse of poverty as an individual problem that can be resolved through self-help and personal responsibility, rather than structural change.

The Girl Effect

Another popular approach to fostering empowerment and poverty alleviation for women and girls in the global South is the Girl Effect. Launched in 2008 by the Nike Foundation in collaboration with other corporate philanthropies, and since 2015 an independent organization, it aims to "rebrand poverty" in a way that takes girls' issues seriously. Nike's savvy advertising campaign for the Girl Effect brings attention to the importance of investing in girls' human capital through education, training, and health interventions. In fact, in the promotional videos, educating girls is posited not only as empowering to the girls themselves but as a solution to global poverty. Education and training, it is argued, will result in reduced fertility, girls' empowerment through paid work once they complete their education, efficiency, economic growth, and better care for the children she will have in the future, thus continuing the positive cycle. Girl Effect posits that it is more than girls who are saved when you give them an education. The girls themselves will save the world through reduced fertility and higher productivity and growth.

Nike's Girl Effect philanthropy is but one example of what feminist political economist Adrienne Roberts has dubbed "transnational business feminism," in which feminist activism has been increasingly corporatized.[17] With the Girl Effect, we can see these transnational business elements at work. The Nike corporation itself launched the project. The project is focused on bottom-line goals, claiming that investing in girls will provide a smart return on investment. Further, like microcredit, Girl Effect embraces a neoliberal solution to poverty focused not on structural change but on self-motivated, empowered individuals producing for the market.

Research on the outcomes of Girl Effect initiatives has shown that it does not achieve its goals when it lands on the ground. Some scholars have shown that Nike-funded programs targeting girls are more focused on brand loyalty and building a customer base for Nike products among the global poor than raising girls out of poverty. Others have shown that only a very narrow category of "girls" can be viewed as eligible for the Girl Effect programs (not too old, not too young, not too educated, not too uneducated, not too poor, not too rich, not pregnant, not married), which limits the impact and success of such programs on the ground. Still others have shown how Girl Effect programs have drawn girls into global financialization and debt, to the benefit of transnational lenders.[18]

While increased attention to the needs of girls in development is a positive development, the way it has been rolled out into policy through philanthropies such as the Girl Effect leaves much to be desired. Of particular concern to many analysts of gender and development policy is the focus that these programs place on achieving instrumental goals of fertility reduction and GDP growth in ways that seem to marginalize broader questions of gender equity. What would happen if the numbers related to productivity and GDP growth did not add up? Would girls' empowerment still be a goal worth pursuing? And what particular ways of thinking about empowerment—as an individualistic exercise, as insertion into the market economy and generating one's own income, as investing income into your children's human capital—are foregrounded in these corporatized development projects, and what ways of thinking about gender equity and empowerment are foreclosed by them?

Empowerment Lite?

While a shift in gender and development away from the strict neoliberalism of SAPs toward more emphasis on women's inclusion, rights, and empowerment is a positive thing, it is also important to note that the change is not as dramatic as it appears. In terms of the priorities of the major development organizations, reflected in spending, personnel investments, and the like, it is clear that gender equity continues to take a far back seat to goals of efficiency and growth in development. The total spending on specific gender empowerment initiatives by the major global development institutions—the World Bank, IMF, USAID, and UNDP—while far greater than in the 1990s, still remains a small fraction of their budgets. The goals achieved have also been more modest than one might imagine from what is celebrated in official documents. The greatest improvements have been in the areas of health—such as maternal mortality declining by a dramatic 37 percent in the last quarter century, and female to male education ratios dramatically shrinking in Sub-Saharan Africa during that same time period. These are certainly important and cannot be discounted. However, in terms of those aspects of change related to economic livelihoods for women, the pace has been slow. Women continue to experience higher rates of poverty, larger burdens of unpaid work, and greater lack of access to and control of resources compared to men.[19]

A further concern, and perhaps an explanation for the slow progress on equity itself, is that interest in gender in development institutions has largely been framed in the most instrumental of terms, as we pointed out in our discussion of the Girl Effect. The focus is on investing in women because it is good for the bottom line, "smart economics." Instead of a wholesale change in approach, increased attention to gender and development over the past couple of decades reflects a slightly reformed version of the neoliberal focus on efficiency that characterized structural adjustment. The dominant idea—roundly critiqued by earlier generations of feminist scholars—continues to be that insertion into wage labor, and the marketization of former nonmarket goods, is liberating to women. As noted feminist development economist Naila Kabeer has argued, women's access to decent work and income can certainly enhance their agency to make choices they value and thus contribute to their empowerment. But the kinds of work that women in the global South often find themselves in are not always decent. They are often precarious and marginalized forms of informal sector work, sex/race/caste segregated work, and highly exploitative.[20]

Unfortunately, "empowerment" as a concept deployed by the World Bank, IMF, Nike Foundation and other mainstream institutions typically refers to women's and girls' ability to unleash their economic potential, without attention to the nature of the economic relations they are drawn into. Nor is attention paid to broader gender power relations beyond those keeping women out of global credit and labor markets. This "empowerment lite," as feminist anthropologist Andrea Cornwall calls it, is one stripped of attention to changing structural relations toward feminist and transformative ends, and instead is focused on integrating women into existing institutions because it is good for growth.[21]

Further, these calls for investing in women because it is good for growth often assume that traditional gender roles will be maintained even as women are being pulled into nontraditional roles as workers and entrepreneurs. For instance, many boosters have supported gender-equity programs with the unproven "ghost statistic" that, once empowered by paid labor, women will spend 90 percent of their earnings on their children's well-being, whereas men, who are supposedly less invested in their children's well-being, spend only 30–40 percent. With this flawed, essentialized notion in mind, policies focus on getting women jobs because they are assumed to be natural carers.[22] As Cornwall puts it, such efforts are "putting them (women) to work for development rather than making development work for *them*."[23]

Other Feminist Challenges to Development: Postcolonial Feminism and LGBTQI Perspectives

Frustration with the failure of successive waves of gender and development policy to come anywhere close to meeting the liberatory ideals of feminism has led some to question the very development project itself. For many, the notion of having global South nations "catch up" to the industrialized countries is both untenable and based on flawed premises. In an era of ecological crisis, the idea that all nations should be industrial, high-consumption economies seems like an undesirable goal. Further, environmental degradation has always fallen hardest on poor women whose livelihoods are affected by dam projects, the effects of global climate change, and rainforest destruction.[24] Instead of helping all women, modernization is likely to hurt many poor women.

The flawed premises of "catching up" also include the assumption that countries in the global South are poor because they have not had enough exposure to Western ideas or the spread of capitalist markets, when in fact the histories of colonialism and capitalism show long and deep encounters. The underlying binary framing of the modern/backward "catching up" model also furthered unhelpful colonial representations of the global South. This contributed to discounting global South women's knowledge and expression of their own needs, instead turning them into "clients" of development while the power to define the problems and their solutions rested with Western development policymakers and practitioners.[25]

This concern emerges from a branch of feminism referred to as postcolonial feminism, which pays attention to the politics of representation in development, particularly how the global South as a whole is typically characterized as inferior, backward, and in need of saving. This is a false and dangerous "single story," as Nigerian author Chimamanda Ngozi Adichie has called it.[26] It reduces the economic, cultural, social, and political heterogeneity of the Two-Thirds World to a single "Third World" defined by what it lacks: technology, industry, modernity, liberty, and wealth. When these politics of representation are trained on poor women in the global South Chandra Mohanty argues, it reduces them to a single type of subject: a helpless victim of local cultures who needs saving. Thus many feminist economists argue that it is vitally important to be attentive to the representational politics of gender and development, lest we reproduce these sorts of narratives where what becomes lost are the needs, desires, and agency of women in the global South themselves.[27]

In addition to an increased emphasis on the flawed colonial assumptions of mainstream gender and development, there have been more scholars questioning the sexuality assumptions of these policies. To a great extent, gender and development theories and policies have tended to assume a heterosexual and cisgender (those whose gender identity matches the one assigned to them at birth) subject, which has invisibilized and/or pathologized affective relationships and identities that do not fit these narrow frames. After all, values about family life have always been embedded in economic development and modernization projects, as they are in economic policy more generally, and the regulation of sexuality in the global South has been a crucial aspect of development since World War II. While much of this regulation has focused on the project of population control, there was also some anxiety about making sure that households conformed to the heterosexual and gender normative ideal of the West.

Since the 1990s, both feminist and LGBTQI activists and scholars have increasingly challenged these biases. There have been efforts to put sexual rights on the table in development, particularly through the work of Outright International. In addition, feminist economists such as Lee Badgett have brought increased attention to the economic costs of discrimination against these groups in development policy contexts. Her research on India, for instance, shows an approximate 3.8 percent GDP loss per year due to stigma and discrimination against LGBTQI individuals in that country.[28] Other work in this area includes challenging the heteronormative assumptions of economic policy in which a particular kind of household is presented as the only legitimate family type, which has all kinds of negative effects on the range of households—female-headed, extended family, same-sex couples, and the like—who do not fit this frame. For example, the economic theories of the household that undergird many gender and development policies present heterosexual coupling as the dominant form of family life and thus a target of policy, and forms outside of it, such as female-headed households, are often viewed as broken versions of what they should be and in need of "fixing" to make them intact again.[29]

Another issue LGBTQI scholars have been tackling in this regard is exposing "pinkwashing," in which countries claim they are committed to sexual rights to signal their modernity and get development funding from the USAID, World Bank, or other agency, while covering up other human rights abuses. Clearly the ways that sexual rights intersect with gender and development are complex, and there is much work that remains to be done in this area. What is clear, however, is that a feminist economics that wants to be truly liberatory must include attention to LGBTQI in their conceptual framework.

Conclusion: Gender, Development, and Feminist Economic Goals

Have the policies and practices associated with economic development contributed to the goals we set out in this book for a well-functioning economy? In terms of provisioning to improve the quality of life, we note that since 1981 (when a consistent series of global poverty statistics was first collected) there has been a decline in global poverty. However, there are still more than a billion people living in extreme poverty, as we discussed in chapter 6, and women are disproportionately represented in that group. Food insecurity and malnutrition remain issues in much of the world, and in recent years the prevalence of malnutrition has been rising in all areas of the global South.[30] On a more positive note, since 1990, life expectancy and literacy rates have been rising alongside gains in income in the developing world, resulting in overall improvements in the Human Development Index for the developing world.[31] Also there has been a significant reduction of 44 percent in maternal mortality worldwide since 1990.[32]

Regarding the question of equity, there are a number of issues to consider, and we will only cover a few here. One startling inequity on the global stage is that the gap between the developed and developing nations is widening when the promise of development economics was a convergence between them, making the world a more unequal place. The one exception here is the region of East Asia, which is catching up with the West. Inequality and the gap between rich and poor within developing countries are also on the rise. In terms of gender equity, women in the developing world have made gains vis-a-vis men in terms of education and access to livelihoods, but the gap in mortality by gender has not closed, and women's share of employment, which rose in the 1970s and 1980s, has lagged in the developing world since 1990.[33] A further point is that intersectional analyses of gender inequality tell us that women who come from the poorest families, women who face structural racism and casteism, disabled women, and LGBTQI persons face greater hurdles because of multiple and overlapping forms of oppression.

Regarding the quality of work life, in the developing world most paid work is informal, meaning without benefits or protections. Women in particular are clustered in informal sector work that is precarious: part-time, insecure, and low-paid. Current efforts by the International Labour Organization to create decent work opportunities for all—work that is productive, secure, fairly paid, includes social protections, is not dangerous—have made some improvements to work life. For instance, there has been a 30 percent reduction in the number of child laborers since 2000. However, there is still room for improvement on that goal.

Insecurities related to poverty, war, crime, religious difference, gender oppression, ethnic conflict, and the like are on the rise in the developing world, which has resulted in patterns of out-migration to escape violence and conflict. Finally, development has shown mixed results in achieving the goal of sustainability. While some efforts to promote sustainable growth have been pursued in developing economies, current methods of resource extraction, industrial growth, and agricultural development result in deforestation, high levels of air and water pollution, and overall environmental degradation that falls hard on the poor, especially poor women. It remains to be seen if the Sustainable Development Goals can help to reverse these trends. There is still a significant amount to be done to achieve the goals of provisioning, equity, decent work, security, and sustainability. This is why gender and development is such an important field for continued activist research in feminist economics today.

9 | Debt, Gender, and Crisis Economics

Although the global financial crisis of 2008 originated in the United States, it caused profound harm to the lives of people around the world. Its effects persist and continue to shape our economic and political environment. Developing countries in the global South are still paying on loans they took out for development purposes in the 1970s; Greece still suffers as a result of the fallout from the 2010 Euro crisis; real income in the United Kingdom continues to decline; in the United States the millions of people who lost their homes to foreclosure still have not recovered their losses; and the Federal Reserve Bank of San Francisco estimates a reduction of about $70,000 in lifetime income for every American.[1]

The conventional story told about the crisis and its aftermath either ignores gender altogether or constructs an essentialist morality tale about testosterone fueled traders run amok on Wall Street. The feminist story that we tell is rather different. Instead of engaging in a debate about biology and gender difference, we examine the dynamics of the 2008 crisis through a critical feminist lens. Following the work of the feminist economist Diane Elson, we conceptualize the economy in terms of three interconnected spheres: the *financial* sphere, where institutions such as banks and investment companies provide financial services for individuals and businesses; the *productive* sphere, where goods and services are produced for sale; and the *reproductive* sphere, where people are reproduced, both daily and intergenerationally, through care, socialization, and education.[2] Conventional accounts of the crisis, whether mainstream or heterodox, examine the connections between the financial sphere and the productive sphere and may include discussions of gender and racial inequality. But the reproductive sphere is mostly taken for granted. A feminist analysis, however, foregrounds social reproduction as the cornerstone on which all other economic activities and functions rest.[3]

The 2008 crisis should not be seen in isolation but as an extension of the debt crises that began in the 1970s.[4] One constant that emerges from this point of view is that generally the people who cause the crises are not the ones who bear the consequences. They are borne by people, families, and communities near the bottom of economic, political, and social hierarchies. They are the ones left to bear the burden of debts for which they were in no way responsible. The question is, who owes what to whom? It is both a simple and a profound question.

Who Owes What to Whom?

To answer this, we begin with financial debts. They are the "common sense" way that people think about debt: as something impersonal and quantifiable.[5] If I borrow $100 from you and promise to return it on a specified date and then do not, I am morally culpable. After all, "surely one has to pay one's debts!"[6] However, not all debts are so simple and not all debts are legitimate: debts that exploit the vulnerability and impoverishment of others are ethically questionable at best, while debts that are the result of loans knowingly given to dictators, or that harm people and the environment, are examples of illegitimate or odious debts.[7] Moreover, there are many debts that entail moral obligations and cannot be fully reduced to dollars and cents.[8] The question of who owes what to whom is both an ethical one and a legal one, and the legal answer may often be at odds with the ethical answer.

For example, by now it is well established that the economic development of Europe required the enslaved labor and expropriation of the natural resources of the new world. Today, by any reasonable moral calculus, the global North owes a huge debt to the global South. At present, however, the South finds itself in the unfortunate position of being a net creditor to the North through payments on its international debt obligations. Women working on the global assembly line in their home countries or migrating to work as maids in the global North and wealthy Gulf states are an integral part of this state of affairs.

The feminist geographer Saskia Sassen has dubbed this the feminization of survival.[9] As we have discussed in previous chapters, the income earned by these women not only supports themselves and their families but is essential to the economic survival of their countries because international debts must be paid in hard currency, generally US dollars.[10] In addition to the gendered human costs, this state of affairs makes no sense economically. It deepens poverty and misery; accelerates income inequality; defers investments in health, education, and infrastructure; and perhaps, most alarmingly, ties our hands with respect to ameliorating climate change. On a personal level, these macro conditions negatively impact people who find themselves pushed into personal indebtedness in order to preserve life itself: housing, food, energy, clothing, medicine, transportation, and education.

We are all familiar with the saying, "they have paid their debt to society." This is generally used in regard to criminals serving their prison time. However, the notion of a debt to society is broader than that. It is that by virtue of being members of a human community we all owe a debt to society and to future generations to provide a just and sustainable environment in which human beings can flourish. Sadly, we have incurred large deficits in this regard and find ourselves facing ever growing debts to the environment, to low-paid care workers, and to all the other varied people and things necessary for social reproduction. A fetish with balanced budgets and unexamined notions about the ethics of debt are major impediments to producing a more just and sustainable—- i.e., feminist—social order.

A feminist ethics of debt also requires understanding that people's subjectivities and sense of self are tied to financial structures and logics. Today many people are only able to maintain their standard of living by relying on debt, credits cards, second mortgages, and even payday loans.[11] This is the "financialization of everyday life."[12] In the financial sphere, however, women are woefully underrepresented in key decision-making positions, and consequently little attention is paid to the gendered (or raced, as people of color are likewise underrepresented) impacts of financial decisions.[13] Moreover, financial illiteracy is correlated with costly credit card behavior, which in turn contributes to amassing crippling levels of consumer debt.[14] Unfortunately, banks and other financial institutions have no incentive to educate borrowers—quite the opposite in fact: they take advantage of borrowers' naivety.

Globalization and Debt

One of the basic principles that emerged in the late 1970s and early 1980s was that state power should protect financial institutions at all costs. As the Marxist scholar David Harvey puts it, "save the banks and put the screws to the people."[15] Until relatively recently these screws were put mainly to people in the global South. That is no longer true. Today many countries in the global North face economic problems that are similar to the ones faced by indebted countries in the global South. These include decreased levels of government spending on health, education, and infrastructure; a dramatic rise in income inequality; and a wealthy elite intent on evading their fair share of the tax burden. Just as economic troubles trapped the global South in a web of debt, the economic problems following the 2008 financial crisis, the great recession, and ongoing economic stagnation have trapped large parts of the global North in a similar situation.

The globalization of debt is, in an ironic sense, a leveling mechanism, a variation on the old "race to the bottom" theme. For example, consider Jamaica, a Caribbean country, and Ferguson, Missouri, a city in the United States. The details are vastly different, but structurally the problems are similar. Jamaica has been in debt since the late 1960s and since then has been subject to the "macroeconomic discipline" of the International Monetary Fund (IMF). Today economic growth is low while poverty, unemployment, and crime are high. Fiscal restraint and public debt reduction are the anchors of the macroeconomic policy imposed on Jamaica by the IMF.

Ferguson is a poor, highly segregated, predominately black city with rampant poverty, high unemployment, and heavy debt obligations stemming from the sale of municipal bonds. Since it cannot run a budget deficit, it is also subject to macroeconomic discipline. For both locales, spending targeted to meet the needs of the local people, especially the poor, takes a back seat to meeting their debt service obligations to traders in global financial markets. Debt, and the austerity mechanisms that accompany it, have become mechanisms for converting the resources of the many—women, racialized minorities, the working poor—into the profits of the few—the financial class. They are the class of people whose income derives from the returns on financial assets: insurance company executives, stockbrokers, investors, and bankers.[16]

The Lehman Sisters Revisited

Popular opinion regards the financial sector as masculine in nature. The willingness to take risks is associated with "manliness," or more formally, hegemonic masculinity, which may be considered the culturally idealized form of manhood.[17] Today it is embodied in wealthy, or at least comfortable, able-bodied white men. For example, consider advertisements for financial services. They depict sober, farsighted, and trustworthy financial advisors carefully guiding hardworking people through the perils and promises of the world of trading and investing. There is, however, another side to this story about masculinity and finance. It is depicted in various US films and documentaries that portray financial traders as grown-up bad boys, fueled by testosterone, drugs, and alcohol, who cast all caution to the wind in their ceaseless pursuit of riches.

This popular depiction of Wall Street, which emerged in the aftermath of the global financial crisis, led many scholars and policymakers to pose the by now well-known rhetorical question: what if the Lehman Brothers had been the Lehman Sisters?[18] Putting the issue this way was attractive to feminists and conservatives alike. It led to another empirical question: are women less risk averse than men? If so, then it was clear where the blame for the financial crisis lay.

The feminist economist Julie Nelson and other feminist political economy scholars took a different view.[19] Nelson carefully examined the studies that claimed that women were more risk averse than men and found that these reports were flawed in their conclusions. Yes, the studies did show that on average women are associated with greater risk aversion. However, this is a statement about averages; the difference is quite small, and women and men are more alike than they are different in regard to risk aversion. Nelson still contends that an increase of women in the higher echelons of Wall Street would be a positive thing. Not because they are essentially more risk averse but because they bring different values and attitudes to the table due to their different social positions. Diverse opinions would go a long way toward stopping the sort of herd mentality that leads to crises. As she puts it,

> [a] leader in the financial industry or its regulation should be prepared to take risks, but also to do so with proper caution and care. When a one-sidedly "macho" culture of finance developed, however, it became all too easy to denigrate appropriate caution as something sissified and weak, while elevating the reckless behavior associated with aggressive masculinity.[20]

Nelson puts her finger on the problem for debt and finance: well-functioning financial markets should distinguish between rational risk taking, which potentially leads to higher profits, and irresponsible gambling, which can lead to ruinous losses.[21] This is precisely what the laws and regulations governing finance are intended to do. However, the complexity of today's financial instruments is such that the boundary between legitimate trading and pure speculation, essentially gambling, is not easy to discern.[22] Nor is the boundary between legal and illegal trading practices.[23]

Still, properly functioning financial markets can be wealth-creating rather than wealth-destroying. In order to function properly, financial markets require oversight not only of the bad boys of Wall Street, but also of the well-dressed patriarchs of the global financial system. The real "wolves of Wall Street" are in fact the top executives of the big investment banks; the top officers of the IMF and other international institutions; the heads of the central banks, especially the US Federal Reserve; the European Central Bank; and the leaders of powerful political entities like the United States and the European Union.[24] They are the ones whose decisions cause crises. They are the ones who bail out the banks and impose austerity on the 99 percent. It is their behavior that needs to be checked if financial markets are to serve public purposes. We agree with the political economist Anne Pettifor's criterion for a well-functioning global financial system as one that will

> . . . ensure that finance or credit are deployed fairly, at sustainable rates of interest, for sound, affordable economic activity, and not for risky and often systematically dangerous speculation.[25]

To her list we would add, promotes investments that valorize social reproduction.

How Will We Pay for It?

Whenever progressives pressure governments for more public spending on the goods and services that benefit the many rather than the few they are met with the response, how will we pay for it? (Although this question is rarely asked in terms of defense spending.) Behind this question is the assumption that governments should be run like households. Just as a household has to balance its budget, so should the government. This view is firmly rooted in nineteenth-century monetary theory—a time when currencies were backed by precious metals (typically gold or silver). Its proponents believe that there is perfect symmetry between national/public debts and household/corporate/private debts. From this (mistaken) view, government (and all government sponsored activities like education, postal delivery, and so on) must be subject to the same requirements as businesses and households—income must equal or exceed expenditures. The books must balance. When debts build up, governments are unable to finance the debt by increasing the money supply, and hard choices have to be made.

However, the government's budget is not like a household budget, because a sovereign government has the power to create money indefinitely. The issue is *not* whether the government is running a deficit but what that money is being spent on and whether there are idle resources in the economy. Governments can channel deficit spending into investments that will pay off in the future: health and education, bridges and roads, clean energy solutions, and computer networks. This is not just a minority point of view. Even the editorial board of the *Financial Times*, a mainstream daily newspaper headquartered in London, states that "[g]reater budget deficits should be welcomed if they finance spending to fit our economies for the future."[26] In contrast, large government debts that are the result of tax cuts for the wealthy, such as the ballooning US deficit run up by the Trump administration, will be a burden on future generations because the spending is directed to enriching the elite rather than to investment in the future of the country.[27]

Now you might ask, what about inflation? What about Weimar Germany in the period preceding World War II? Prices doubled every three days and the currency collapsed. There are many other examples, including Confederate dollars in the United States during the Civil War and more recently Zimbabwe in 2007–2008, where prices doubled every two days. These are all examples of hyperinflation, inflation that is out of control and destroys the currency because people no longer have faith in its value. There is no doubt that this is a serious problem. However, hyperinflation is not caused by deficit spending. It is caused by structural shocks to economies and political systems such as war and civil unrest. In ordinary times, it is the responsibility of the government to manage the supply of money and credit and to direct it toward productive uses. Ann Pettifor makes this point when she argues that democracies must, and can, reclaim control over money production and restrain the unregulated finance sector so as to serve the interests of the many as well as the health of the environment.[28]

A last thought on inflation. The conservative economist Milton Friedman once quipped that inflation is like a few drinks at a cocktail party. It lubricates the social fabric. The trick is knowing when to stop. Much like a leader in the temperance movement, he advocated strict control of the supply of money and credit. He knew, of course, that inflation hurts lend-ers and helps borrowers because it lowers the real interest rate; borrowers can repay their debts with money that is worth less than it was when they borrowed it.[29] It is not at all surprising to us that the financial class has a vested interest in not letting the cocktail party get out of hand. But they go too far. The specter of inflation upholds the fiction that money is a scarce commodity and deficit spending is reckless and irresponsible, something advocated only by soft-hearted and soft-headed economists and activists. We beg to disagree. Money is not a scarce commodity; it is social con-struction and can be managed for the benefit of the common good.

Common Causes and Common Solutions

As we discussed in chapter 6, in 1971 the United States abandoned the gold standard, one of the major pillars of the Bretton Woods agreements. Since then the world has seen a series of major debt crises: the Third World debt crisis, the US Savings and Loan crisis, the Peso and Asian financial crises, the global financial crisis and ensuing Great Recession, and the Euro cri-sis, to name some of the better known.[30] These debt crises fall into two camps. In the global South, they were the result of a combination of devel-opment strategies financed by international borrowing that became unsustainable in the face of rising interest rates and changes in the struc-ture of the global economy. They culminated in draconian IMF and World Bank-led Structural Adjustment Policies (SAPs). In the global North, debt crises resulted in large part from the adoption of neoliberal financial poli-cies that radically deregulated the financial sector, culminating in fiscal austerity policies.

Despite their differences, they have an underlying common cause and common policy response. The common cause was an excess of liquidity in financial markets—banks were flush with cash and looking for places to lend it—which fueled unsustainable bubbles. Financial bubbles that are not supported by the underlying value of the assets are not sustainable. What causes bubbles? One explanation is that when economic times are good, the demand for credit increases as expectations about the future become increasingly positive. Individuals, businesses, and corporations borrow in order to invest in the latest "in" thing, be it tulips in Holland in the early seventeenth century, real estate in Thailand, or mortgage-backed securities in the United States in the early twenty-first century.

This explanation was articulated in economics by Hyman Minsky, building on John Maynard Keynes's distinction between enterprise (what we are calling productive investment) and speculation. Speculation, according to Keynes, refers to the activity of forecasting the psychology of the market, while enterprise refers to the forecasting of the prospective yield of assets over their life span. In other words, speculation is buying stock in a company not because you think the earnings of the company will increase but because you think that the market thinks that the stock price will rise. As the organization of financial markets improves, the predominance of speculation increases. Keynes famously argues,

> Speculators may do no harm as bubbles on a steady stream of enterprise. But the position is serious when enterprise becomes the bubble on a whirlpool of speculation. When the capital development of a country becomes a by-product of the activities of a casino, the job is likely to be ill-done.[31]

When bubbles burst, as they always do, the people who caused the bubble and enjoyed the temporary riches are rarely the same people who are left to pick up the tab.

As discussed above, the common solution imposed by the IMF and other international financial institutions was, and continues to be, to provide bailout funds to soothe the fears of the national and transnational investors and to impose belt-tightening measures, such as SAPs in the global South and fiscal austerity measures in the global North. As we discussed in chapter 6, austerity includes cutbacks in government spending on social welfare programs; elimination of subsidies on basic commodities, energy, and housing; tax increases for the working and middle class; and decreases in the real minimum wage. SAPs include a poisonous combination of austerity mixed with changes in the structures of the economy such as privatization and liberalization. Austerity and SAPs are both extremely unpopular among the vast majority of people. Decreased spending puts a damper on growth that makes recessions worse and thus contributes to the debt problem rather than fixing it.[32] Why in the world would any sane economist advocate for them?

The mainstream rationale is that they will restore investor confidence, improve economic efficiency, and spur economic growth, but decades of experience and research on this topic suggests a very different outcome. Austerity measures, we have learned, cause other crises: in living standards, in the availability of decent work, and in the provision of public services and welfare support. Moreover, crises destabilize politics and lead to the rise of populism and nationalism.[33] Most importantly, they shift the burden of debt from the financial class, famously called the "one percent," to the rest of society. The consequences of austerity on the lives of ordinary people, especially the poor, who constitute the majority of people in the world, have been disastrous. Women, especially poor women, bear the brunt of the consequences because they are the ones who pick up the slack when subsidies are eliminated, food prices rise, wages fall, and taxes increase.

Deregulating Financial Markets

The 2008 financial crisis sent shock waves through global financial systems and marked a turning point in the global economy. As in previous debt crises, the policy solution was to bail out the financial sector and impose austerity on the rest of us. The difference is that by then, policymakers knew better; they knew that austerity is the wrong answer. So why do they continue? There are many reasons, chief among them is that the immense wealth of the financial class translates into political power. Another reason is the hold that neoliberalism has on the mainstream of the economics profession and therefore on policymakers.

The principles of neoliberalism were put into practice in the United States and the United Kingdom under the leadership of President Reagan and Prime Minister Margaret Thatcher, respectively. Speaking the rhetoric of freedom and choice, they prepared the soil for the liberalization of financial markets that was to come. Many serious economists, political theorists, and political scientists who did not drink the Kool-Aid saw the writing on the wall and argued for continued, different, and better regulation of the financial sector. Sadly, they were a minority voice. Guided by neoliberal economic rhetoric and funded by wealthy donors such as the Koch brothers, policymakers in the United States relentlessly pursued the deregulation of financial markets while at the same time dismantling the social safety nets characteristic of the "golden age of capitalism."

The deregulation, or liberalization, of financial markets gave capital the ability to cross international borders, and this subsequently weakened the power of labor unions in the United States.[34] During the late 1980s, various books and articles chronicled what was called the "deindustrialization of America."[35] As manufacturing jobs moved from the global North to the global South, real wages stagnated, and income inequality widened dramatically. Politicians and government officials responded not by taking steps to decrease inequality but by providing easy credit so that consumers could maintain their standard of living by increasingly relying on debt.[36] A working paper by economists Michael Kumhof and Romain Rancière shows that high-income households were able to recycle part of their additional income back to the rest of the population by way of loans.[37] Without a reasonable prospect of wage growth and increase in the incomes of poor and middle-income households, the debt became unsustainable. This unsustainable debt created the excess liquidity in the same way that "petro dollars" created the excess liquidity that led to the Third World debt crisis. Protecting the interests of the investor class, this time through deregulation, was again the priority.

The neoliberal zeal for financial deregulation began with the Savings and Loan (S&L) crisis that started in the mid-1970s. S&Ls were specialized banks whose purpose was to increase home ownership by funding mortgages. This funding was obtained by offering higher rates on savings accounts than other commercial banks. This sanguine arrangement began to break down in 1973, as inflation reared its ugly head. As we discussed above, lenders are hurt by inflation because it lowers the real interest rate. The S&Ls were trapped into long-term mortgages at already relatively low-interest rates and constrained by federal regulations from raising the rate of interest that they paid to depositors.[38] As their depositors fled in search of higher returns, the S&Ls teetered on the brink of insolvency.

The policy response was deregulation. A variety of measures was passed that effectively loosened or removed regulatory constraints on the ability of commercial banks to engage in the sort of speculation characteristic of investment banks. These three were the most salient: In 1980, the Depository Institutions Deregulation and Monetary Control Act was passed, which among other things removed the ceilings on interest rates. The Garn-St. Germain Depository Institutions Act was passed in 1982, which deregulated the S&Ls and allowed banks to provide adjustable rate mortgages. Finally, in 1999, the Gramm-Leach-Bliley Act was passed. It repealed the Glass-Steagall Act of 1933.[39] The purpose of Glass-Steagall was to prevent runs on banks that were endemic during the Great Depression. It separated commercial banking from investment banking and created the Federal Deposit Insurance Corporation (FDIC) to insure deposits.

Glass-Steagall had been so weakened by the time it was repealed that its repeal was more symbolic than anything else. Nevertheless, many were horrified that this last piece of legislation guarding the stability of the financial system was being dismantled, even in the face of clear evidence of the potentially disastrous consequences. These consequences arise not because the banks are allowed to take on more risk but rather because the deposits remain insured by the federal government. This shifting of risk distorts incentives, prevents the financial sector from allocating resources in a productive manner, and "exposes the whole economy to major—or systemic—risks, costs, and losses."[40]

The Subprime Crisis

The enthusiasm for financial deregulation as the answer to the S&L crisis set the stage for the emergence of an unregulated subprime mortgage market. (A subprime mortgage is a one that is granted to people whose poor credit scores would not allow them to take out conventional mortgages.) The development of new financial instruments based on securitization facilitated the market for high-risk mortgages.[41] Securitization allows lenders to sell their loans to third parties, generally large Wall Street firms such as Bear Stearns, Goldman Sachs, and Lehman Brothers, which repackage them into discrete bundles, mortgage backed securities (MBS), to be resold to investors. This allowed subprime lenders to effectively rid themselves of the default risk associated with their subprime loans, because the risk of default was transferred from them to Wall Street firms and then to investors. The risk to investors, at the bottom of the chain, was supposed to be eliminated by pooling: if some borrowers did not pay, the payments from other loans in the pool would cover the losses.[42]

The good old days depicted in the classic movie *It's a Wonderful Life* were over (if they had ever really existed). The original lender-borrower relationship was a thing of the past. Now no one really knew who was responsible for the mortgages or even which mortgages were in which package.[43] Since the packages are immediately resold, the creditworthiness of the mortgage holders mattered little to anyone. Growth seemed to be all that mattered: the more mortgages sold, the higher the profits. Wall Street investment firms provided both the financial backing and the sheen of respectability necessary to create the economic behemoth that triggered the worst economic crisis since the Great Depression.[44]

Since profits of the subprime lenders depended on volume, they targeted populations that had previously been excluded from the housing market and neighborhoods that had been previously "red-lined."[45] On the positive side, this allowed people who were previously excluded from home ownership to obtain mortgages.[46] Although the fight against redlining was central to many black social movements, and both radicals and liberals in the women's movement championed an end to sex discrimination in credit markets, the unethical and often fraudulent practices by which these loans were sold offset any benefits.[47] Financial journalists have documented the ways that lenders targeted borrowers who had scant financial knowledge and thus were easy prey for unethical bait and switch tactics.[48] Examples include offering adjustable rate mortgages (ARMS) that started at low rates of interest but could rise to unsustainable levels, pushing second mortgages that were in excess of the borrowers' ability to pay given their incomes, and disguising the true costs of mortgages when all fees and points were factored in.

Dean Baker, a US policy economist, has argued that many people saw what was coming. That banks were issuing fraudulent mortgages and Wall Street was securitizing them as fast as they could get them was an open secret.[49] However, Alan Greenspan, then the chair of the Federal Reserve, denies knowing anything about the flood of junk mortgages or the bubble in the housing market. It is as if he really did believe that risk had been eliminated from financial markets, that clever financial engineering had created high-yield but completely safe investments from risky pools of mortgages.[50] You could, in effect, get your money for nothing.[51] This brings to mind Marx's commentary on the practices of the English East India Company,

> The monopolies of salt, opium, betel and other commodities, were inexhaustible mines of wealth. The employees themselves fixed the price and plundered at will the unhappy Hindus. The Governor-General took part in this private traffic. His favourites received contracts under conditions whereby they, *cleverer than the alchemists, made gold out of nothing.* Great fortunes sprang up like mushrooms in a day.[52]

Just as the fortunes of the employees of the East India Company were created out of the expropriation of Indian resources and the exploitation of the Indian people, Wall Street fortunes were created out of the losses suffered by people whose mortgages ended up "under water," or who lost their homes to foreclosures.[53] While subprime mortgages generated an estimated $100 billion in revenues for lenders in the mid-2000s, their gain was based on the dispossession of women and racialized minorities from their homes and wealth.[54]

Signs of trouble were apparent in 2007 as the subprime mortgage market faltered. The bubble burst on September 14, 2008, when Lehman Brothers, one of the world's largest investment firms, announced that it was filing for bankruptcy. Defaults on subprime mortgages had reached a level where they were becoming impossible to ignore, and it became apparent that Lehman's assets were not worth the paper they were printed on. It did not take long for the Lehman collapse to spread to the other financial giants in the United States and around the world. This crisis, however, was unlike the others that preceded it. The financial journalist John Lanchester describes it this way:

> [I]t was like the tide going out everywhere on Earth simultaneously. People had lived through crises before . . . but what happened in those cases was that capital fled from one place to another. No one had ever lived through, and no one thought possible, a situation where all the credit simultaneously disappeared from everywhere and the entire system teetered on the brink.[55]

The policy response (no surprise here) was to provide massive bailouts to the banks, first in the United States and then in other countries, in order to prevent the collapse of the international financial system. The system did not collapse, but many people lost their homes and often their life savings. The US economy was plunged into a recession so deep that it was called the "Great Recession."

The harmful effects of the collapse of the subprime housing market were not spread equally among all US citizens. Feminist political economist Adrienne Roberts and others document the dynamics of gender, race, and class in the subprime crisis. Although growing numbers of women have purchased their own homes, the targeting of women for subprime loans prevented them from using their homes as wealth-building assets the way that men with similar levels of income are able to do. Interestingly this is not dependent on class. Women earning below the median income are 3.3 percent more likely to receive subprime loans than similarly situated men; women whose incomes are double the median are nearly 50 percent more likely to receive subprime mortgages than men.[56]

Race is another important factor. While an African American woman is 5.7 percent more likely to receive a subprime mortgage than an African American man, that number rises to 256.1 percent when she is compared to a white man.[57] In terms of households, Hispanics lost an average of 66 percent net worth between 2005 and 2009, black households lost 53 percent, and white households lost 16 percent.[58]

The racialized effect of predatory lending practices on communities is likewise pernicious. Subprime lending is five times higher in African American neighborhoods than in white ones. Moreover, it has been estimated that the high concentration of foreclosures in African American and Latinx communities resulted in "neighborhood blight" and loss of much needed tax revenues. African Americans and other people of color lost $164 billion of wealth, and foreclosures destroyed $1.86 trillion in the value of surrounding homes.

The Euro Crisis and Beyond

The financial crisis soon spread to Europe. The Euro crisis was marked by the 2009 announcement by Prime Minister George Papandreou that Greece had understated its budget deficit.[59] The financial community was not amused, and Greece found itself shut out from borrowing in international financial markets. By 2010 it was on the verge of bankruptcy, an event that could have sparked a new financial meltdown. If Greece were monetarily sovereign, then the solution would have been much easier. It could have either devalued its currency to increase tourism and trade or it could have paid its debts by increasing the money supply. As a member of the Eurozone it could do neither.

Greece's situation was, in some ways, analogous to the situation that New York City found itself in 1975. The economic base of the city had been eroding for several years as a result of capitalist restructuring, deindustrialization, and suburbanization. If adequate federal funding had been available, expanding public employment and public provisions could have provided a solution to the city's short-run debt problems. However, the federal funding was not forthcoming and New York City's budget deficit increased. In 1975 the city went into bankruptcy. The terms of the bailout were such that the bondholders had first claim on city tax revenues and whatever was left over was used for essential city services. The power of the unions was broken, wages were frozen, and large cuts were made to spending on education, health, and transportation. David Harvey adds, "[t]he final indignity was the requirement that municipal unions should invest their pension funds in city bonds . . . [t]his amounted to a coup by the financial institutions against the democratically elected government of New York City, and it was every bit as effective as the military coup that had earlier occurred in Chile."[60] In the midst of a fiscal crisis, when public provisioning was desperately needed in order to meet the needs of the poor, the elderly, and the middle classes, income, wealth, and power were instead redistributed to the upper classes.

Just as New York City had no choice but to accept the terms of the bailout, Greece's only solution was to accept the bailout from the "Troika," a colloquial expression for the European Central Bank (ECB), Germany, and the IMF. They were also forced to accept the austerity measures that came with it. The effects on Greek citizens were devastating. They were asked to pay higher taxes, do without public services, and accept lower wages and pensions. Energy costs skyrocketed, and the Greek standard of living fell precipitously. Despite the fact that Greece's woes were due to the machinations of financial elites, in the popular media and official circles its shaky financial status was laid squarely on the shoulders of its "lazy" and "irresponsible" people.[61]

The Greek people did not take this sitting down. Their protests destabilized the government, and the Troika's austerity measures worsened Greece's already deep recession. There seemed to be no satisfactory solution. As the situation wore on other countries were "drawn into the muck."[62] Portugal had a large budget deficit and an uncompetitive economy; Ireland had experienced a real estate boom and bust resulting in massive bank bailouts; Spain also experienced a real estate boom and bust and shaky banks; and Italy had a large budget deficit and an unstable government.

These countries became known by the unflattering acronym PIIGS. They were, in some form or another, subjected to the fiscal discipline imposed by austerity. The acronym reflects something of the old-fashioned paternalistic contempt shown by the elite for the poor. Their economic problems are their own fault; they have been profligate and undisciplined spenders who need to be taught a stern lesson by the patriarchs of the global financial system. It is reminiscent of the language used to talk about the starving Irish peasants during the hell of the famine years. Like the Irish before them, the PIIGS needed discipline. The unruly, feminized poor needed the strict guidance and discipline of the patriarchal financial class.

Conclusion

We have come full circle. The financial elites have caused a huge mess. Income and wealth inequality are both at all-time highs. The elites have not been held accountable nor have they had to bear the losses. There were a few token exceptions, Bernie Madoff most famously, and a few individual brokers and firms, but by and large the financial class remains in the catbird's seat. What comes next? What would feminist alternatives to austerity entail? First and foremost, social reproduction and care work would be the number one priority. This involves persuading governments of the importance of investing in social infrastructure: in health, education, childcare, housing, and eldercare. Ruth Pearson and Diane Elson argue that such investments benefit all people, not just the privileged few, and ensure the health of the economy in the long run. For example,

> . . . public investment in the social infrastructure—skilled and trained teachers, health and social care workers as well as schools, hospitals, clinics and day care centres—also delivers benefits to the economy in the short, medium and long term. Research indicates that, for example, additional investment in affordable childcare services would enable more women to remain in or re-enter the labour force after maternity, improve intellectual development of otherwise marginalised or vulnerable children.[63]

They go on to say that similar arguments can be made about investment in quality health services and eldercare. These are not just issues that pertain to the quality of life of particular populations, although that in itself is important. Pearson and Elson also note a direct link to the productivity of the workforce and the prospects for long-term sustainable growth. Neoliberal ideology that makes the individual rather than the collective responsible for economic destiny is based on misleading and inaccurate assumptions about how economies work. This harkens back to the early Marxist-feminist scholarship we cited in previous chapters, which brought to the fore the crucial role that unpaid reproductive labor played in capitalism. It is both painfully obvious, and bears repeating: economic well-being is about the well-being of people who have to be birthed, fed, clothed, housed, and nurtured. The intergenerational and daily reproduction of the economy depends on this first and foremost.

There is, however, another issue that also bears consideration. As we discussed above, more and more people are depending on credit to finance not only future human capital investments—buying a house, pursuing a college degree, and so forth—but also for maintaining their daily standard of living. One consequence is that many, perhaps most, people in the middle and working classes find themselves trapped in webs of debt. The philosopher Maurice Lazzarato argues that today the debtor/creditor relationship has replaced the worker/capitalist relationship of Marx's day.[64] Similarly, Silvia Federici writes that the "new 'debt economy' [that] has come into existence is changing not only the architecture of capitalist accumulation but the form of the class relationship and debt itself."[65] Federici goes on to say that one of the pernicious effects of debt is that it is now used by governments and financiers not only to accumulate wealth but to undermine social solidarity and efforts to create alternatives to capitalism.

Jason Hickel makes a similar point in regard to global South debt. He argues that structural adjustment policies, which forced indebted countries to cut social spending, privatize assets, devalue their currencies, and radically deregulate their economies, effectively halted the progress they were making toward becoming economically prosperous and politically independent countries. We quote, "[w]hat they failed to accomplish through piecemeal coups and covert intervention, the debt crisis did for them in one small swoop."[66] Or as Federici puts it, "due to the 'debt crisis,' the gains obtained by anticolonial struggle were nullified and a new economic order was forced into existence that has condemned entire populations to a poverty never before experienced."[67] Many people who attempt to migrate in an effort to escape impoverishment and better provide for their families who stay behind, find themselves trapped in massive debt to smugglers, regardless of whether their attempts were successful or not.[68]

What has happened to people in the global North may be less dire at this point, but it is only a matter of degree. Many in the 99 percent find themselves locked into lifetimes of debt repayments that most likely can never be repaid.[69] In the United States, students today graduate with so much debt that they cannot qualify for mortgages to buy their own homes. Subprime mortgage debts remain on the books, not of the banks, which were bailed out, but on the people who managed to avoid foreclosures.[70]

Creating a path forward will be a difficult task. Because, as Federici points out, one important difference between debt today and in the past is that the creditor is "no longer the local shopkeeper or neighbor but the banker and, due to the high interest rates, debt, like a cancer, with time continuously increases."[71] Most importantly though, according to Federici,

[a] new class relation is produced where the exploiters are more hidden, more removed, and the mechanisms of exploitation are far more individualized and guilt inducing. Instead of work, exploita-

tion, and above all "bosses," so prominent in the world of smoke-stacks, we now have debtors confronting not an employer but a bank and confronting it alone, not as part of a collective body and collective relationship, as was the case with wage workers.[72]

There is only one workable answer to the problem of debt in the twenty-first century and that is debt forgiveness. This was the message of Jubilee 2000 and is the message of many antidebt movements today, such as Strike Debt. So what holds progressives back? We think that at least part of the answer comes down to shame; we as individuals in a neoliberal world have internalized the message, "but surely one must pay one's debts." This is a particular trap for women for many reasons ranging from economic—the wage and wealth gap—to psychological—financial independence is indispensable to freedom and autonomy. "Lean in" feminism has schooled us well in the neoliberal creed of personal responsibility and economic independence.

While on a personal level these values may be all well and good (who does not want to be financially independent?), on a collective level they will not work. We need an end to individual shame and to place an emphasis on collective solutions.[73] Consider this message from *The Debt Resister's Operations Manual*,

> Because there is so much shame, frustration and fear surrounding our debt, we seldom talk about it openly with others. An initial step in building a debt resistance movement involves sharing the myriad ways debt affects us, both directly and indirectly. You are encouraged to share your experience at Debt Stories, occupiedstories.com/strikedebt. Remember, you are not a loan![74]

This and other efforts are already taking place. Although they were not as successful as they hoped, Jubilee 2000 did raise awareness of the unsustainability of global South debt. The campaign against "odious debts" continues. It is becoming the norm rather than the exception to call for an end to student debt in the United States. Hopefully, we will see similar campaigns in relationship to medical debt. The people of Greece continue to protest the Troika's policies, the economies of Portugal and Ireland have recovered despite austerity measures, Chileans are taking to the streets to protest inequality, and the indigenous peoples of Ecuador have led a successful effort against IMF-imposed SAPs. Not all debts are legitimate and not all debts should be repaid. Who owes what to whom? That is the question. As feminists we think that the answer entails looking beyond the money figures on accounting ledgers and looking instead at where real value is created. Although the financial, productive, and reproductive spheres of the economy are intimately woven together in everyone's daily life, social reproduction is the cornerstone.

10 | Creating Feminist Economic Futures

The feminist vision of the economy we have presented in this book has aimed to both interpret the economy and change it.[1] Theorizing the economy differently, we believe, contributes to the creation of equitable feminist futures. We want to be clear, though, in what we mean by "equitable." The vision of feminism that animates our work is not the "lean in" feminism that is focused on women achieving corporate success, but rather a more transformative feminism for the 99 percent. Rather than seeing the integration of women into the business-as-usual economy as the goal, ours is a feminist approach that seeks to dismantle the hierarchies that exist in the current economic system, ones founded on gender, class, race, nation, sexual orientation, religion, and other power dynamics. It is also a feminism that defines the goals of the economy around provisioning for human needs in ways that support the flourishing of human life, rather than defining the economy's achievements by per-capita GDP, profits, and the growth of the market economy.

We acknowledge the diversity of economic practices, both market and nonmarket, that contribute to survival and well-being. As such, ours is a feminist vision of the economy that presents a significant challenge to the market-centered approach of mainstream, neoclassical economics. Although mainstream economics has lost some of its allure in the wake of its inability to solve the financial crises, growing inequality, and the threat of climate change that beset the world today, it still retains some power to shape policy and public opinion. However, the world is increasingly searching for new ways to understand and restructure our economic systems toward more sustainable, equitable outcomes. Feminist economics has much to add to that effort. We therefore conclude this book by elaborating on the list of feminist aspirations that we introduced at the beginning and that we believe are crucial and interconnected components for achieving an improved quality of life for all.

Aspirations for Feminist Futures

An Egalitarian Division of Labor

As we have shown throughout this book, current divisions of labor repro-duce inequalities and interfere with the goals of provisioning and human flourishing that we hold for the economy. The gender division of labor that associates production in the market with masculinity and social repro-duction and care in the household with femininity, for instance, creates all kinds of inequities. While unequal divisions of labor in the home are changing, women still take on the vast majority of unpaid care work, which results in an enormous human cost to those who perform this work. Further, the undervaluation of feminized care work—both in its unpaid and paid forms—has resulted in its overall depletion and a crisis of care.[2] In the paid labor force there is occupational segregation that, gener-ally speaking, has resulted in a view of "women's work" as natural, unskilled, and less important than work associated with men—a value hierarchy that holds regardless of the actual gender of the person doing the work. This gender coding is further influenced by other categories of social difference, especially race and class. Those fortunate enough to match the characteristics needed to claim masculinity, whiteness, hetero-sexuality, markers of class privilege such as higher education, and other key characteristics have the easiest access to the most privileged positions in the labor market.

Divisions of labor, in their many various manifestations—manual and mental, global South and global North, rural and urban, agriculture and manufacturing, productive and reproductive—mark, and thereby value and devalue, human beings. Moreover, the value assigned by society to the people doing the work partly determines the value of the work. Care work is a good example. Over the last forty years in the United States, upper- and middle-class women of European descent have been urged to stay home after giving birth if they want to be considered "good mothers." Meanwhile, society views poor women of color on welfare who want to stay home with their children as lazy and irresponsible, and policy man-dates force them to go back to work shortly after giving birth or risk losing their benefits.[3] Poor mothers who provide childcare for the children of the affluent typically do not make enough money to adequately care for their own children. Migrant care workers who are mothers often do not get to see their own children for years at a time when working abroad. The dif-ference in these experiences lies in the power dynamics and cultural rep-resentations of those doing the care work and those getting the care.

We imagine different and more equitable systems of division, representation, and valorization of labor. These would acknowledge the inherent value of human labor and challenge stereotypes that connect the worth of one's work to social location. As feminist economists, a key factor for us is the need to recognize and value social reproduction in both its unpaid and paid forms and its important contribution to human well-being and flourishing. Counting unpaid domestic and care work in GDP, as we discussed in chapter 3, represents one such effort. Decentering the capitalist labor market in discussions of work, as the feminist geographer J. K. Gibson-Graham has done, is another way forward. Gibson-Graham's community economies framework recognizes the diverse locations and practices of production and reproduction and focuses on the work of families, community groups, cooperatives, social networks, and the like.[4] This makes visible a whole range of economic activities typically ignored by mainstream economists. Feminist economists such as Nancy Folbre, Julie Nelson, and others have called for the institution of a social wage for both unpaid and paid care workers in order to recognize the high value of their contributions to society.[5] We imagine extending this idea beyond care to include all kinds of work that are not currently valued by the market yet necessary for social provisioning.

Global gendered divisions of labor are also inequitable. Therefore the factors that contribute to these divisions, particularly those that "make women's wages cheap" in transnational garment production, informalized manufacturing, migration to perform care work, and other global economic contexts, must be addressed. One strategy for addressing women's exploitation in transnational production, for instance, has been to pressure global supply chain manufacturers to provide decent wages and working conditions. One example of activism around these concerns is antisweatshop campaigns, such as the Worker's Rights Consortium in the United States and the Clean Clothes Campaign in the United Kingdom, both of which monitor the global garment industry. Achieving a more equitable outcome regarding global gender divisions of labor would also include pushing back against flexibilized, informalized labor conditions through both policy shifts and grassroots organizing. The work of the Self-Employed Women's Association (SEWA) on this issue was described in chapter 7. SEWA has organized 1.5 million informal sector workers and provided them with childcare, health, legal and other supports, and shown us a successful example of a grassroots effort. At the policy level, the informal economies expert Martha Chen has suggested that governments focus on creating more formal jobs, regulating informal sector enterprises and extending labor and legal protections to informal sector workers.[6]

A central issue that fuels the global gender division of labor is the widening inequality between wealthy and poor countries, making global redistribution another key goal. Also central is the character of current structural adjustment and austerity policies for indebted countries, which have led nations in the global South to cut social service supports, promote unregulated export manufacturing, and/or encourage women's outmigration for remittance revenue as part of a debt repayment plan. Along with many other feminist economists and civil society groups, such as ActionAid, we call for alternatives to the flawed and disastrous structural adjustment and austerity policies currently prescribed by the International Monetary Fund and the World Bank.

With regard to global care work specifically, the focus on privatized solutions to care crises has also fueled social inequalities and divisions that Shellee Colen has called "stratified reproduction," in which some people can afford to nurture their children, while others cannot.[7] Thus, in our estimation, any solution to the global gender division of labor must include a reconceptualization of care as a social, not private, responsibility.

An Egalitarian Division of Income and Wealth

According to a report on global economic inequality issued by Oxfam International in January 2020, the twenty-two richest men in the world have more wealth than all of the women in Africa. Women and girls perform billions of hours of unpaid care work every day, contributing far more to the economic well-being of the planet than the global tech industry that made so many of those rich men wealthy in the first place. Precisely because of these care work responsibilities, women remain at the bottom of the economic ladder. Government support for childcare, health care, clean water, sanitation, and other vital public services could both reduce women's workloads and improve their quality of life. But unfortunately the funds to support these services are either insufficient or not available. In short, the Oxfam report makes a compelling case for both tackling inequalities in the global economy and recognizing the centrality of gender bias in structuring inequities in our current global system.[8]

Oxfam's perspective on the crucial need to address the gendered elements of poverty and inequality is not, however, widely shared among mainstream economists. This is not because economists have never thought about poverty. Questions about poverty have certainly been a central part of the economics tradition. The economic and social upheavals of the transition from feudalism to capitalism, for instance, led many early economists to think about the relationship between progress and poverty and to imagine that the state had some role in alleviating the more brutal consequences of economic change.[9] As the field progressed through the nineteenth century, economists and politicians pointed to the newly discovered laws of economics to support claims that there was nothing to be done, lest one interfere with the natural workings of the free market.[10] This sentiment is eerily similar to conservative UK Prime Minister Margaret Thatcher's now infamous slogan, "There is no alternative" (TINA). Drawing on the neoliberal economic ideas that gained precedence while she was in power in the 1980s, what Thatcher meant was that the market economy is the only economic system that works and that a market distribution of income is the only option.

We, along with a whole range of critical economists of various stripes, argue that in fact there is an alternative to our currently unequal system. Poverty and inequality are not the unavoidable but unfortunate results of otherwise well-functioning economies. They are instead better understood as the results of conscious decisions. They can be markedly reduced, and the means to do so are at hand. Of course, the causes of poverty and inequality are complex. The factors that contribute to poverty include unequal access to resources and opportunities, discrimination, poor health, vulnerability to violence, geography, environmental crises and natural disasters, fluctuating costs of basic needs, indebtedness, and more. As we argued in chapter 5, poverty is not simply a material condition but a social one, and a feminist approach to reducing poverty would of necessity require a multidimensional lens.

Given the lack of attention to social reproduction in mainstream antipoverty analysis, feminist economists have long argued for policies that put it near the top of the agenda. They therefore advocate for policies that support social reproductive work, either through state subsidies for family needs or policies that provide direct support for families struggling to balance care and paid work at the margin of poverty. Additionally, the disproportionate representation of poor women in low-wage work calls for interventions that provide good jobs at living wages for workers.

Social movement efforts to address poverty in the United States that incorporate some of these insights include the Universal Living Wage campaign to raise the minimum wage to cover basic living standards. Mothering Justice, a group in Detroit that is empowering mothers to shape antipoverty policies while simultaneously challenging the negative stereotypes of poor mothers of color that haunt US policy debates, is another example. The National Welfare Rights Organization, a group advocating for assistance for single mothers, has been effectively leading antipoverty initiatives since the 1970s. Housing rights organizations, food justice movements, and immigrant rights movements are just a few of the ongoing efforts aimed at reducing poverty and increasing well-being.

Feminist economists have also brought significant attention to the ways that austerity programs in both the global North and especially the global South have exacerbated women's poverty. These programs have undermined the provision of public services to support social reproduction, reduced protections for workers, gutted social security for aging populations, cut social spending on the poor, and otherwise are contributing to a misery projected to impact 5.8 billion people on the planet by the year 2021.[11] After a few decades of austerity, the failure of these programs to achieve their stated goal of growth and stability and eventually reduce poverty is clear. Numerous social movements around the globe continue to challenge these policies.

Decent Work and Ample Time

According to the International Labor Organization (ILO), decent work is work that pays a fair income, provides security in the workplace and social protection for families, offers prospects for personal development and social integration, gives people the freedom to express their concerns and to organize and participate in the decisions that affect their lives, and ensures equal treatment for all women and men.[12] People may want more than this. They may want work that gives meaning to their lives, some degree of social prestige, and personal satisfaction.

These are all aspects of work that do not have to be tied to paid jobs. Lola Weikal, in *The Life and Times of Rosie the Riveter*, says, quoting an old Yiddish proverb, "work makes life sweet."[13] However, that work does not necessarily have to be the work that pays the bills. "What's your day job?" is a common question asked of young artists, actors, and musicians. People build rich lives around any number of things including parenting, activism, and volunteer work. The key here is in having ample time for these other pursuits. The demand of personal time in capitalist economies has a long history. In Karl Marx's time, workers were required to work for fourteen to sixteen hours a day, six days a week at meager wages and in unsafe conditions. Marx noted that not only did such long hours not allow time for leisure and education, but even worse, workers were unable to get adequate sleep and were deprived of fresh air, sunlight, and nutritious diets.

Conditions on the sugar and cotton plantations were even more horrendous. In both cases, workers' lives were cut short by such draconian conditions.[14] That an eight-hour day and a forty-hour week are now the norm in most industrial economies in the world, and living wages are a commonly accepted goal, is thanks to the continuous struggles of the labor movement.

That movement, however, is part of the twentieth century, not the twenty-first. The amount of dead-end jobs is increasing, not decreasing, as global North countries continue to move toward flexible labor markets and the dismantling of social protections. The progressive labor economist Guy Standing calls the social class of workers in these dead-end jobs the *precariat*. Their lives are characterized by chronic insecurity, low incomes, lack of benefits, and precarious employment. It actually is unskilled labor in the sense that the only skill required is the capacity for obedience to the dictates of bosses. It is a heterogeneous group—composed of migrants, temporary workers, single mothers, retired people, and others. Unlike the old proletariat, for the new precariat work is simply a job—necessary to survive, but not something that creates a sense of identity and opportunity for solidarity. Packing shelves, serving drinks, sweeping floors, or washing dishes for low wages are not routes to happiness or satisfaction. Standing argues that it is this latter characteristic of the precariat that makes them a potentially transformative class. They are not burdened by false consciousness and misplaced loyalties.[15]

To realize the transformative potential of the precariat requires a new strategy. The old strategies were predicated on a proletariat, and, as we discussed above, a national rather than a global economic structure. It will not work anymore. We must also grapple with the fact that economic restructuring and technological change have led to a decline in the demand for laborers. Put quite simply, there will not be enough jobs for everyone. And the jobs that do exist in the precariat do not typically pay a living wage. Decoupling paid labor from personal income may be imperative for the future survival of many on the planet. Relatedly, there is a need to halt or at least slow down climate change, which requires that we separate economic well-being from growth in national income. There is also a persuasive case to be made for averting climate change through degrowth or scaling down the material throughput of the economy.[16] Providing a universal basic income (UBI), an income paid to individuals regardless of their family relationships, their income level, or their employment status may be an important step toward this goal.[17] As always, the devil is in the details, but this does not change the fact that the imperative will not go away.

In addition to universal basic income, Standing argues that we need to end moralistic social policies and instead provide basic human rights for everyone. We agree and would add that this includes an immediate end to the attack on women's reproductive rights.[18] Standing goes on to argue that we should redefine the right to work as the right to choose jobs that are commensurate with one's abilities and aspirations and to provide adequate time for leisure and recuperation.[19] With the emergence of the precariat, the issue of shorter hours has taken on a new urgency. Kathi Weeks is likewise an advocate for UBI and shorter working hours. According to her, it is not that we need more "family time" but rather that we need time to think of ways to create spaces in which to create "new subjectivities, new work and non-work ethics, and new practices of work and sociality."[20]

Environmental Sustainability

Since its inception, industrialization and capitalism have gone hand in hand with the exploitation of the natural environment: mining, logging, and quarrying scar the earth. The sulfurous skies hanging over the world's mega cities, poisoned rivers running through the northeastern United States, and deforestation in the Amazon River basin are just three examples. Today climate change poses an existential threat to everyone. As we write this (in late 2019), nearly the entire continent of Australia is beset by horrific wildfires that are destroying forests, animals, and animal habitats. Hurricanes, tornadoes, typhoons, floods, and other natural disasters have increased in size and intensity. The consequences of climate change are no longer in the future. They are in the here and now. Even the most neoclassical of economists recognizes that climate change is real and that something needs to be done, although there is much disagreement about whether "green growth" is even possible. We will not go into those debates here. Our point is that even the most conservative proposals, such as the Paris Accords, are proving exceptionally difficult to achieve, not because of lack of scientific consensus, but because of the undue influence of powerful transnational corporate interests whose profitability depends on resource extraction, agribusiness, and a host of other environmentally destructive policies.

In addition to necessary economic, political, and technical interventions—such as new measures of economic performance that consider environmental damage—changing this pattern of devastating environmental destruction requires a fundamental change in national and international priorities. This in turn requires rethinking the relationship between humans and the environment, between private property and communal property, and between ownership and use. The concept of the commons, natural and cultural resources that are not owned privately but rather belong to us all, is the thread that ties these things together. Stephen Healy and Katherine Gibson, geographers and founding members of the Community Economies Research Network, argue that from our atmosphere to the open ocean, from languages to the rule of law, use without ownership underpins human experience. These resources and properties are necessarily shared because they cannot be wholly appropriated or completely enclosed; they are part of the commons and need to be cared about and cared for.[21] Similarly, Silvia Federici argues that the commons is the thread that connects all histories of class struggle and continues today in the global South and the global North and in urban and rural areas. Moreover, women have historically been at the forefront of the struggles over caring for the commons. This should come as no surprise. Since women were, and still are, the ones primarily responsible for social reproduction, they are most affected by the harms from climate change, the degradation of natural systems, and the dangers of toxic pollutants.

In many countries in Africa women are at the forefront of struggles to get back communal land rights; in South America they are the vanguard fighting against transnational mining companies and agribusinesses; and in the United States they are leaders in campaigns to ensure safe drinking water for impoverished urban communities. Now it is important to stress that we are not making an essentialist argument here about women being naturally more caring or closer to nature. We are saying, however, that women's social position allows them to see the contradictions that arise from the separation of production and social reproduction that characterizes capitalist economies. As the feminist sociologist Joan Acker puts it, production is organized around goals of capital accumulation, not around meeting the reproductive and survival needs of people.[22]

Federici argues in a similar vein that the distancing between production, reproduction, and consumption allows us to ignore the conditions under which what we eat and wear are produced, their social and environmental costs, and the damage to populations on whom the waste is unloaded. Such distancing is not so easy, however, for poor people in the global South, many of whom rely directly on natural resources like arable land, forests, rivers, and fisheries for their daily sustenance. Nor is it so easy for poor people in the global North, whose communities have been the cruel victims of environmental racism.

Debt forgiveness and an end to austerity measures are also crucial components in taking back the commons. Poor global South countries are still living under the conditions imposed by the IMF and other international financial institutions. We have known for many years now that the need to service their international debt obligations quite literally forces many countries to increase extractive activities, such as logging and mining, which leads to deforestation and mining pollution as well as a reduction in and degradation of the land that is necessary for the survival of ordinary people.[23] Austerity policies that demand cutbacks in government spending inevitably result in cutbacks in environmental protections. In Greece, for example, the cuts in public spending demanded following the Euro crisis have exacerbated air pollution in large cities; increases in the price of heating oil have led people to heat by wood instead (a far more polluting source of fuel), and the need to generate economic growth has opened the door to destructive gold mining operations.[24] Rethinking the capitalist logic of debt, a logic that transfers resources from the poor to the rich and causes untold environmental harm, is part of a feminist rethinking of the commons.

Caring for oneself, for others, and for the nonhuman world is a feminist strategy for slowing down climate change and alleviating environmental harms. Care in this sense is not a description of tender feelings, rather it is an assemblage of practices such as cooperation and sharing. It means refusing to base our life on the suffering of others and, in Silvia Federici's words, living according to a principle of cooperation and responsibility to each other and to the earth, the forests, the seas, and the animals. Environmental issues cannot be separated from issues of social reproduction. As Cinzia Arruza, Tithi Bhattacharya, and Nancy Fraser, authors of *Feminism for the 99%: A Manifesto*, put it, social justice, the well-being of human communities, and the sustainability of nonhuman nature are inextricably bound together. The liberation of women and the preservation of our planet from ecological disaster go hand in hand.[25]

Concluding Remarks

The world we live in today is much different from the one we inhabited in 2006, when *Liberating Economics* was first published. The horrifying consequences of climate change, the residue from the 2008 financial crisis and ongoing financialization of the economy, and the refugee crises on the southern borders of the United States and Europe were then only dimly coming into view. They are firmly center stage today, and the responses from our political and economic leaders are failing to address them.

Rather than progressive, egalitarian, and humane responses, what is emerging in some quarters is the worst sort of populism, racism, and even in some cases, fascism. There is Donald Trump in the United States, Boris Johnson in the United Kingdom, Jair Bolsanaro in Brazil, Vladimir Putin in Russia, Narendra Modi in India, and Recep Tayyip Erdogan in Turkey. The depressing list goes on. The economics profession has not done much better. Although some lip service is paid to heterodox schools and pluralism in economic methodology, the top academic departments in the country remain firmly ensconced in the glass castle of promarket deductive reasoning and high theory.

Things are not hopeless. This is also a time of prodigious change and energy. The critical interventions and social movements we have mentioned in this chapter and throughout the book demonstrate that it is possible to think outside the dominant gender-biased and market-centered model to foster economies that work for everyone. Acknowledging the connections and mediating between the productive and the reproductive sphere are essential to these efforts.

We close with one last example. In India, a group of ordinary Muslim women of the Shaheen Bagh neighborhood occupied a Delhi street to protest the Modi government's new law, the Citizen Amendment Act, which makes Hinduism the basis for acquiring Indian citizenship. The protest was initially sparked by a video of a young, head-covered woman from Jamia Milia Islamia University fiercely trying to guard a fellow male student from brutal assault by the Delhi police.[26] It became an iconic image of defiance during the cold Delhi winter of 2019, challenging age-old narratives of women's vulnerability and male physical supremacy.[27] The women of Shaheen Bagh, most of whom had never before engaged in protests, are now living on the street to protest while also cooking, cleaning, and educating their children. They have been supported by many other activist women and men of various faiths who provide them with water, tea, and food.[28] Reminiscent of Occupy Wall Street, the site has become a place of communal living, teaching, and making art. It has also become the epicenter of protest all over India.[29]

What was it that prompted these ordinary Muslim women to leave the relative safety and comfort of their homes for the bitter cold of the street? Irfanullah Farooqi, an Indian sociology professor, argues that from their socially marginalized position, these women saw the pathologically inhumane ways that the state encroached on their domestic lives.[30] In other words, their marginalized position as women and as Muslims, mainly responsible for social reproduction, facilitated their awareness of the real dangers that fascism, racism, and populism posed to their lives. In our current times, it is almost inevitable that more people on the margins will come face to face with the contradiction between the imperatives necessary for social reproduction and the accumulation of profit. While many have called for a return to the national demand management and social protection policies that were the hallmark of the period roughly from the end of World War II to the middle of the 1970s to smooth out this contradiction, we take a different view. Not only were these initiatives flawed in their time, they cannot work in today's financialized and globalized economies.

Today debt, both personal and sovereign, is an important part of global governance. Sovereign debt obligations undermine the ability of states to make needed social investments in schools, health services, public transportation, green technologies, and childcare and eldercare. Similarly, personal obligations of debt ensure that people are unable to risk losing their sources of income no matter how miserable they are. Again, this demonstrates the contradiction between the imperatives necessary for social reproduction and the need for the accumulation of profit by the elite.

Things must change. An economic system that simultaneously withdraws public support for social reproduction while at the same time forcing people into precarious work is not sustainable. As Arruza, Bhattacharya, and Fraser put it, such a system will deplete the very social capacities on which it depends. The open question is what will replace it? One important take away from Federici's *Caliban and the Witch* is that contrary to the story told by the British political economists of the time, the transition from feudalism to capitalism was not inevitable but was the outcome of significant struggles between the peasants and the ruling classes, the violent displacement and enslavement of the people of the new world, and the brutal subjugation of women. What the outcome of this historical conjuncture may be has yet to be determined. What we do know is that it will require a feminist economics for the 99 percent. That is, a feminist economics that can address the intersectional gender inequities that negatively impact a whole diversity of people around the globe. It is our hope that this book can contribute to building solidarity between all who can benefit from these struggles for gender justice and creating solutions that will realize our vision of feminist futures.

Notes

CHAPTER 1

1. Oxfam, "An Economy that Works for Women," 2017, https://www.oxfam.org/en/research/economy-works-women

2. Ariane Hegewisch and Heidi Hartmann, "Gender Wage Gap: 2018 Earnings Differences by Race and Ethnicity," Institute for Women's Policy Research, March 7, 2019, https://iwpr.org/publications/gender-wage-gap-2018

3. M. V. Lee Badgett, Soon Kyu Choi, and Bianca D. M. Wilson, "LGBT Poverty in the United States: A Study of Differences Between Sexual Orientation and Gender Identity Groups," Williams Institute UCLA, October 2019, https://williamsinstitute.law.ucla.edu/wp-content/uploads/National-LGBT-Poverty-Oct-2019.pdf

4. UN Women, "Progress of the World's Women 2015/2016: Transforming Inequalities, Realizing Rights," https://www.unwomen.org/en/digital-library/publications/2015/4/progress-of-the-worlds-women-2015

5. United Nations, "Introduction to Gender and Climate Change," https://unfccc.int/topics/gender/the-big-picture/introduction-to-gender-and-climate-change

6. Jacob Mincer and Solomon Polachek, "An Exchange: The Theory of Human Capital and the Earnings of Women: Women's Earnings Reexamined," *Journal of Human Resources* 13, no. 1 (Winter 1978): 118–34; Gary S. Becker, "Human Capital, Effort, and the Sexual Division of Labor," *Journal of Labor Economics* 3, no. 1 (1985): 33–58.

7. Marianne A. Ferber and Julie A. Nelson, "Introduction: The Social Construction of Economics and the Social Construction of Gender," in *Beyond Economic Man: Feminist Theory and Economics*, eds. Marianne A. Ferber and Julie A. Nelson (Chicago: University of Chicago Press, 1993), 1–22.

8. Lourdes Benería, "Towards a Greater Integration of Gender in Economics," *World Development* 23 (1995): 1839–50.

9. Adam Smith, *An Inquiry into the Nature and Causes of the Wealth of Nations*, vol. 1 (Chicago: University of Chicago Press, [1776] 1976), chap. 2.

10. Nancy Folbre, *The Invisible Heart: Economics and Family Values* (New York: The New Press, 2001).

11. Julie A. Nelson, *Feminism, Objectivity, and Economics* (New York: Routledge, 1996).

12. It should be noted that other nonmainstream schools of thought, such as behavioral economics, Marxian economics, and Austrian economics, are also critical of *Homo economicus*.

13. Robert H. Frank, Thomas Gilovich, and Dennis T. Regan, "Does Studying Economics Inhibit Cooperation?" *Journal of Economic Perspectives* 7, no. 2 (1993): 159–71.

14. Joan Scott, "Gender: A Useful Category of Historical Analysis," *American Historical Review* 91 (December 1986): 1053–75.

15. The work of feminist historian Carroll Rosenberg-Smith, *Disorderly Conduct: Visions of Gender in Victorian America* (Oxford: Oxford University Press, 1986), remains the classic work on these topics.

16. Paula Giddings, *When and Where I Enter: The Impact of Black Women on Race and Sex in America* (New York: William Morrow, 1984).

17. See Michèle A. Pujol, *Feminism and Anti-Feminism in Early Economic Thought* (Aldershot: Edward Elgar, 1992); Ulla Grapard, "Robinson Crusoe: The Quintessential Economic Man," *Feminist Economics* 1, no. 1 (1995): 33–52; and RhondaWilliams, "Race, Deconstruction, and the Emergent Agenda of Feminist Economic Theory," in *Beyond Economic Man: Feminist Theory and Economics*, eds. Marianne A. Ferber and Julie A. Nelson (Chicago: University of Chicago Press, 1993), 144–52.

18. Sandra Harding, "Can Feminist Thought Make Economics More Objective?" *Feminist Economics* 1, no. 1 (1995): 7–32; Helen Longino, *Science as Social Knowledge: Values and Objectivity in Scientific Inquiry* (Princeton: Princeton University Press, 1990); and Lynn Hankison-Nelson, *Who Knows: From Quine to a Feminist Empiricism* (Philadelphia: Temple University Press, 1994).

19. Diana Strassman, "Not a Free Market: The Rhetoric of Disciplinary Authority in Economics," in *Beyond Economic Man: Feminist Theory and Economics*, 54–68.

20. Pujol, *Feminism and Anti-Feminism in Early Economic Thought*.

21. Nancy Folbre, "The Unproductive Housewife: Her Evolution in British Economic Thought," *Signs* 16, no. 3 (1991): 463–84.

22. Pujol, *Feminism and Anti-Feminism in Early Economic Thought*.

23. William Darrity Jr., ed., *Economics and Discrimination* (Cheltenham and Northampton: Edward Elgar, 1995). See also Mark Haller, *Eugenics: Hereditarian Attitudes in American Thought* (New Brunswick: Rutgers University Press, 1984). Haller discusses the role of Irving Fisher, a prominent American economist, as the head of propaganda of the American Eugenics Association.

24. Angela Y. Davis, *Women, Race and Class* (New York: Vintage, 1983), and S. Charusheela, "Empowering Work? Bargaining Models Reconsidered," in *Toward a Feminist Philosophy of Economics*, eds. Drucilla K. Barker and Edith Kuiper (London and New York: Routledge, 2003), 287–303.

25. Cinzia Arruzza, Tithi Bhattacharya, and Nancy Fraser, "Notes for a Feminist Manifesto," *New Left Review* 114 (November/December 2018), 117.

26. S. Charusheela, "Intersectionality," in *The Handbook of Research on Gender and Economic Life*, eds. Deborah M. Figart and Tonia L. Warnecke (Cheltenham and Northampton: Edward Elgar, 2013).

27. Julie A. Nelson, "Feminism and Economics," *Journal of Economic Perspectives* 9 no. 2 (1995): 131–48.

28. J. K. Gibson-Graham, Jenny Cameron, and Stephen Healy, *Take Back the Economy: An Ethical Guide for Transforming our Communities* (Minneapolis: University of Minnesota Press, 2013). The authors note the similarity to the feminist slogan, Take Back the Night, while also noting that it is about questioning the strategies that people employ

to make the economy something that actually benefits people and the planet. https://anthroprospective.com/katherine-gibson-helps-to-build-resilient-economies-2

CHAPTER 2

1. Heidi I. Hartmann, "The Family as the Locus of Gender, Class, and Political Struggle: The Example of Housework," in *Feminism and Methodology*, ed. Sandra Harding (Bloomington and Indianapolis: Indiana University Press, 1987), 109–34.

2. This changed with the launch of the "New Home Economics" at the University of Chicago, which opened the black box of the family to economic analysis in the 1970s. See Gary S. Becker, *A Treatise on the Family* (Cambridge: Harvard University Press, 1991).

3. See Stephanie Coontz, *Marriage, a History: From Obedience to Intimacy, or How Love Conquered Marriage* (New York: Penguin, 2006), and Marilyn Yalom, *The History of the Wife* (New York: Harper Collins, 2001).

4. Coontz, *Marriage, a History*.

5. See Maurice Dobb, *Studies in the Development of Capitalism* (New York: International, 1964), and Silvia Federici, *Caliban and the Witch: Women, the Body, and Primitive Accumulation* (New York: Autonomedia, 2004) for more detailed accounts.

6. Rodney Hilton, ed., *The Transition from Feudalism to Capitalism* (London: Verso, [1976] 1985); Maurice Dobb, *Studies in the Development of Capitalism* (New York: International Press, 1946).

7. Jane Humphries, "Enclosures, Common Rights, and Women: The Proletarianization of Families in the Late Eighteenth and Early Nineteenth Centuries," *Journal of Economic History* 50 (March 1990): 17–42.

8. Federici, *Caliban and the Witch*, 73.

9. Federici, *Caliban and the Witch*.

10. Nancy Folbre, "The Unproductive Housewife: Her Evolution in Nineteenth-Century Economic Thought," *Signs* 13, no. 3 (Spring 1991): 463–84.

11. Humphries, "Enclosures, Common Rights, and Women: The Proletarianization of Families in the Late Eighteenth and Early Nineteenth Centuries."

12. Peter Dorman et al., "Debating Markets," *Feminist Economics* 2, no. 1 (Spring 1996): 69–85.

13. Marilyn Yalom, *The History of the Wife*, 188–89.

14. There is a large literature on "the cult of domesticity." For one interesting discussion see Carroll Rosenberg-Smith, *Disorderly Conduct: Visions of Gender in Victorian America* (New York: Alfred A. Knopf, 1985).

15. Nancy Folbre, "Socialism, Feminist and Scientific," in *Beyond Economic Man: Feminist Theory and Economics*, eds. Marianne A. Ferber and Julie A. Nelson (Chicago: University of Chicago Press, 1993), 94–110.

16. Jane Humphries, "Female Headed Households in Early Industrial Britain: The Vanguard of the Proletariat?" *Labor History Review* 63 (Spring 1998): 31–65.

17. Naomi Gertsel and Harriet Engel Gross, "Gender and Families in the United States: The Reality of Economic Dependence," in *Women: A Feminist Perspective*, ed. Jo Freeman (Mountain View: Mayfield, 1995), 92–127.

18. Michele Pujol, *Feminism and Anti-Feminism in Early Economic Thought* (Northampton: Edward Elgar Publishing, 1998); Nancy Folbre, *Greed, Lust and Gender* (Oxford: Oxford University Press).

19. Among the noteworthy documents expressing outrage at the reigning gender order are Mary Wollstonecraft's *A Vindication of the Rights of Woman*, first published in 1792, and *The Declaration of Sentiments* by Elizabeth Cady Stanton and Lucretia Mott, a report of the Seneca Falls Women's Rights Convention in 1848. These and others are available in Alice S. Rossi, ed., *The Feminist Papers: From Adams to de Beauvoir* (New York: Columbia University Press, 1973).

20. Marilyn Yalom, *History of the Wife* (New York: Harper Collins, 2001), 188–89.

21. Folbre, "Socialism, Feminist and Scientific." Seeing that these demands were too much for even the most radical men, feminist leaders backed off and focused instead on the much narrower demand for women's formal legal equality with men as represented by the right to vote.

22. Michel Pujol, *Feminism and Anti-Feminism in Early Economic Thought*. Also see Jane Humphries, "Female Headed Households in Early Industrial Britain: The Vanguard of the Proletariat?" *Labor History Review* 63 (Spring 1998): 31–65.

23. Deborah M. Figart, Ellen Mutari, and Marilyn Power, *Living Wages, Equal Wages: Gender and Labor Market Policies in the United States* (New York: Routledge, 2002), chap. 5, 67–90.

24. Figart, Mutari and Power, *Living Wages, Equal Wages*.

25. Figart, Mutari and Power, *Living Wages, Equal Wages*.

26. See Dorman et al., "Debating Markets."

27. D'Vera Cohn, Gretchen Livingston, and Wendy Wang, Pew Research Foundation, "After Decades of Decline, A Rise in Stay-at-Home Mothers," https://www.pewsocialtrends.org/2014/04/08/after-decades-of-decline-a-rise-in-stay-at-home-mothers

28. Gary S. Becker, *A Treatise on the Family*.

29. For further discussion see Hartmann, "The Family as the Locus of Gender, Class, and Political Struggle." Also see Harriet Fraad, Stephen Resnick, and Richard Wolff, *Bringing It All Back Home: Class, Gender, and Power in the Household* (London: Pluto Press, 1994); and Arlie R. Hochschild and Ann Machung, *The Second Shift* (New York: William Morrow, 1990).

30. See Arlie R. Hochschild and Ann Machung, *The Second Shift*.

31. Wendy Wang, Pew Research Foundation, "For Young Adults, the Ideal Marriage Meets Reality," https://www.pewresearch.org/fact-tank/2013/07/10/for-young-adults-the-ideal-marriage-meets-reality

32. Pew Research Foundation, "Raising Kids and Running a Household: How Working Parents Share the Load," https://www.pewsocialtrends.org/2015/11/04/raising-kids-and-running-a-household-how-working-parents-share-the-load

33. Sharon J. Bartley, Priscilla W. Blanton, and Jennifer L. Gilliard, "Husbands and Wives in Dual-Earner Marriages: Decision-Making, Gender Role Attitudes, Division of Household Labor and Equity," *Marriage and Family Review* 37, no. 4 (2005): 69–94.

34. Kevin Matos, Families and Work Institute, "Modern Families: Same and Different Sex Couples Negotiating the Home," http://www.familiesandwork.org/downloads/modern-families.pdf

35. Barbara Ehrenreich, "Maid to Order," in *Global Woman: Nannies, Maids, and Sex*

Workers in the New Economy, eds. Barbara Ehrenreich and Arlie R. Hochschild (New York: Metropolitan Books, 2003), 85–103.

36. In 1900, 44 percent of African American women worked in private household service, and another 44 percent worked in agriculture. See Teresa Amott and Julie Matthaei, *Race, Gender, and Work: A Multicultural Economic History of Women in the United States*, rev. ed. (Boston: South End Press, 1996), 157.

37. Gretchen Livingston, Pew Research Foundation, "About One-Third of US Children Are Living with an Unmarried Parent," https://www.pewresearch.org/fact-tank/2018/04/27/about-one-third-of-u-s-children-are-living-with-an-unmarried-parent

38. See Kevin Matos, *Modern Families*.

39. Nancy Fraser, *Justice Interruptus: Critical Reflections on the "Postsocialist" Condition* (London and New York: Routledge, 1997), 41–68.

40. See Gary S. Becker, *A Treatise on the Family*.

41. Bina Agarwal, "'Bargaining' and Gender Relations: With and Beyond the Household," *Feminist Economics* 3 (Spring 1997): 1–50; Notburga Ott, "Fertility and Division of Work in the Family: A Game Theoretic Model of Household Decisions," in *Out of the Margin: Feminist Perspectives on Economics*, eds. Edith Kuiper and Jolande Sap (New York and London: Routledge, 1995), 80–99.

42. Notburga Ott, "Fertility and Division of Work in the Family."

43. Michael Bittman et al., "When Does Gender Trump Money? Bargaining and Time in Household Work," *American Journal of Sociology* 109, no. 1 (2003): 186–214.

44. Aliya Hamid Rao, "Even Breadwinning Wives Don't Get Equality at Home," *Atlantic*, May 12, 2019. https://www.theatlantic.com/family/archive/2019/05/breadwinning-wives-gender-inequality/589237

45. M. V. Lee Badgett, "Gender, Sexuality, and Sexual Orientation: All in the Feminist Family?" *Feminist Economics* 1 (Spring 1995): 121–40.

46. Alyssa Schneebaum, "The Economics of Same-Sex Couple Households: Essays on Work, Wages and Poverty" (PhD diss., University of Massachusetts Amherst, 2013).

CHAPTER 3

1. Marilyn Waring, *If Women Counted: A New Feminist Economics* (London: MacMillan Press, 1989); Deborah Budlender, "Statistical Evidence on Care and Non-Care Work across Six Countries," *UNRISD Gender and Development Program*, Paper No. 4, 2008.

2. Yun-Ae Yi, "Margaret G. Reid: Life and Achievements," *Feminist Economics* 2, no. 3 (1996): 17–36.

3. Gary S. Becker is an important exception. His book, *A Treatise on the Family* (Cambridge: Harvard University Press, 1981), provides a neoclassical economic analysis of the family and household production.

4. Waring, *If Women Counted*; Lourdes Benería, "Accounting for Women's Work: The Progress of Two Decades," *World Development* 20 (November 1992): 1547–60.

5. UN Women, "Redistribute Paid Work," https://www.unwomen.org/en/news/in-focus/csw61/redistribute-unpaid-work

6. Ester Boserup, *Women's Role in Economic Development* (New York: Allen and Unwin, 1970).

7. Diane Elson, "Male Bias in Macroeconomics: The Case of Structural Adjustment," in *Male Bias in the Development Process* (Manchester: University of Manchester Press, 1991); Isabella Bakker, *The Strategic Silence: Gender and Economic Policy* (London: Zed Press, 1994).

8. Barbara Bergmann, "The Only Ticket to Equality: Total Androgyny, Male Style," *Journal of Contemporary Legal Issues* 9 (1998): 75–86.

9. Linda Hirshman, *Get to Work: A Manifesto for Women of the World* (New York: Viking, 2006).

10. Nancy Folbre and Julie A. Nelson, "For Love or Money—or Both?" *Journal of Economic Perspectives* 14, no. 4 (2000): 123–40. For a discussion of the racialized aspects of this issue see Drucilla K. Barker and Susan F. Feiner, "Affect, Race and Class: An Interpretive Reading of Caring Labor," *Frontiers: A Journal of Women's Studies* 30, no.1 (2000): 41–54.

11. Susan Himmelweit, "The Discovery of 'Unpaid Work': The Social Consequences of the Expansion of 'Work,'" *Feminist Economics* 1, no. 2 (1995): 1–19.

12. Arlie Hochschild and Barbara Ehrenreich, *Global Woman: Nannies, Maids, and Sex Workers in the New Economy* (New York: Henry Holt, 2003).

13. Maria Dalla Costa and Selma James, *The Power of Women and the Subversion of the Community* (Bristol: Falling Wall Press, 1975); Silvia Federici, *Revolution at Point Zero: Housework, Reproduction and Feminist Struggle* (Oakland: Common Press, 2012). The original essay, "Wages Against Housework," was published in 1975.

14. Maxine Molyneux, "Beyond the Domestic Labor Debate," *New Left Review* 116 (1979): 3–27.

15. Federici, *Revolution at Point Zero*, 16.

16. Federici, Revolution at Point Zero, 16.

17. For further discussion of the revolutionary aspect of the Wages for Housework movement see Kathi Weeks, *The Problem with Work: Feminism, Marxism, Antiwork Politics, and Postwork Imaginaries* (Durham: Duke University Press, 2011), chap. 3.

18. Bruce Pietrykowski, *Work* (Cambridge: Polity Press, 2019), 54.

19. Pietrykowski, *Work,* 53.

20. Ehrenreich and Hochschild, *Global Woman*; Evelyn Nakano Glenn, *Forced to Care* (Cambridge: Harvard University Press, 2012).

21. Glenn, *Forced to Care.*

22. Glenn, *Forced to Care.*

23. Pietrykowski, *Work,* 56–57.

24. Diane Elson, "The Social Content of Macroeconomic Policies," *World Development* 28, no. 7 (2000): 1347–64.

25. Catherin Hoskyns and Shirin M. Rai, "Recasting the Global Political Economy: Counting Women's Unpaid Work," *New Political Economy* 12, no. 3 (2007): 277–317.

26. Guy Standing, "Care Work: Overcoming Insecurity and Neglect," in *Care Work: The Quest for Security,* ed. Mary Daly (Geneva: International Labour Office, 2001), 15–31.

27. Silvia Federici, *Revolution at Point Zero* (Brooklyn, Autonomedia 2012), 116.

28. Liz O'Donnell, "The Crisis Facing America's Working Daughters," *Atlantic,* February 9, 2009, https://www.theatlantic.com/business/archive/2016/02/working-daughters-eldercare/459249

29. O'Donnell, "The Crisis Facing America's Working Daughters."

30. Agneta Stark, "Warm Hands in Cold Age: On the Need of New World Order of Care," *Feminist Economics* 11, no. 2 (July 2005): 7–36.

31. Liz O'Donnell, "The Crisis Facing America's Working Daughters."

32. Gun-Britt Trydegård, "Care work in Changing Welfare States: Nordic Care Workers' Experiences," *European Journal of Aging* 9, no. 2 (June 2012): 119–29.

33. Agneta Stark, "Warm Hands in Cold Age: On the Need of New World Order of Care," *Feminist Economics* 11, no. 2 (July 2005): 7–36.

34. Susan C. Eaton, "Eldercare in the United States: Inadequate, Inequitable, but Not a Lost Cause," *Feminist Economics* 11, no. 2 (July 2005): 37–51.

35. Federici, *Revolution at Point Zero*, 119.

36. Ann Crittenden, *The Economic Consequences of Motherhood: Why the Most Important Job in the World Is Still the Least Valued* (New York: Henry Holt, 2000), 5, 87–108.

37. Michelle J. Budig and Paula England, "The Wage Penalty for Motherhood," *American Sociological Review* 66 (April 2001): 204–25.

38. Claire Cain Miller, "The 10-Year Baby Window That Is Key to the Women's Pay Gap," *New York Times,* April 9, 2018, https://www.nytimes.com/2018/04/09/upshot/the-10-year-baby-window-that-is-the-key-to-the-womens-pay-gap.html. The study cited by the article is Yoon Kyung Chung, Barbara Downs, Danielle H. Sandler, and Robert Sienkiewicz, "The Parental Gender Earnings Gap in the United States," Working Papers 17–68, Center for Economic Studies, US Census Bureau (November 2017).

39. Joan Williams, *Unbending Gender: Why Family and Work Conflict and What to Do about It* (New York: Oxford University Press, 2001).

40. Randy Albelda and Chris Tilly, *Glass Ceilings and Bottomless Pits* (Cambridge: South End Press, 1997).

41. Catalyst, University of Michigan Business School and Center for the Education of Women, "Women and the MBA: Gateway to Opportunity," 2000, http://www.umich.edu/~cew/mbafacts.pdf

42. Betty Friedan, *The Feminine Mystique* (New York: W. W. Norton, 1963).

43. Deb Figart and Ellen Mutari, "Work Time Regimes in Europe: Can Flexibility and Gender Equity Co-exist?" *Journal of Economic Issues* 34, no. 4 (November 2000): 847–71.

44. Martha Bailey, Tanya Byker, Elena Patel, and Shanthi Ramnath, "The Long Term Effects of California's 2004 Paid Family Leave Act on Women's Careers: Evidence from U.S. Tax Data." NBER Working Paper No. 26416, October 2019, https://www.nber.org/papers/w26416.pdf

45. Andrea Rangecroft, "Where Dads Are Encouraged to Take Months Off Work," BBC News Magazine, January 6, 2016, https://www.bbc.com/news/magazine-35225982

46. Claire Cain Miller, "The 10-Year Baby Window," *New York Times,* April 9, 2018, https://www.nytimes.com/2018/04/09/upshot/the-10-year-baby-window-that-is-the-key-to-the-womens-pay-gap.html

47. Barbara Bergmann, "Watch Out for Family Friendly Policies," *Dollars and Sense* 215 (January–February 1998): 10–11.

48. Silvia Federici, *Revolution at Point Zero.*

49. Pietrykowski, *Work*, 63.

50. Christine Bauhart and Wendy Harcourt, eds., *Feminist Political Ecology and the Economics of Care: In Search of Economic Alternatives* (London: Routledge, 2018).

51. J. K. Gibson-Graham, Jenny Cameron, and Stephen Healy, "Commoning as Post-capitalist Politics," in *Releasing the Commons: Rethinking the Futures of the Common,* eds. A. Amin and P. Howell (London: Routledge, 2006), 192–212.

CHAPTER 4

1. World Bank, "Labor Force, Female (% of Total Labor Force)," https://data.world-bank.org/indicator/SL.TLF.TOTL.FE.ZS

2. World Economic Forum, "The Global Gender Gap Report 2018," http://www3.weforum.org/docs/WEF_GGGR_2018.pdf

3. Wyndham Robertson, "The Long Shadow of 'Help Wanted—Female,'" *New York Times,* November 29, 2018, https://www.nytimes.com/2018/11/29/opinion/help-wanted-female-classifieds.html

4. Bruce Pietrykowski, *Work* (Cambridge: Polity Press, 2019), 55–56.

5. Deborah M. Figart, Ellen Mutari, and Marilyn Power, *Living Wages, Equal Wages* (New York and London: Routledge, 2002).

6. Teresa Amott and Julie Matthaei, eds., *Race, Gender and Work: A Multi-Cultural Economic History of the United States, rev. ed.* (Brooklyn: South End Press, 1999).

7. United States Department of Labor, Bureau of Labor Statistics, "Changes in Women's Labor Force Participation in the 20th Century," https://www.bls.gov/opub/ted/2000/feb/wk3/art03.htm?view_full

8. Claudia Koonz, *Mothers in the Fatherland: Women, the Family, and Nazi Politics* (New York: St. Martin's Press, 1988).

9. The labor force participation rate is defined as the number of workers who are employed or actively seeking employment divided by civilian working-age population.

10. Howard N. Fullerton Jr., "Labor Force Participation: 75 Years of Change, 1950–98 and 1998–2025," *Monthly Labor Review* 122 (1999): 3.

11. US Department of Labor, Bureau of Labor Statistics (BLS), *Report on the American Workforce* (1999).

12. Bureau of Labor Statistics, "Married Mothers Less Likely to Participate in Labor Force in 2017 than Other Moms," *Economics Daily,* April 26, 2018, https://www.bls.gov/opub/ted/2018/married-mothers-less-likely-to-participate-in-labor-force-in-2017-than-other-moms.htm

13. Becky Pettit and Jennifer Hook, "The Structure of Women's Employment in Comparative Perspective," *Social Forces* 84, no. 2 (2005): 779–801.

14. Barbara Bergmann, *The Economic Emergence of Women* (New York: Basic Books, 1986).

15. Claudia Goldin, *Understanding the Gender Gap: An Economic History of American Women* (New York: Oxford University Press, 1990).

16. Randy Albelda and Chris Tilly, *Glass Ceilings and Bottomless Pits* (Brooklyn: South End Press, 1997), and Joni Seager, *The State of Women in the World Atlas: New Revised Second Edition* (London: Penguin Books, 1997).

17. Betty Friedan, *The Feminine Mystique* (New York: W.W. Norton and Co., 1963).

18. The term wage gap is somewhat of a misnomer. Technically, if a woman earns $.75 for every $1 a man earns, the wage ratio is 75 percent, and the wage gap is 25 percent.

However, in order to be consistent with nontechnical usage, we refer to the wage ratio as the wage gap.

19. Deborah M. Figart, "Wage Gap," in *The Elgar Companion to Feminist Economics*, eds. Janice Peterson and Margaret Lewis (Cheltenham and Northampton: Edward Elgar, 1999), 746–49.

20. Ariane Hegewish and Emma William-Baron, "The Gender Wage Gap 2016; Differences by Gender, Race and Ethnicity," *Institute for Women's Policy Research Fact Sheet, September 13, 2017,* https://iwpr.org/publications/gender-wage-gap-2016-earnings-dif ferences-gender-race-ethnicity

21. Organization for Economic Cooperation and Development (OECD), "Labor Force Participation Rate by Sex and Age Group," *OECD Stat,* https://stats.oecd.org/ index.aspx?queryid=54741

22. US Department of Labor, Bureau of Labor Statistics, "Highlights of Women's Earnings 2017," https://www.bls.gov/opub/reports/womens-earnings/2017/home.htm

23. US Department of Labor, "Highlights."

24. United States Department of Labor, Bureau of Labor Statistics, "Highlights of Women's Earnings in 2018," https://www.bls.gov/opub/reports/womens-earnings/2018/ pdf/home.pdf

25. American Association of University Women, "Graduating to a Pay Gap: The Earnings of Women and Men One Year after Graduation," https://www.aauw.org/re search/graduating-to-a-pay-gap

26. Francine D. Blau and Lawrence M. Kahn, "The Gender Wage Gap: Extent, Trends, and Explanations," *Journal of Economic Literature* 55, no. 3 (2017): 789–865.

27. Judith Warner, Nora Ellmann, and Diana Boesch, "The Women's Leadership Gap," Center for American Progress, https://www.americanprogress.org/issues/women/ reports/2018/11/20/461273/womens-leadership-gap-2

28. Mariam K. Chamberlain, "Glass Ceiling," in *The Elgar Companion to Feminist Economics,* eds. Janice Peterson and Margaret Lewis (Cheltenham and Northampton: Edward Elgar, 1999), 396–401.

29. Frances K. Conley, *Walking Out on the Boys* (New York: Farrar, Straus and Gir-oux, 1998).

30. Ha Yan, "A Day in the Life of a Surgical Intern: Women in Surgery," *The Lancet,* March 3, 2018, https://doi.org/10.1016/S0140-6736(18)30436-7

31. United States Department of Labor, Bureau of Labor Statistics, *Highlights of Women's Earnings 2017* (2018).

32. Officially, these are called Construction and Extraction Occupations. Bureau of Labor Statistics, *Highlights of Women's Earnings in 2018,* https://www.bls.gov/opub/re ports/womens-earnings/2018/home.htm

33. Elise Shaw, Anne Hegewisch, Emma Williams-Baron, and Barbara Gault, Institute for Women's Policy Research, "Undervalued and Underpaid in America: Women in Low-Wage, Female-Dominated Jobs," https://iwpr.org/wp-content/uploads/wpal limport/files/iwpr-export/publications/D508%20Undervalued%20and%20Underpaid. pdf

34. Amott and Matthaei, *Race, Gender, and Work.*

35. Mary C. King, "Black Women's Labor Market Status: Occupational Segregation in the United States and Great Britain," *Review of Black Political Economy* 24, no. 1 (Sum-

mer 1995): 23–40. King points out that in Great Britain the term *black* refers to people of Indian, Pakistani, and Bengali ancestry as well as those of African descent from Africa or the Caribbean. King uses black in the American sense to refer to people of African descent.

36. Jean L. Pyle points this out in her discussion of the differences in natalist policies directed toward ethnic Malay women and ethnic Chinese women in Singapore. Jean L. Pyle, "Women, the Family, and Economic Restructuring: The Singapore Model?" *Review of Social Economy* 55 (Summer 1997): 215–23.

37. Seager, *The State of Women in the World Atlas*, 64.

38. Solomon W. Polachek, "Human Capital and Gender Earning Gap: A Response to Feminist Critiques," in *Out of the Margin: Feminist Perspectives on Economics*, eds. Edith Kuiper and Jolande Sap (London and New York: Routledge, 1995), 61–89.

39. Carnegie Mellon University, "Brains of Girls and Boys Are Similar, Producing Equal Math Ability," www.sciencedaily.com/releases/2019/11/191108074852.htm

40. Marianne Bertrand and Sendhil Mullainathan, "Are Emily and Greg More Employable than Lakisha and Jamal? A Field Experiment on Labor Market Discrimination," *American Economic Review* 94, no. 4 (2004): 991–1013.

41. Joyce Jacobsen, *The Economics of Gender* (Malden: Blackwell, 1998).

42. Rhonda Williams and William E. Spriggs, "How Does It Feel to Be Free? Reflections on Black-White Economic Inequality in the Era of 'Color-Blind' Law," *Review of Black Political Economy* 27 (Summer 1999): 9–21.

43. Jane Humphries, "Economics, Gender, and Equal Opportunities," in *The Economics of Equal Opportunities*, eds. Jane Humphries and Jill Rubery (Manchester: Equal Employment Opportunities Commission, 1995), 55–79.

44. Bergmann, *The Economic Emergence of Women*.

45. Bruce Pietrykowski, "The Return to Caring Skills," *Feminist Economics* 23, no. 4 (2017): 34–61.

46. Figart, Mutari, and Power, *Living Wages, Equal Wages*.

47. Myra H. Strober and Carolyn L. Arnold, "The Dynamics of Occupational Segregation among Bank Tellers," in *Gender in the Workplace*, eds. Clair Brown and Joseph Pechman (Washington, DC: Brookings Institute, 1987), 107–58.

48. Asaf Levanon, Paula England, and Paul Allison, "Occupational Feminization and Pay: Assessing Causal Dynamics Using 1950–2000 U.S. Census Data," *Social Forces* 88, no. 2 (December 2009): 865–91, https://doi.org/10.1353/sof.0.0264

49. Bruce Pietrykowski, *Work* (Cambridge: Polity, 2019), 58–59.

50. Richard Anker, "Theories of Occupational Segregation by Sex: An Overview," in *Women, Gender, and Work*, ed. Martha Fetherolf Loutfi (Geneva: International Labour Office, 2001): 129–65.

51. Bergmann, *The Economic Emergence of Women*, and Susan Eisenberg, "Still Building the Foundation: Women in the Construction Trades," *Working USA* 2, no.1 (1998): 23–25.

52. Corinne Bendersky, "Making U.S. Fire Departments More Diverse and Inclusive," *Harvard Business Review*, https://hbr.org/2018/12/making-u-s-fire-departments-more-diverse-and-inclusive

53. Paul Demko, "Burned," *City Pages* 22 (January 2001).

54. Figart, Mutari, and Power, *Living Wages, Equal Wages*.

55. Figart et al, *Living Wages*. See also Olga Alonso-Villar and Corel del Rio, "Occu-

pational Segregation of African American Women in the United States," *Feminist Economics* 23, no. 1 (2017): 108–34.

56. *Automobile Workers. v. A. Johnson Controls*, 499 US. 187 (1991).

57. Kimberlé Crenshaw, "Demarginalizing the Intersection of Race and Sex: A Black Feminist Critique of Antidiscrimination Doctrine, Feminist Theory and Antiracist Politics," *University of Chicago Legal Forum* 1989, Article 8.

58. Bergmann, *The Economic Emergence of Women*.

59. Minnesota Department of Employee Relations, "Guide to Understanding Pay Equity Compliance and Computer Reports" (October 2000).

60. "Raise the Minimum Wage," https://raisetheminimumwage.com

61. Laura Huizar and Tsedeye Gebresalassie, National Employment Law Project, "What a $15 Minimum Wage Means for Women and Workers of Color," https://www.nelp.org/wp-content/uploads/Policy-Brief-15-Minimum-Wage-Women-Workers-of-Color.pdf

62. See http://www.livingwagecampaign.org

63. Figart, Mutari, and Power, *Living Wages, Equal Wages*.

64. Guy Standing, *A Precariat Charter: From Denizens to Citizens* (London: Bloomsbury, 2014), chap. 1.

CHAPTER 5

1. Diana M. Pearce, "The Feminization of Poverty: Women, Work, and Welfare," *Urban and Social Change Review* 11 (1978): 28–36.

2. UNICEF Office of Research, "Fairness for Children: A League Table of Inequality in Child Well-Being in Rich Countries," *Innocenti Report Card no. 13* (2016), https://www.unicef-irc.org/publications/pdf/RC13_eng.pdf

3. Spotlight on Poverty and Opportunity, "Poverty Next Door: Income Inequality in America and Pathways to Positive Change," https://spotlightonpoverty.org; Anthony Harkins and Meredith McCarroll, eds., *Appalachian Reckoning: A Region Responds to "Hillbilly Elegy"* (Morgantown: West Virginia University Press, 2019).

4. United States Census Bureau, "Income and Poverty in the United States: 2018," https://www.census.gov/data/tables/2019/demo/income-poverty/p60-266.html

5. United States Census Bureau, "Income and Poverty.".

6. Institute for Women's Poverty Research, "Poverty, Gender and Public Policies," https://iwpr.org/wp-content/uploads/wpallimport/files/iwpr-export/publications/D505-Poverty,%20Gender,%20and%20Public%20Policies.pdf

7. Cornell University, "Disability Statistics," http://www.disabilitystatistics.org/reports/acs.cfm?statistic=7. This data estimates the poverty of noninstitutionalized persons age twenty-one to sixty-four who lived below the poverty line in 2017.

8. Raj Chetty, Nathaniel Hendren, Patrick Kline, Emmanuel Saez, and Nicholas Turner, "Is the United States Still a Land of Opportunity? Recent Trends in Intergenerational Mobility," *American Economic Review Papers and Proceedings* 104, no. 3 (2014): 141–47.

9. Chetty et al., "Is the United States Still a Land of Opportunity?"

10. M. V. Lee Badgett, Soon Kyu Choi, and Biana Wilson, *LGBT Poverty in the United States: A Study of Differences between Sexual Orientation and Gender Identity Groups*,

Williams Institute, https://williamsinstitute.law.ucla.edu/wp-content/uploads/National-LGBT-Poverty-Oct-2019.pdf

11. Constance F. Citro and Robert T. Michael, eds., *Measuring Poverty: A New Approach* (Washington, DC: National Academic Press, 1995).

12. United States Census, "Supplemental Poverty Measure," https://www.census.gov/topics/income-poverty/supplemental-poverty-measure.html

13. Barbara Bergmann and Trudi Renwick, "A Budget-Based Definition of Poverty with an Application to Single-Parent Families," *Journal of Human Resources* 29 (Winter 1993): 1–24.

14. In Western Europe this question is answered by defining the poverty line as 50 percent of median income. Thus a decent standard of living is one that enables people to be a part of the middle class.

15. Economic Policy Institute, "Family Budget Calculator," https://www.epi.org/resources/budget

16. The interested reader might want to take the poverty tour presented on the web page of the US Catholic Bishops, http://www.usccb.org/about/catholic-campaign-for-human-development/povertyusa

17. Shahra Razavi, *Gendered Poverty and Well Being* (Malden, MA: Blackwell, 2000).

18. Amartya Sen, *Development as Freedom* (Oxford: Oxford University Press, 1999).

19. Chetty et al., "Is the United States Still a Land of Opportunity."

20. Sylvia Chant, ed., *The International Handbook of Gender and Poverty: Concepts, Research, Policy* (Northampton, MA: Edward Elgar Publishing, 2010).

21. Chant, *The International Handbook of Gender and Poverty.*

22. Center for Poverty Research, University of California, Davis, "Who Are the Working Poor in America?" https://poverty.ucdavis.edu/faq/who-are-working-poor-america

23. Ana María Claver Muñoz and Cristina Rovira Izquierdo, "Raising Their Voices against Precariousness: Women's Experiences of In-Work Poverty in Europe," Oxfam International, https://www.oxfam.org/en/research/raising-their-voices-against-precariousness-womens-experiences-work-poverty-europe

24. Robert Kuttner, "The Market for Labor," in *Everything for Sale: The Virtues and Limits of Markets* (Chicago: University of Chicago Press, 1999), 68–109.

25. Jane Falkingham, Maria Evandrou, and Athnina Vlachantoni, "Gender, Poverty and Pensions," in *The International Handbook of Poverty: Concepts, Research and Policy*, ed. Sylvia Chant (Northampton, MA: Edward Elgar, 2010), 232–40.

26. Randy Albelda, "Different Anti-Poverty Programs, Same Single-Mother Poverty: Fifteen Years of Welfare Reform," *Dollars and Sense* 298 (January/February 2012), http://www.dollarsandsense.org/archives/2012/0112albelda.html

27. Karen Christopher, "Single Motherhood, Employment, or Social Assistance: Why Are U.S. Women Poorer than Women in Other Affluent Nations?" *Journal of Poverty* 6 (2002): 61–80.

28. Gøsta Esping-Andersen, *The Three Worlds of Welfare* (Princeton: Princeton University Press, 1990).

29. Ann Schola Orloff, "Gender and the Social Rights of Citizenship," *American Sociological Review* 58 (1993): 303–28; Ruth Lister, *Feminist Perspectives* (London: Macmillan, 1997); and Diane Sainsbury, *Gender, Equality, and Welfare States* (Cambridge: Cambridge University Press, 1996).

30. Diana Sainsbury, *Gender, Equality, and Welfare States*, and "Gender and Social Democratic Welfare States," in *Gender and Welfare State Regimes*, ed. Diane Sainsbury (Oxford: Oxford University Press, 1999), 75–116.

31. Randy Albelda and Chris Tilly, *Glass Ceilings and Bottomless Pits: Women's Work, Women's Poverty* (Brooklyn, NY: South End Press, 1999).

32. In 1939 the Social Security Act was amended to add dependents and survivors benefits for widows and children of breadwinners.

33. Albelda, "Different Anti-Poverty Programs."

34. Randy Albelda, "Fallacies of Welfare-to-Work Policies," *Lost Ground: Welfare Reform, Poverty, and Beyond*, eds. Randy Albelda and Ann Withhorn (Cambridge: South End Press, 2002), 79–94.

35. Kathryn Edin and H. Luke Shaefer, *$2.00 a Day: Living on Almost Nothing in America* (Boston: Houghton Mifflin Harcourt, 2015).

36. Albelda, "Different Anti-Poverty Programs."

37. Heather Han, Monica Rahacek, and Julia Isaacs, "Improving Child Care Subsidy Programs," February 2018, Urban Institute, https://www.urban.org/sites/default/files/publication/96376/improving_child_care_subsidy_programs.pdf

38. Han et al., "Improving Child Care Subsidy Programs."

39. Jamila Michener and Margaret Teresa Brower, "What's Policy Got to Do with It?: Race, Gender and Economic Inequality in the United States," *Daedelus* (Winter 2020), https://www.amacad.org/publication/race-gender-economic-inequality-united-states

40. Ann Cammett, "Welfare Queens Redux: The Criminalizing of Black Mothers in the Age of Neoliberalism," *Southern California Interdisciplinary Law Journal* 25 (2016): 363–94.

41. Howard Schneider, "4 in 10 Americans Can't Fund a $400 Emergency Expense without Borrowing, Fed Survey Finds," *Business Insider*, May 22, 2018, https://www.businessinsider.com/4-in-10-adults-lack-400-cash-for-unexpected-expense-fed-survey-shows-2018-5

42. Lawrence M. Berger, Maria Cancian, and Katherine Magnuson, "Anti-Poverty Policy Initiatives for the United States," *Russell Sage Foundation Journal of the Social Sciences* 14, no. 3 (February 2018): 1–19.

43. Berger et al., "Anti-Poverty Policy Initiatives for the United States."

44. L. Randall Wray, Stephanie A. Kelton, Pavlina R. Tcherneva, Scott Fullwiler, and Flavia Dantas, "Guaranteed Jobs Through a Public Service Employment Program," Levy Economics Institute of Bard College Policy Note, http://www.levyinstitute.org/pubs/pn_18_2.pdf

45. Wray et al., "Guaranteed Jobs Through a Public Service Employment Program."

46. William Darity, "A Direct Route to Full Employment," *Review of Black Political Economy* 37, no. 3 (2010): 179–81.

47. Pavlina Tcherneva and L. Randall Wray, "Gender and the Job Guarantee: The Impact of Argentina's Jefes Program on Females Heads of Poor Households," Levy Institute Working Paper #50, December 2005.

48. Milton Friedman, *Capitalism and Freedom* (Chicago: University of Chicago Press, 1992).

49. Evelyn Forget, *Basic Income for Canadians: The Key to a Healthier, Happier, More Secure Life for All* (Winnipeg: University of Manitoba Press, 2018).

50. Kathi Weeks, *The Problem with Work: Feminism, Marxism, Antiwork Politics, and Postwork Imaginaries* (Durham: Duke University Press, 2011), 137–50.

CHAPTER 6

1. Sydney W. Mintz, *Sweetness and Power: The Place of Sugar in Modern History* (New York: Penguin Books 1986), chap. 3.

2. Marian Vasile, "The Gender of Silk," *Journal of Research in Gender Studies* 31, no. 1 (2013): 102–7.

3. David Graeber, *Debt: The First 5,000 Years* (Brooklyn and London: Melville House, 2011), 311.

4. Mintz, *Sweetness and Power*, chap. 2.

5. Eric Hobsbawm, *Industry and Empire* (London: The Penguin Group, 1968, 1999).

6. See Ester Boserup, *Women's Role in Economic Development* (London: Allen and Unwin, 1970), for a discussion of the African case, and Bina Agarwal, *A Field of One's Own* (Cambridge: Cambridge University Press, 1998), for a discussion of South Asia. These books provide ample evidence of the problems created by the imposition of Western norms on African and Asian agricultural communities.

7. Thomas Jefferson, Notes on the State of Virginia, p. 64. The Federalist Papers Project. www.thefederalistpapers.org

8. Cynthia Enloe, *Beaches and Bases: Making Feminist Sense of International Politics* (Berkeley: University of California Press, 1989, 2000), 49.

9. The countries of Latin America gained independence much earlier, in the late eighteenth and early nineteenth centuries.

10. Sunil Kukreja, "The Two Faces of Development," in *Introduction to International Political Economy*, 2nd ed., eds. David N. Balaam and Michael Veseth (Upper Saddle River: Prentice Hall, 2001), 320–45.

11. For example, in 1954 the democratic government of Guatemala was brought down when it attempted to redistribute some of the land of the United Fruit Company to landless peasants. In 1953, the United States supported Mohammed Reza Pahlavi, Shah of Iran, in order to prevent the nationalization of Iran's oil industry.

12. The World Bank, http://iresearch.worldbank.org/PovcalNet/povDuplicateWB.aspx.

13. Jason Hickel, *The Divide: A Brief Guide to Global Inequality and its Solutions* (London: William Heinemann 2017), 35.

14. Jason Hickel, "A Response to Max Roser: How Not to Measure Global Poverty," February 6, 2019, https://www.jasonhickel.org/blog/2019/2/6/response-to-max-roser

15. Oxfam International, "Why the Majority of the World's Poor Are Women," 2019, https://www.oxfam.org/en/even-it/why-majority-worlds-poor-are-women

16. Oxfam International, "Why the Majority of the World's Poor Are Women."

17. Lant Pritchett, "Divergence Big Time," *Journal of Economic Perspectives* 11, no. 3 (1997): 3–17.

18. Measured in 1985 USD.

19. Branko Milanovic, *Global Inequality: A New Approach for the Age of Globalization* (Cambridge and London: Harvard University Press, 2016).

20. Milanovic, *Global Inequality*.

21. The World Bank Group, "Poverty and Shared Prosperity," 2016, https://openknowledge.worldbank.org/bitstream/handle/10986/25078/9781464809583.pdf

22. Jason Hickel, "Is Global Inequality Getting Better or Worse: A Critiques of the World Bank's Convergence Narrative," *Third World Quarterly* 38, no. 10 (2017): 1–15.

23. Jason Hickel, "Global Inequality May Be Much Worse Than We Think," *The Guardian*, April 2016, https://www.theguardian.com/global-development-professionals-network/2016/apr/08/global-inequality-may-be-much-worse-than-we-think

24. *Who's Counting? Marilyn Waring On Sex, Lies & Global Economics*, Terrance Nash, Director, BullFrog Films, 1995.

25. United Nations, "Introduction to Gender and Climate Change," 2019, https://unfccc.int/topics/gender/the-big-picture/introduction-to-gender-and-climate-change

26. The Women's Environment and Development Organization (WEDO), "Gender, Climate Change and Human Security: Lessons from Senegal," in *The Women, Gender and Development Reader*, eds. Nalini Visvanathan, Lynn Duggan, Nan Wiegersma, and Laurie Nisonoff (London: Zed Books, 2011), 317–26.

27. Seema Arora-Jonsson, "Virtue and Vulnerability: Discourses on Women, Gender and Climate Change," *Global Environmental Climate Change* 21, no. 2 (2011): 744–51.

28. Lindsey Dillon et al. "The Environmental Protection Agency in the Early Trump Administration: Prelude to Regulatory Capture," *American Journal of Public Health* 108, no. S2 (April 1, 2018): S89–94.

29. Jason Hickel, *The Divide*, chap. 7.

30. James Ford, "Living with Climate Change in the Arctic," Worldwatch Institute, *World Watch Magazine* 18, no. 5 (September/October 2005), http://www.worldwatch.org/node/584

31. David Harvey, *A Brief History of Neoliberalism* (Oxford: Oxford University Press, 2005).

32. Teresa Amott and Julie Matthaei, *Race, Gender and Work: A Multi-Cultural Economic History of Women in the United States*, rev. ed. (Boston: South End Press, 1996).

33. Amott and Matthaei, Race, Gender and Work.

34. Amott and Matthaei, Race, Gender and Work, 2.

35. Ricardo French-Davis, *Economic Reforms in Chile: From Dictatorship to Democracy* (Ann Arbor: University of Michigan Press, 2002).

36. The term "hot money" refers to investing in the financial assets of a foreign country, such as stocks or bonds that can be sold quickly and are short-term attempts to make money through speculation rather than make long-term investments in the economy. See J. B. Maverick, "Foreign Portfolio vs. Foreign Direct Investment: What's the Difference?" Investopedia, April 18, 2019, https://www.investopedia.com/ask/answers/060115/what-difference-between-foreign-portfolio-investment-and-foreign-direct-investment.asp

37. Guy Standing, "Global Feminization Through Flexible Labor: A Theme Revisited," *World Development* 27, no. 3 (1999): 583–602.

38. V. Spike Peterson, *A Critical Rewriting of Global Political Economy: Integrating Reproductive, Productive and Virtual Economies* (London and New York: Routledge, 2003), 62. Guy Standing makes a similar argument in "Global Feminization Through Flexible Labor."

39. Lourdes Benería, "Structural Adjustment Policies," in *The Elgar Companion to Feminist Economics*, eds. Janice Peterson and Margaret Lewis (Cheltenham and Northhampton: Edward Elgar, 1999), 687–95.

40. The loans were made by official lenders such as the World Bank and other government development banks, as well as private commercial banks.

41. United Nations, Global Issues, Water, https://www.un.org/en/sections/issues-depth/water

42. Adrienne Roberts, "Privatizing Social Reproduction: The Primitive Accumulation of Water in an Era of Neoliberalism," *Antipode* 40, no. 4 (2008): 535–60.

43. Roberts, "Privatizing Social Reproduction."

44. M. Barlow and T. Clark, *Blue Gold: The Battle Against Corporate Theft of the World's Water* (Toronto: McClelland & Stewart, 2003), 59.

45. Melissa Denchak, "Flint Water Crisis: Everything You Need to Know," National Resource Defense Council, 2018, https://www.nrdc.org/stories/flint-water-crisis-everything-you-need-know

46. United Nations Committee on the Elimination of Discrimination against Women (CEDAW), "Privatization and Its Impact on the Right to Education of Women and Girls," July 7, 2014, https://ppp.worldbank.org/public-private-partnership/sites/ppp.worldbank.org/files/documents/Privatizationpercent20and%20its%20Impact%20on%20the%20Right%20to%20Education%20of%20Women%20and%20Girls.pdf

47. This is the doctrine of comparative advantage. It is important to note that costs refer not only to the explicit dollar costs of production but also to opportunity costs. The opportunity cost of producing one good is the most highly valued alternative foregone. In other words, the opportunity cost of producing steel is in the value of the labor resources and manufacturing resources taken from other activities.

48. Women's Environment and Development Organization, "WEDO Primer: Women and Trade," November 1999, http://www.wedo.org/wp-content/uploads/genderagendawto_primer.htm

49. Rachel L. Wellhausen, "Recent Trends in Investor–State Dispute Settlement," *Journal of International Dispute Settlement* 7 (January 2016): 117–35.

50. Investor-State Dispute Settlement Platform, "Key Cases," April 2019, https://isds.bilaterals.org/?-key-cases

51. Stephanie Daniel Roth, "People Power in Romania Stopped a Mining Project, Now Corporation is Suing for Billions of Dollars," Investor-State Dispute Settlement Platform, December 2019, https://isds.bilaterals.org/?people-power-in-romania-stopped-a

52. Investor-State Dispute Settlement Platform, "Key Cases."

53. Robin Morgan, *Sisterhood Is Global* (New York: Anchor Press/Doubleday, 1984).

54. Drucilla K. Barker and Edith Kuiper, "Gender, Class and Location in the Global Economy," in *Handbook of Feminist Theory*, eds. Ania Plomien, Clare Hemmings, Marsha Henry, Mary Evans, Sadie Wearing, and Sumi Madhok (Thousand Oaks, CA: Sage, 2014), 500–15.

55. Barker and Kuiper, "Gender, Class and Location."

CHAPTER 7

1. Paul Krugman, "In Praise of Cheap Labor," *Slate Magazine*, March 21, 1997, https://slate.com/business/1997/03/in-praise-of-cheap-labor.html

2. Guy Standing, "Global Feminization through Flexible Labor: A Theme Revisited," *World Development* 27 (March 1999): 583–602.

3. Saskia Sassen, "Counter Geographies of Globalization: The Feminization of Survival," in *Feminist Post-Development Thought: Rethinking Modernity, Post-Colonialism and Representation*, ed. K. Saunders (London: Zed, 2002), 89–104.

4. Lamia Karim, "Disposable Bodies," *Anthropology Now* 6, no. 1 (Spring 2014): 52–63.

5. Gladys Lopez-Acevedo and Raymond Robertson, *Stitches to Riches? Apparel Employment, Trade and Economic Development in South Asia* (Washington, DC: World Bank, 2016), https://www.worldbank.org/en/region/sar/publication/stitches-to-riches-apparel-employment-trade-and-economic-development-in-south-asia

6. Krugman, "In Praise of Sweatshop Labor."

7. "Bangladesh Export Processing Zones Authority," https://www.bepza.gov.bd

8. Cynthia Enloe, *Bananas, Beaches and Bases: Making Feminist Sense of International Politics* (Berkeley: University of California Press, 2014).

9. Leslie Salzinger, *Genders in Production: Making Workers in Mexico's Global Factories* (Berkeley: University of California Press, 2003).

10. Laura Villadiego, "The Gender Gap in Electronics Factories: Women Exposed to Chemicals and Lower Pay," *Equal Times*, December 22, 2017, https://www.equaltimes.org/the-gender-gap-in-the-electronics#.XOmEY9NKgk4

11. Teri L. Caraway, *Assembling Women: The Feminization of Global Manufacturing* (Ithaca: Cornell University Press, 2007).

12. Ruth Pearson, "'Nimble Fingers' Revisited: Reflection on Women and the Third World Industrialisation in the Late Twentieth Century," in *Feminist Visions of Development: Gender Analysis and Policy,* eds. Cecile Jackson and Ruth Pearson (London and New York: Routledge, 1998), 171–88.

13. Enloe, *Bananas, Beaches and Bases.*

14. Juanita Elias, *Fashioning Inequality: The Multinational Company and Gendered Employment in a Globalizing World* (Aldershot, UK: Ashgate Publishing, 2004).

15. V. Spike Peterson, "Rethinking Theory: Inequalities, Informalization and Feminist Quandaries," *International Feminist Journal of Politics,* 14, no. 1 (2012), 5–35.

16. International Labour Organization, *Women and Men in the Informal Economy: A Statistical Picture* (Geneva: International Labour Office, 2018), https://www.ilo.org/wcmsp5/groups/public/---dgreports/---dcomm/documents/publication/wcms_626831.pdf

17. International Labour Organization, *Women and Men in the Informal Economy.*

18. Ceyhun Elgin and Adem Yavuz Elveren, "Informality, Inequality and Feminization of Labor," *Political Economy Research Institute working paper series*, https://www.peri.umass.edu/component/k2/item/1170-informality-inequality-and-feminization-of-labor

19. James Heintz, *Globalization, Economic Policy and Employment: Poverty and Gender Implications* (Geneva: International Labour Office, 2006).

20. UN Women, "Progress of the World's Women: Transforming Economies, Realizing Rights," https://www.unwomen.org/en/digital-library/publications/2015/4/progress-of-the-worlds-women-2015

21. SEWA website, http://www.sewa.org

22. WIEGO, "Empowering Informal Workers, Securing Informal Livelihoods," http://www.wiego.org/informal-economy/links-growth

23. Rahel Kunz, "Remittances in the Global Political Economy," in *Handbook on the international political economy of gender*, eds. Juanita Elias and Adrienne Roberts (Cheltenham, UK: Edward Elgar Publishing, 2018).

24. Human Rights Watch, "I Already Bought You: Abuse and Exploitation of Female

Migrant and Domestic Workers," https://www.hrw.org/report/2014/10/22/i-already-bought-you/abuse-and-exploitation-female-migrant-domestic-workers-united

25. Shellee Colen, "'Like a Mother to Them': Stratified Reproduction and West Indian Childcare Workers and Employers in New York City," in *Conceiving the New World Order: the Global Politics of Reproduction*, eds. Faye Ginsburg and Rayna Reiter (Berkeley: University of California Press, 1995).

26. Martin F. Manalansan, "Queering the Chain of Care Paradigm," *Scholar and Feminist Online* 16, no. 3 (2008), http://sfonline.barnard.edu/immigration/manalansan_01.htm

27. See for instance Valerie Francisco-Menchavez, *The Labor of Care: Filipina Migrants and Transnational Families in the Digital Age* (Champaign: University of Illinois press, 2018).

28. Amnesty International, *Sex Workers at Risk: A Research Summary on Human Rights Abuses Against Sex Workers*, Amnesty International, https://www.amnestyusa.org/reports/sex-workers-at-risk-a-research-summary-of-human-rights-abuses-against-sex-workers

29. Coalition against Trafficking in Women letter in response to *Sex Workers at Risk*, http://catwinternational.org/Content/Images/Article/621/attachment.pdf

30. Wendy Chapkis, *Live Sex Acts: Women Performing Erotic Labor* (London and New York: Routledge, 1996).

31. Jean L. Pyle, "Sex, Maids, and Export Processing: Risks and Reasons for Gendered Global Production Networks," *International Journal of Politics, Culture, and Society* 15 (September 2001): 55–76.

32. Kamala Kempadoo, "Introduction: Globalizing the Sex Worker's Rights," in *Global Sex Workers: Rights, Resistance, and Redefinition*, eds. Kamala Kempadoo and Jo Doezema (New York and London: Routledge, 1998), 204–9.

33. See Londa Schiebinger's historical analysis of the simultaneous emergence of gender and race ideology in *Nature's Body* (Boston: Beacon Press, 1995).

34. The National Herald staff, "Greek Economic Crisis Drove More Women into Prostitution," https://www.thenationalherald.com/203788/greek-economic-crisis-drove-more-women-into-prostitution

35. The National Herald, "Greek Economic Crisis."

36. Leah Platt, "Regulating the Global Brothel," *American Prospect*, December 19, 2001, https://prospect.org/features/regulating-global-brothel

37. "Challenging Corporate Power: Struggles for Women's Rights, Economic and Gender Justice," https://www.awid.org/publications/challenging-corporate-power-struggles-womens-rights-economic-and-gender-justice

CHAPTER 8

1. "Inaugural Address of Harry S. Truman," https://avalon.law.yale.edu/20th_century/truman.asp

2. Evan Andrews, "Why Are Countries Classified as First, Second, Third World?" https://www.history.com/news/why-are-countries-classified-as-first-second-or-third-world

3. Chandra Mohanty, "One Third/Two-Thirds Worlds," in *Beyond Borders: Thinking*

Critically about Global Issues, ed. Paula S. Rothenberg (New York: Worth Publishers, 2006): 41–43.

4. Margaret Snyder and Mary Tadesse, *African Women and Development* (London: Zed Books, 1995).

5. Ester Boserup, *Women's Role in Economic Development* (New York: St. Martin's Press, 1970).

6. Lourdes Benería and Gita Sen, "Class and Gender Inequalities and Women's Role in Economic Development," *Feminist Studies* 8, no. 1 (Spring 1982): 157–76.

7. Adele Mueller, *Peasants and Professionals: The Social Organization of Women in Development Knowledge* (Toronto: University of Toronto Press, 1987), 1–2.

8. Chandra Mohanty, "Under Western Eyes: Feminist Scholarship and Colonial Discourses," *boundary 2* 12, no. 3 (Spring/Autumn 1984): 333–358.

9. Isabella Bakker, *The Strategic Silence* (London: Zed Press, 1995); Diane Elson, "Gender Awareness in Modeling Structural Adjustment," *World Development* 23, no. 11 (November 1995): 1851–68.

10. Marilyn Waring, *If Women Counted: A New Feminist Economics* (New York: Harper Collins, 1990).

11. Amartya Sen, *Development as Freedom* (New York: Alfred A. Knopf, 1999).

12. Edith Kuiper and Drucilla K. Barker, *Feminist Economics and the World Bank* (Abingdon: Routledge Press, 2006).

13. Radhika Balakrishnan, James Heintz, and Diane Elson, *Rethinking Economic Policy for Social Justice: The Radical Potential of Human Rights* (Abingdon: Routledge Press, 2016).

14. "Progress of the World's Women: Families in a Changing World, 2019–2020," http://www.unwomen.org/en/digital-library/progress-of-the-worlds-women

15. Kate Bedford, *Developing Partnerships: Gender, Sexuality and the Reformed World Bank* (Minneapolis: University of Minnesota Press, 2009).

16. Lamia Karim, *Microfinance and Its Discontents* (Minneapolis: University of Minnesota Press, 2011); Ha-Joon Chang and Milford Bateman, "The Microfinance Illusion," *SSRN Electronic journal*, https://papers.ssrn.com/sol3/papers.cfm?abstract_id=2385174

17. Adrienne Roberts, "The Political Economy of 'Transnational Business Feminism,'" *International Feminist Journal of Politics* 17, no. 2 (2015): 209–31.

18. Lindsey Hayhurst, "Corporatising Sport, Gender and Development: postcolonial IR Feminisms, Transnational Private Governance and Global Corporate Social Engagement," *Third World Quarterly* 32, no. 3 (2011): 531–49; Kathryn Moeller, *The Gender Effect* (Berkeley: University of California Press, 2017).

19. UNICEF, "Gender Equality Overview," https://data.unicef.org/topic/gender/overview

20. Naila Kabeer, "Gender Equality, Economic Growth, and Women's Agency: The 'Endless Variety' and 'Monotonous Similarity' of Patriarchal Constraints," *Feminist Economics* 22, no. 1 (2016): 295–321.

21. Andrea Cornwall, "Women's Empowerment: What Works?" *Journal of International Development* 28, no. 3 (2016): 342–59.

22. Kathryn Moeller, "The Ghost Statistic that Haunts Women's Empowerment," *New Yorker*, January 4, 2019, https://www.newyorker.com/science/elements/the-ghost-statistic-that-haunts-womens-empowerment

23. Cornwall, "Women's Empowerment: What Works?"

24. Christine Bauhardt and Wendy Harcourt, eds., *Feminist Political Ecology and the Economics of Care* (Abingdon: Routledge, 2018).

25. Adele Mueller, *Peasants and Professionals*; Marianne Marchand and Jane Parpart, eds., *Feminism, Postmodernism, Development* (Abingdon: Routledge, 1995).

26. See for instance Adichie's TED talk "The Danger of a Single Story," https://www.ted.com/talks/chimamanda_adichie_the_danger_of_a_single_story?language=en

27. S. Charusheela and Eiman Zein-Elabdin, eds., *Postcolonialism Meets Economics* (Abingdon: Routledge, 2003).

28. Lee Badgett et al., "The Relationship between LGBT Inclusion and Economic Development," USAID and Williams Institute Report, October 2014.

29. Suzanne Bergeron, "Economics, Performativity, and Social Reproduction in Global Development," *Globalizations* 8, no. 2 (Spring 2011): 151–61.

30. Hunger Notes, "2018 World Hunger and Poverty Facts and Statistics," https://www.worldhunger.org/world-hunger-and-poverty-facts-and-statistics

31. United Nations Development Report, "Human Development Index Trends, 1990–2017," http://hdr.undp.org/en/composite/trends

32. World Health Organization, "Maternal Mortality," https://www.who.int/newsroom/fact-sheets/detail/maternal-mortality

33. Stephanie Seguino, "Global Trends in Gender Equality," *Journal of African Development* 18 (2016): 1–30.

CHAPTER 9

1. John W. Schoen, "Financial Crisis of 2008 Is Still Taking a Bite Out of Your Paycheck 10 Years Later," CNBC, September 12, 2018, https://www.cnbc.com/2018/09/11/financial-crisis-of-2008-still-taking-bite-out-of-your-paycheck-report.html

2. Earlier work by Elson and others only distinguished between the monetized and nonmonetized spheres of the economy. Diane Elson, "Gender and the Global Economic Crisis in Developing Countries: A Framework for Analysis," *Gender and Development* 18, no. 2 (July 2010): 201—12.

3. For example, the feminist economist Stephanie Seguino analyzes the gender and ethical implications of the demand side problems caused by the crisis. Stephanie Seguino, "The Global Economic Crisis, Its Gender Implications and Policy Responses," *Gender and Development* 18, no. 2 (July 2010): 79–199.

4. David Harvey, *The Enigma of Capital and the Crises of Capitalism* (Oxford: Oxford University Press, 2010).

5. David Graeber, *Debt: The First 5,000 Years* (Brooklyn and London: Melville House, 2012).

6. David Graeber, *Debt*, 2. This came up in the context of a conversation between the author and an attorney who provided legal advice for antipoverty foundations in London.

7. Jubilee Australia, "Digging to the Roots of Poverty," https://www.jubileeaustralia.org/illegitimate-debt

8. David Graeber, *Debt*.

9. Saskia Sassen, "Women's Burden: Counter-geographies of Globalization and the Feminization of Survival," *Journal of International Affairs* 53, no. 2 (2000): 503–24.

10. A hard currency is one that has the confidence of international investors and businesses because they hold their value. Dollars, Euros, and Yen are three examples. International debts must be repaid in hard currency. The US dollar is unique because it is the world's foreign reserve currency.

11. Gary Dymski, Jesus Hernandez, and Lisa Mohanty, "Race, Gender, Power, and the US Subprime Mortgage and Foreclosure Crisis: A Meso Analysis," *Feminist Economics* 19, no. 3 (2013): 124–51.

12. Ruth Pearson and Diane Elson, "Transcending the Impact of the Financial Crisis in the United Kingdom: Towards Plan F—A Feminist Economic Strategy," *Feminist Review* 109 (2015): 8—30.

13. Pearson and Elson, "Transcending."

14. Brett Theodos, Emma Kalish, Signe-Mary McKernan, and Caroline Ratcliffe, "Do Financial Knowledge, Behavior, and Well-Being Differ by Gender?" Urban Institute, 2014, https://www.urban.org/sites/default/files/publication/22456/413077-Do-Financial-Knowledge-Behavior-and-Well-Being-Differ-by-Gender-.PDF; Gary R. Mottola, "In Our Best Interest: Women, Financial Literacy, and Credit Card Behavior," Washington, DC: FINRA Investor Education Foundation, 2012, http://citeseerx.ist.psu.edu/viewdoc/download?doi=10.1.1.352.8088&rep=rep1&type=pdf

15. David Harvey, *The Enigma of Capital: and the Crises of Capitalism*, 2nd ed. (Oxford: Oxford University Press, 2010), 10.

16. Drucilla K. Barker, "The Real Wolves of Wall Street: Examining Debt, Austerity, and Accountability Through the Lens of Primitive Accumulation," *International Critical Thought* 8, no. 4 (2018): 535–52.

17. R. W. Connell and James W. Messerschmidt, "Hegemonic Masculinity: Rethinking the Concept," *Gender and Society* 19, no. 6 (December 2005): 829–59.

18. For a provocative account see Elizabeth Prügl, "'Lehman Brothers and Sisters': Revisiting Gender and Myth After the Financial Crisis," in *Scandalous Economics: Gender and the Politics of Financial Crises*, eds. Aida A. Hozic and Jaqui True (New York: Oxford University Press, 2016), 21–40.

19. Julie A. Nelson, *Gender and Risk-Taking: Economics, Evidence, and Why the Answer Matters* (London and New York: Routledge, 2017), 123. See also Elizabeth Prügl, "'Lehman Brothers and Sisters': Revisiting Gender and Myth After the Financial Crisis," in *Scandalous Economics*, 21–40, and Irene van Staveren, "The Lehman Sisters Hypothesis," *Cambridge Journal of Economics* 38, no. 5 (September 2014): 995–1014.

20. Julie A. Nelson, *Gender and Risk-Taking*, 123.

21. David Graeber also makes this point in *Debt*.

22. This point is made by both Marieke de Goede, *Virtue, Fortune, and Faith: A Genealogy of Finance* (Minneapolis: University of Minnesota Press, 2005), and Miranda Joseph, *Debt to Society: Accounting for Life under Capitalism* (Minneapolis: University of Minnesota Press, 2014).

23. de Goede, *Virtue, Fortune and Faith*.

24. Drucilla K. Barker, "The Real Wolves," 19.

25. Ann Pettifor, *The Production of Money: How to Break the Power of Bankers* (London and New York: Verso Books, 2017), 5.

26. The Editorial Board, "Governments Must Learn to Love Borrowing Again," *Financial Times*, December 8, 2019, https://www.ft.com/content/f320e1ce-1828-11ea-8d73-6303645ac406?segmentid=acee4131-99c2-09d3-a635-873e61754ec6

27. There is a school of economics, Modern Monetary Theory, that argues that deficits do not matter as long as the economy is below full employment. We are not engaging with this here. For us, the central question to consider is how is the money being spent? For further discussion of this point of view see Ann Pettifor, "'Deficit Financing' or 'Deficit-Reduction Financing'?" Prime Economics, October 2, 2018, http://www.primeeconomics.org/articles/deficit-financing-or-deficit-reduction-financing

28. Ann Pettifor, *The Production of Money*.

29. The real interest rate is the nominal interest rate adjusted for inflation.

30. By the time this book goes to print, it is highly likely that another crisis will have occurred.

31. John Maynard Keynes, *The General Theory of Employment, Interest and Money* (New York: Harcourt, Brace and Company, 1964), 159.

32. Victoria Chick and Ann Pettifor with Geoff Tilley, "The Economic Consequences of Mr Osborne, Updated," *Prime Economics*, March 15, 2016, http://static1.squarespace.com/static/541ff5f5e4b02b7c37f31ed6/t/56ec3ccaa3360c829bb2a001/1458322639033/The+Economic+Consequences+of+Mr+Osborne+2016+final+v2.pdf

33. Chick and Pettifor, "The Economic Consequences of Mr. Osborne".

34. Under the Bretton Woods system, capital controls limited the international mobility of capital. It was difficult for fund managers to move money from country to country in order to seek higher returns. However, when the United States went off the gold standard, this regulation was no longer workable and had to be dismantled.

35. Barry Bluestone and Bennett Harrison, *The Deindustrialization of America* (New York: Basic Books, 1982).

36. Raghuram G. Rajan, *Fault Lines: How Hidden Fractures Still Threaten the World Economy* (Princeton: Princeton University Press, 2011).

37. Michael Kumhof and Romain Rancière, "Inequality, Leverage and Crises IMF Working Paper," November 2010, https://www.imf.org/external/pubs/ft/wp/2010/wp10268.pdf

38. This is Regulation Q, a part of the Glass Steagall Act.

39. Matthew Sherman, "A Short History of Financial Deregulation in the United States," Center for Economic and Policy Research, July 2009, http://cepr.net/documents/publications/dereg-timeline-2009-07.pdf

40. Ann Pettifor, *The Production of Money*, 30.

41. Investopedia, "Subprime Lender," reviewed by Jason Fernando, updated October 24, 2019, https://www.investopedia.com/terms/s/subprimelender.asp

42. Michael W. Hudson, *The Monster: How a Gang of Predatory Lenders and Wall Street Bankers Fleeced America-and Spawned a Global Financial Crisis* (New York: Times Books, Henry Holt and Company, 2010). Michael W. Hudson is a financial journalist, not to be confused with Michael Hudson, the heterodox, financial economist.

43. There were rare exceptions. The medical doctor turned hedge-fund manager, Michael Burry, did investigate what is in the CDOs, saw the large number of subprime mortgages, and recognized the consequences. He predicted the housing market would default when the interest on the adjustable rate mortgages rose. His story is documented in the biopic *The Big Short*.

44. Michael W. Hudson, *The Monster*.

45. Redlining was the technically illegal practice of denying mortgages to people living in neighborhoods on the basis of race, rather than the borrowers' credit worthiness.

46. John V. Duca, "Subprime Mortgage Crisis: 2007—2010," Federal Reserve History, 2013, https://www.federalreservehistory.org/essays/subprime_mortgage_crisis

47. Adrienne Roberts, "Financing Social Reproduction: The Gendered Relations of Debt and Mortgage Finance in Twenty-first-century America," New Political Economy 18, no. 1 (2013): 21–42.

48. Michael W. Hudson, Monster. See also John Lanchester, "After the Fall," London Review of Books 40, no. 13 (July 2018): 3–8.

49. Dean Baker, "Alan Greenspan Owes America an Apology," Guardian, March 28, 2013, https://www.theguardian.com/commentisfree/2013/oct/28/alan-greenspan-housing-market-crisis

50. John Lanchester, "After the Fall."

51. For an interesting and generally accessible articulation of this position see Marieke deGoede, Virtue, chap. 5, "Regulation and Risk in Capital Markets."

52. Karl Marx, Capital, vol. 1 (London: Verso, 1990), 917, emphasis ours.

53. Drucilla K. Barker, "The Real Wolves."

54. Kendra Strauss, "Accumulation and Dispossession: Lifting the Veil on the Subprime Mortgage Crisis," Antipode 14, no. 1 (2009): 10–14.

55. John Lanchester, "After the Fall," 3–8.

56. Allen J. Fishbein and Patrick Woodall, "Women Are Prime Targets for Subprime Lending: Women are Disproportionately Represented in High-Cost Mortgage Market," The Consumer Federation of America, Washington, DC, 200, 3–4, https://consumerfed.org/pdfs/WomenPrimeTargetsStudy1206062.pdf. Cited in Roberts, "Financing Social Reproduction."

57. Fishbein and Woodall, "Women Are Prime Targets for Subprime Lending."

58. Paul Taylor, Rakesh Kochhar, Richard Fry, Gabriel Velasco, and Seth Motel, "Twenty-to-One: Wealth Gap Rises to Record Highs between Whites, Blacks and Hispanics," Pew Research Center, Washington, DC, 2011, 5, https://www.pewresearch.org/wp-content/uploads/sites/3/2011/07/SDT-Wealth-Report_7-26-11_FINAL.pdf. Cited in Roberts, "Financing Social Reproduction."

59. As the facts unfolded, it was revealed that Goldman Sachs had engaged in some fancy financial shenanigans to help Greece hide its increasing debt. See Alan S. Blinder, After the Music Stopped: The Financial Crisis, the Response, and the Work Ahead (New York: Penguin Press, 2013), 414.

60. David Harvey, A Brief History of Neoliberalism, 44.

61. Anna M. Agathangelou, "Global Rascality of Capitalism and 'Primitive' Accumulation: Unmaking the Death Limit?" in Scandalous Economics, eds. Aida A. Hozic and Jaqui True (New York: Oxford University Press, 2016), 205–30.

62. Agathangelou, "Global Rascality of Capitalism and 'Primitive' Accumulation," 418.

63. Pearson and Elson, "Transcending."

64. Maurice Lazzarato, The Making of Indebted Man, trans. Joshua David Jordan (Cambridge: Semiotext(e), 2012).

65. Silvia Federici, "From Commoning to Debt: Financialization, Microcredit, and the Changing Architecture of Capital Accumulation," 61, in Re-Enchanting the World: Feminism and the Politics of the Commons (Oakland: PM Press, 2019), 60–74.

66. Jason Hickel, The Divide: A Brief Guide to Global Inequality and its Solutions (London: William Heinemann, 2017), 155.

67. Federici, "From Commoning," 61.

68. Julia O'Connell Davidson, "Troubling Freedom: Migration, Debt, and Modern Slavery," *Migration Studies* 1, no. 2 (2013): 176–95.

69. Lisa Adkins, "What Can Money Do? Feminist Theory in Austere Times," *Feminist Review* 109, no. 1 (February 2015): 31–48. She is talking specifically about women.

70. Michael Hudson, "The Coming Savings Write-downs," *Counterpunch*, July 29, 2019, https://www.counterpunch.org/2019/07/29/the-coming-savings-writedowns

71. Federici, 64. The reason that debt builds up like this is explained by compound interest. This occurs when previous interest is added to the principal amount. It is basically interest on interest. Over time, compounding rewards savers and hurts borrowers. See Investopedia, Compound Interest, reviewed by Julia Kagan, https://www.investopedia.com/terms/c/compoundinterest.asp. For a more detailed explanation, including the history, see Michael Hudson, *The Bubble and Beyond: Fictitious Capital, Debt Deflation and Global Crisis* (Dresden: Islet-Verl, 2012), chap. 2.

72. Federici, "From Commoning," 64.

73. One of our graduate students wrote an anthropology thesis on payday lenders. One of the most remarkable findings was their difficulty in finding people who would talk about it. The shame and secrecy attached to having resorted to payday loans was astonishing. See Arya Novinbakht, *The Walking Debt: Surviving an Outbreak of Predatory Lending* (University of South Carolina, Master's thesis, 2018). Retrieved from https://scholarcommons.sc.edu/etd/4748

74. Strike Debt/Occupy Wall Street, *The Debt Resisters' Operations Manual* (September 2012), vi, https://strikedebt.org/The-Debt-Resistors-Operations-Manual.pdf

CHAPTER 10

1. Here we are paraphrasing a famous statement by Karl Marx, "Philosophers have hitherto only *interpreted* the world in various ways; the point is to *change* it." Karl Marx, Theses on Feuerbach, 1845. https://www.marxists.org/archive/marx/works/1845/theses

2. Shirin M. Rai, Catherine Hoskyns, and Dania Thomas, "Depletion: The Cost of Social Reproduction," *International Feminist Journal of Politics* 16, no. 1 (2014): 86–105.

3. Susan Douglas and Meredith Michaels, *The Mommy Myth* (New York: Simon and Schuster, 2004).

4. J. K. Gibson-Graham, *The End of Capitalism (As We Knew It)* (Oxford: Blackwell Publishers, 1996).

5. Nancy Folbre and Julie A. Nelson, "For Love or Money—Or Both?" *Journal of Economic Perspectives* 14, no. 4 (Fall 2000): 123–40.

6. Martha Alter Chen, "The Informal Economy: Definitions, Theories and Policies," WIEGO Working Paper No. 1, August 2012, https://www.wiego.org/sites/default/files/migrated/publications/files/Chen_WIEGO_WP1.pdf

7. Shellee Colen, "'Like a Mother to Them': Stratified Reproduction and West Indian Childcare Workers and Employers in New York," in *Conceiving the New World Order: The Global Politics of Reproduction*, eds. Faye D. Ginsburg and Rayna Rapp (Berkeley: University of California Press, 1995), 78–102.

8. Oxfam International, *Time to Care*, https://www.oxfam.org/en/research/time-care

9. Karl Polanyi, *The Great Transformation: The Political and Economic Origins of Our Time* (Boston: Beacon Press, 1944, 1957, 2001), chaps. 7–9.

10. Polyani, *The Great Transformation*.

11. Isabel Ortiz and Matthew Cummins, "Austerity, the New Normal: A Renewed Washington Consensus 2010–24," Initiative for Policy Dialogue Working Paper, October 2019, http://policydialogue.org/files/publications/papers/Austerity-the-New-Normal-Ortiz-Cummins-6-Oct-2019.pdf

12. ILO, *Decent Work*, https://www.ilo.org/global/topics/decent-work/lang--en/index.htm

13. *The Life and Times of Rosie the Riveter* is a documentary film, directed by Connie Field, about the lives of women in the defense industry during World War II.

14. Karl Marx, *Capital*, vol. 1, chap. 10, section 5, Marxist Archive, https://www.marxists.org/archive/marx/works/1867-c1/ch10.htm#S5

15. Standing, *A Precariat Charter: From Denizens to Citizens* (London: Bloomsbury, 2014), chap. 1.

16. Jason Hickel, "DeGrowth: A Theory of Radical Abundance," *Real-World Economics Review* 87 (2019): 54–68, and Juliet B. Schor and Andrew K. Jorgenson, "Is It Too Late for Growth?" *Review of Radical Political Economics* 51, no. 2 (2019): 320–29. *Throughput* refers to the amount of matter and energy involved in each stage of economic cycle: extraction, production, consumption, and disposal.

17. Kathi Weeks, *The Problem with Work: Feminism, Marxism, Antiwork Politics, and Postwork Imaginaries* (Durham and London: Duke University Press, 2011), 138–39.

18. Guy Standing, *A Precariat Charter*.

19. Standing, *A Precariat Charter*.

20. Weeks, *The Problem with Work*, 174.

21. The Community Economies Research Network (CERN) is an international network of researchers, activists, artists, and others who are interested in ways of enacting new visions of the economy. Stephen Healy and Katherine Gibson, "Commoning Social Life. Essay for the Institute for Culture and Society's Annual Report," 2017, https://www.communityeconomies.org/index.php/publications/articles/commoning-social-life

22. Joan Acker, "Gender, Capital, and Globalization," *Critical Sociology* 30, no. 1 (2004): 17–41.

23. Dzodzi Tsikata, "Effects of Structural Adjustment, Third World Network," Fall 1995, Global Policy Forum, https://www.globalpolicy.org/component/content/article/218/46625.html

24. Joseph N. Lekakis and Maria Kousis, "Economic Crisis, Troika and the Environment in Greece," *South European Society and Politics* 18, no. 3 (2013): 305–31.

25. Chinzia Arruzza, Tithi Bhattacharya, and Nancy Fraser, *Feminism for the 99%: A Manifesto* (London and New York: Verso, 2019), 46–49.

26. NDTV, Delhi, reported by Mariyam Alavi, edited by Deepshikha Ghosh, "Thought Cops Wouldn't Attack Women: Jamia Student Seen in Viral Video," December 17, 2019, https://www.ndtv.com/delhi-news/jamia-millia-islamia-student-seen-in-viral-video-thought-cops-wouldnt-attack-women-2149942

27. Rafia Kazim, "At Shaheen Baugh, Muslim Women Take Their Place as Heroes of the Movement," *The Wire*, January 30, 2020, https://thewire.in/women/shaheen-bagh-muslim-women

28. Bagh Irfanullah Farooqi, "Citizenship as Participation: Muslim Women Protestors of Shaheen," *Economic and Political Weekly* LC no. 4 (January 25, 2020), https://www.epw.in/system/files/pdf/2020_55/4/CM_LV_4_250120_Irfanullah%20Farooqi.pdf

29. Farooqi, "Citizenship as Participation."

30. Farooqi, "Citizenship as Participation."

Select Bibliography

BOOKS, JOURNAL ARTICLES, AND BOOK CHAPTERS

Adkins, Lisa. "What Can Money Do? Feminist Theory in Austere Times." *Feminist Review* 109, no. 1 (February 2015): 31–48.

Agarwal, Bina. *A Field of One's Own.* Cambridge: Cambridge University Press, 1998.

Agathangelou, Anna M. "Global Rascality of Capitalism and 'Primitive' Accumulation: Unmaking the Death Limit?" In *Scandalous Economics*, edited by Aida A. Hozic and Jaqui True, 205–330. New York: Oxford University Press, 2016.

Albelda, Randy, and Chris Tilly. "Fallacies of Welfare-to-Work Policies." In *Lost Ground: Welfare Reform, Poverty, and Beyond*, edited by Randy Albelda and Ann Withhorn, 79–94. Cambridge: South End Press, 2002.

Albelda, Randy, and Chris Tilly. *Glass Ceilings and Bottomless Pits.* Cambridge: South End Press, 1997.

Alonso-Villar, Olga, and Coral Del Río. "The Occupational Segregation of African American Women: Its Evolution From 1940 to 2010." *Feminist Economics* 23, no. 1 (2017): 108–34.

Amott, Teresa, and Julie Matthaei. *Race, Gender, and Work: A Multicultural Economic History of Women in the United States.* Rev. ed. Boston: South End Press, 1996.

Anker, Richard. "Theories of Occupational Segregation by Sex: An Overview." In *Women, Gender, and Work*, edited by Martha Fetherolf Loutfi, 129–56. Geneva: International Labour Office, 2001.

Argawal, Bina. "'Bargaining' and Gender Relations: With and Beyond the Household." *Feminist Economics* 3 (Spring 1997): 1–51.

Arora-Jonsson, Seema. "Virtue and Vulnerability: Discourses on Women, Gender and Climate Change." *Global Environmental Change* 21, no. 2 (May 2011): 744–51.

Arruzza, Cinzia, Tithi Bhattacharya, and Nancy Fraser. *Feminism for the 99 Percent: A Manifesto.* London and Brooklyn, NY: Verso, 2019.

Badgett, M. V. Lee. "Gender, Sexuality, and Sexual Orientation: All in the Feminist Family?" *Feminist Economics* 1 (Spring 1995): 121–40.

Bakker, Isabella. *The Strategic Silence: Gender and Economic Policy.* London: Zed Press, 1994.

Balakrishnan, Radhika, James Heintz, and Diane Elson. *Rethinking Economic Policy for Social Justice: The Radical Potential of Human Rights.* New York: Routledge, 2016.

Balamm, David N., and Michael Veseth. *Introduction to International Political Economy.* 2nd ed. Upper Saddle River, NJ: Prentice-Hall, 2001.

Barker, Drucilla K. "The Real Wolves of Wall Street: Examining Debt, Austerity, and Accountability through the Lens of Primitive Accumulation." *International Critical Thought* 8, no. 4 (October 2, 2018): 535–52.

Barker, Drucilla K., and Edith Kuiper, eds. *Feminist Perspectives on the World Bank: History, Theory and Policy.* London and New York: Routledge, 2006.

Barker, Drucilla K., and Edith Kuiper. "Gender, Class and Location in the Global Economy." In the *Handbook of Feminist Theory,* edited by Ania Plomien, Clare Hemmings, Marsha Henry, Mary Evans, Sadie Wearing, and Sumi Madhok, 500–15. New York and Newbury Park: Sage Publishing, 2014.

Barker, Drucilla K., and Edith Kuiper, eds. *Toward a Feminist Philosophy of Economics.* New York and London: Routledge, 2003.

Barker, Drucilla K., and Susan F. Feiner. "Affect, Race, and Class: An Interpretive Reading of Caring Labor." *Frontiers: A Journal of Women Studies* 30, no. 1 (2009): 41–54.

Barlow, Maude, and Tony Clarke. *Blue Gold: The Battle against Corporate Theft of the World's Water.* Toronto: McClelland & Stewart, 2003.

Bartley, Sharon J., Priscilla W. Blanton, and Jennifer L. Gilliard. "Husbands and Wives in Dual-Earner Marriages: Decision-Making, Gender Role Attitudes, Division of Household Labor, and Equity." *Marriage & Family Review* 37, no. 4 (September 26, 2005): 69–94.

Bauhardt, Christine, and Wendy Harcourt, eds. *Feminist Political Ecology and the Economics of Care: In Search of Economic Alternatives.* 1New York: Routledge, 2018.

Becker, Gary S. "Human Capital, Effort, and the Sexual Division of Labor." *Journal of Labor Economics* 3, no. 1, part 2 (1985): 33–58.

Becker, Gary S. *A Treatise on the Family.* Cambridge: Harvard University Press, 1993.

Bedford, Kate. *Developing Partnerships: Gender, Sexuality, and the Reformed World Bank.* Minneapolis: University of Minnesota Press, 2009.

Beenstock, Michael, and Peter Warburton. "The Market for Labor in Interwar Britain." *Explorations in Economic History* 28, no. 3 (July 1991): 287–308.

Benería, Lourdes. "Accounting for Women's Work: The Progress of Two Decades." *World Development* 20, no. 11 (1992): 1547–60.

Benería, Lourdes. "Structural Adjustment Policies." In *The Elgar Companion to Feminist Economics,* edited by Janice Peterson and Margaret Lewis, 687–95. Cheltenham and Northampton: Edward Elgar, 1999.

Benería, Lourdes. "Towards a Greater Integration of Gender in Economics." *World Development* 23 (November 1995): 1839–50.

Benería, Lourdes, and Gita Sen. "Accumulation, Reproduction, and Women's Roles in Economic Development." *Signs* 7 (Winter 1981): 279–98.

Benería, Lourdes, and Gita Sen. "Class and Gender Inequalities and Women's Role in Economic Development: Theoretical and Practical Implications." *Feminist Studies* 8, no. 1 (1982): 157.

Berger, Lawrence M., Maria Cancian, and Katherine Magnuson. "Anti-Poverty Policy Initiatives for the United States." *Russell Sage Foundation Journal of the Social Sciences* 14, no. 3 (February 2018): 1–19.

Bergeron, Suzanne. "Economics, Performativity, and Social Reproduction in Global Development." *Globalizations* 8, no. 2 (April 2011): 151–61.

Bergmann, Barbara. *The Economic Emergence of Women.* New York: Basic Books, 1986.

Bergmann, Barbara. "Feminism and Economics." *Academe* (September–October 1983): 22–26.

Bergmann, Barbara. "The Only Ticket to Equality: Total Androgyny, Male Style." *Journal of Contemporary Legal Issues* 9 (1998): 75–86.

Bergmann, Barbara. "Watch out for Family Friendly Policies." *Dollars and Sense* 215 (January–February 1998): 10–11.

Bergmann, Barbara, and Trudi Renwick. "A Budget-Based Definition of Poverty with an Application to Single-Parent Families." *Journal of Human Resources* 29 (Winter 1993): 1–24.

Bertrand, Marianne, and Sendhil Mullainathan. "Are Emily and Greg More Employable Than Lakisha and Jamal? A Field Experiment on Labor Market Discrimination." *American Economic Review* 94, no. 4 (2004): 991–1013.

Bittman, Michael, Paula England, Liana Sayer, Nancy Folbre, and George Matheson. "When Does Gender Trump Money? Bargaining and Time in Household Work." *American Journal of Sociology* 109, no. 1 (July 2003): 186–214.

Blau, Francine D., and Lawrence M. Kahn. "The Gender Wage Gap: Extent, Trends, and Explanations." *Journal of Economic Literature* 55, no. 3 (2017): 789–865.

Blinder, Alan S. *After the Music Stopped: The Financial Crisis, the Response, and the Work Ahead.* New York: Penguin Press, 2013.

Bluestone, Barry, and Bennett Harrison. *The Deindustrialization of America: Plant Closings, Community Abandonment, and the Dismantling of Basic Industry.* New York: Basic Books, 1982.

Boserup, Ester. "Economic Change and the Roles of Women." In *Persistent Inequalities: Women and World Development,* edited by Irene Tinker, 14–26. New York and Oxford: Oxford University Press, 1990.

Boserup, Ester. *Women's Role in Economic Development.* London: Allen and Unwin, 1970.

Budig, Michelle J., and Paula England. "The Wage Penalty for Motherhood." *American Sociological Review* 66 (April 2001): 204–25.

Cammett, Ann, "Welfare Queens Redux: The Criminalizing of Black Mothers in an Age of Neoliberalism," *Southern California Interdisciplinary Law Journal* 25 (2016): 363–94.

Caraway, Teri L. *Assembling Women: The Feminization of Global Manufacturing.* Ithaca: Cornell University Press, 2007.

Chamberlain, Mariam K. "Glass Ceiling." In *The Elgar Companion to Feminist Economics,* edited by Janice Peterson and Margaret Lewis, 396–401. Cheltenham and Northampton: Edward Elgar, 1999.

Chant, S. *The International Handbook of Gender and Poverty.* Cheltenham: Edward Elgar, 2010.

Chapkis, Wendy. *Live Sex Acts: Women Performing Erotic Labor.* London and New York: Routledge, 1996.

Charusheela, S. "Empowering Work? Bargaining Models Reconsidered." In *Toward a Feminist Philosophy of Economics,* edited by Drucilla K Barker and Edith Kuiper, 287–303. London and New York: Routledge, 2003.

Charusheela, S. "Intersectionality." In *The Handbook of Research on Gender and Economic Life,* edited by Deborah M. Figart and Tonia L. Warnecke. Cheltenham and Northampton: Edward Elgar, 2013.

Charusheela, S., and Eiman Zein-Elabdin, eds. *Postcolonialism Meets Economics.* Abingdon: Routledge, 2003.

Chetty, Raj, Nathaniel Hendren, Patrick Kline, Emmanuel Saez, and Nicholas Turner. "Is the United States Still a Land of Opportunity? Recent Trends in Intergenerational Mobility." *American Economic Review* 104, no. 5 (May 2014): 141–47.

Christopher, Karen. "Single Motherhood, Employment, or Social Assistance: Why Are U.S. Women Poorer Than Women in Other Affluent Nations?" *Journal of Poverty* 6, no. 2 (March 2002): 61–80.

Citro, Constance F., and Robert T. Michael, eds. *Measuring Poverty: A New Approach.* Washington, DC: National Academies Press, 1995.

Colen, Shellee. "'Like a Mother to Them': Stratified Reproduction and West Indian Childcare Workers and Employers in New York City." In *Conceiving the New World Order: The Global Politics of Reproduction,* edited by Faye Ginsburg and Rayna Reiter, 78–102. Berkeley: University of California Press, 1995.

Collins, Patricia Hill. *Black Feminist Thought: Knowledge, Consciousness, and the Politics of Empowerment.* New York: Routledge, 1990.

Connell, R. W., and James W. Messerschmidt. "Hegemonic Masculinity: Rethinking the Concept." *Gender & Society* 19, no. 6 (December 2005): 829–59.

Coontz, Stephanie. *Marriage, a History: How Love Conquered Marriage.* New York: Penguin Books, 2006.

Coontz, Stephanie. *The Way We Never Were: American Families and the Nostalgia Trap.* New York: Basic Books, 2000.

Cornwall, Andrea. "Women's Empowerment: What Works?" *Journal of International Development* 28, no. 3 (April 2016): 342–59.

Crenshaw, Kimberlé. "Demarginalizing the Intersection of Race and Sex: A Black Feminist Critique of Antidiscrimination Doctrine, Feminist Theory and Antiracist Politics." *University of. Chicago Legal Forum* vol. 1989, article 8.

Crittenden, Ann. *The Economic Consequences of Motherhood: Why the Most Important Job in the World Is Still the Least Valued.* New York: Henry Holt, 2000.

Dalla Costa, Mariarosa, and Selma James. *The Power of Women and the Subversion of the Community.* Bristol: Falling Wall Press, 1975.

Darrity, William, Jr., ed. "A Direct Route to Full Employment." *Review of Black Political Economy* 37, no. 3–4 (January 2010): 179–81.

Darrity, William, Jr., ed. *Economics and Discrimination.* Cheltenham and Northampton: Edward Elgar, 1995.

Davis, Angela. *Women, Race & Class.* New York: Vintage, 1983.

de Beauvoir, Simone. *The Second Sex.* New York: Alfred A. Knopf, 1993 [1949].

Dillon, Lindsey, Christopher Sellers, Vivian Underhill, Nicholas Shapir, Jennifer Liss Ohayon, Marianne Sullivan, Phil Brown, Jill Harrison, Sara Wylie, and the "EPA Under Siege" Writing Group. "The Environmental Protection Agency in the Early Trump Administration: Prelude to Regulatory Capture." *American Journal of Public Health,* 108 (2018): 589–94.

Dobb, Maurice. *Studies in the Development of Capitalism.* New York: International Publishing, 1946.

Dorman, Peter, Nancy Folbre, Donald McCloskey, and Tom Weisskopf. "Debating Markets," edited by Tom Weisskopf and Nancy Folbre. *Feminist Economics* 2 (Spring 1996): 69–85.

Douglas, Susan J., and Meredith W. Michaels. *The Mommy Myth: The Idealization of Motherhood and How It Has Undermined Women.* New York: Free Press, 2004.

Dymski, Gary, Jesus Hernandez, and Lisa Mohanty. "Race, Gender, Power, and the US

Subprime Mortgage and Foreclosure Crisis: A Meso Analysis." *Feminist Economics* 19, no. 3 (July 2013): 124–51.

Eaton, Susan C. "Eldercare in the United States: Inadequate, inequitable, but Not a Lost Cause." *Feminist Economics* 11, no. 2 (2005): 37–51.

Edin, Kathryn, and H. Luke Shaefer. *$2.00 a Day: Living on Almost Nothing in America.* Boston: Houghton Mifflin Harcourt, 2015.

Ehrenreich, Barbara. "Maid to Order." In *Nannies, Maids and Sex Workers in the New Economy,* edited by Barbara Ehrenreich and Arlie R. Hochschild, 85–103. New York: Metropolitan Books, 2003.

Ehrenreich, Barbara. *Nickel and Dimed: On (Not) Getting by in America.* New York: Henry Holt, 2002.

Ehrenreich, Barbara, and Arlie Hochschild, eds. *Global Woman: Nannies, Maids, and Sex Workers in the New Economy.* New York: Henry Holt, 2002.

Eisenberg, Susan. "Still Building the Foundation: Women in the Construction Trades." *Working USA* 2, no. 1 (1998): 23–25.

Elias, Juanita. *Fashioning Inequality: The Multinational Company and Gendered Employment in a Globalizing World.* Aldershot and Burlington, VT: Ashgate, 2004.

Elson, Diane. "Gender Awareness in Modeling Structural Adjustment." *World Development* 23, no. 11 (November 1995): 1851–68.

Elson, Diane. "Gender and the Global Economic Crisis in Developing Countries: A Framework for Analysis." *Gender & Development* 18, no. 2 (July 2010): 201–12.

Elson, Diane. "Male Bias in Macroeconomics: The Case of Structural Adjustment." In *Male Bias in the Development Process,* edited by Diane Elson, 164–90. Manchester and New York: Manchester University Press, 1991.

Elson, Diane. "The Social Content of Macroeconomic Policies." *World Development* 28, no. 7 (2000): 1347–64.

Elson, Diane, and Nilufer Cagatay. "The Social Content of Macroeconomic Policies." *World Development* 28, no. 7 (July 2000): 1347–64.

Enloe, Cynthia H. *Bananas, Beaches and Bases: Making Feminist Sense of International Politics.* Berkeley: University of California Press, 2000 [1989].

Esping-Andersen, Gøsta. *The Three Worlds of Welfare Capitalism.* Princeton: Princeton University Press, 1990.

Falkingham, Jane, Maria Evandrou, and Athnina Vlachantoni. "Gender, Poverty and Pensions." In *The International Handbook of Poverty: Concepts, Research and Policy,* 232–40. Northampton, MA: Edward Elgar, 2010.

Federici, Silvia. *Caliban and the Witch.* 2nd. rev. ed. New York: Autonomedia, 2014.

Federici, Silvia. *Re-Enchanting the World: Feminism and the Politics of the Commons.* Oakland: PM Press, 2019.

Federici, Silvia. *Revolution at Point Zero: Housework, Reproduction, and Feminist Struggle.* Oakland: PM Press, 2012.

Feiner, Susan F., ed. *Race and Gender in the American Economy: Views from across the Spectrum.* New York: Prentice-Hall, 1994.

Ferber, Marianne A., and Julie A. Nelson. "Introduction: The Social Construction of Economics and the Social Construction of Gender." In *Beyond Economic Man: Feminist Theory and Economics,* edited by Marianne A. Ferber and Julie A. Nelson, 1–22. Chicago: University of Chicago Press, 1993.

Figart, Deborah M. "Wage Gap." In *The Elgar Companion to Feminist Economics,* edited by Janice Peterson and Margaret Lewis, 746–49. Cheltenham and Northampton: Edward Elgar, 1999.

Figart, Deborah M., and Ellen Mutari. "Work Time Regimes in Europe: Can Flexibility and Gender Equity Coexist?" *Journal of Economic Issues* 34, no. 4 (2000): 847–71.

Figart, Deborah M., Ellen Mutari, and Marilyn Power. *Living Wages, Equal Wages: Gender and Labor Market Policies in the United States.* New York: Routledge, 2002.

Folbre, Nancy. *Greed, Lust & Gender: A History of Economic Ideas.* Oxford and New York: Oxford University Press, 2009.

Folbre, Nancy. *The Invisible Heart: Economics and Family Values.* New York: New Press, 2001.

Folbre, Nancy. "Socialism, Feminist and Scientific." In *Beyond Economic Man: Feminist Theory and Economics*, edited by Marianne A. Ferber and Julie A. Nelson, 94–110. Chicago: University of Chicago Press, 1993.

Folbre, Nancy. "The Unproductive Housewife: Her Evolution in British Economic Thought." *Signs* 16, no. 3 (April 1991): 463–84.

Folbre, Nancy. *Who Pays for the Kids: Gender and the Structures of Constraint.* London and New York: Routledge, 1994.

Folbre, Nancy, and Julie A. Nelson. "For Love or Money—or Both?" *Journal of Economic Perspectives* 14, no. 4 (2000): 123–40.

Forget, Evelyn L. *Basic Income for Canadians: The Key to a Healthier, Happier, More Secure Life for All.* Toronto: James Lorimer & Company, 2018.

Fraad, Harriet, Stephen Resnick, and Richard Wolff. *Bringing It All Back Home: Class, Gender, and Power in the Household.* London: Pluto Press, 1994.

Francisco-Menchavez, Valerie. *The Labor of Care: Filipina Migrants and Transnational Families in the Digital Age.* Champaign: University of Illinois Press, 2018.

Frank, Robert H., Thomas Gilovich, and Dennis T. Regan. "Does Studying Economics Inhibit Cooperation?" *Journal of Economic Perspectives* 7, no. 2 (1993): 159–71.

Fraser, Nancy. *Justice Interruptus: Critical Reflections on the "Postsocialist" Condition.* London and New York: Routledge, 1997.

Fraser, Nancy, Tithi Bhattacharya, and Cinzia Arruzza. "Notes for a Feminist Manifesto." *New Left Review* 114 (2018): 113–34.

French-Davis, Ricardo. *Economic Reforms in Chile: From Dictatorship to Democracy.* Ann Arbor: University of Michigan Press, 2002.

Friedan, Betty. *The Feminine Mystique.* New York: W. W. Norton, 1963.

Friedman, Milton, and Rose D. Friedman. *Capitalism and Freedom.* Chicago: University of Chicago Press, 1982.

Fullerton, Howard N., Jr. "Labor Force Participation: 75 Years of Change, 1950–98 and 1998–2025." *Monthly Labor Review* 122, no. 3 (1999): 3–12.

Gertsel, Naomi, and Harriet Engel Gross. "Gender and Families in the United States: The Reality of Economic Dependence." In *Women: A Feminist Perspective*, edited by Jo Freeman, 92–127. Mountain View: Mayfield, 1995.

Gibson-Graham, J. K. *The End of Capitalism (as We Knew It): A Feminist Critique of Political Economy.* Oxford: Blackwell Publishers, 1996.

Gibson-Graham, J. K., Jenny Cameron, and Stephen Healy. "Commoning as a Postcapitalist Politics." In *Releasing the Commons*, edited by Ash Amin and Phillip Howell, 191–212. New York: Routledge, 2016.

Gibson-Graham, J. K., Jenny Cameron, and Stephen Healy. *Take Back the Economy: An*

Ethical Guide for Transforming Our Communities. Minneapolis: University of Minnesota Press, 2013.

Giddings, Paula. *When and Where I Enter: The Impact of Black Women on Race and Sex in America*. New York: Harper Collins, 2007 [1984].

Ginsburg, Faye D., and Rayna R. Reiter, eds. *Conceiving the New World Order: The Global Politics of Reproduction*. Berkeley: University of California Press, 1995.

Glenn, Evelyn Nakano. *Forced to Care: Coercion and Caregiving in America*. Cambridge, MA: Harvard University Press, 2010.

Goede, Marieke de. *Virtue, Fortune and Faith: A Genealogy of Finance*. Minneapolis: University of Minnesota Press, 2005.

Goldin, Claudia. *Understanding the Gender Gap: An Economic History of American Women*. New York: Oxford University Press, 1990.

Graeber, David. *Debt: The First 5,000 years of History*. Brooklyn and London: Melville House, 2012.

Grapard, Ulla. "Robinson Crusoe: The Quintessential Economic Man." *Feminist Economics* 1 (Spring 1995): 33–52.

Haller, Mark. *Eugenics: Hereditarian Attitudes in American Thought*. New Brunswick, NJ: Rutgers University Press, 1984.

Harding, Sandra. "Can Feminist Thought Make Economics More Objective?" *Feminist Economics* 1 (Spring 1995): 7–32.

Harkins, Anthony, and Meredith McCarroll, eds. *Appalachian Reckoning: A Region Responds to 'Hillbilly Elegy.'* Morgantown: West Virginia University Press, 2019.

Hartmann, Heidi I. "The Family as the Locus of Gender, Class, and Political Struggle: The Example of Housework." In *Feminism and Methodology*, edited by Sandra Harding, 109–34. Bloomington and Indianapolis: Indiana University Press, 1987.

Harvey, David. *A Brief History of Neoliberalism*. Oxford: Oxford University Press, 2005.

Harvey, David. *The Enigma of Capital: And the Crises of Capitalism*. Oxford and New York: Oxford University Press, 2010.

Hayhurst, Lyndsay M. C. "Corporatising Sport, Gender and Development: Postcolonial IR Feminisms, Transnational Private Governance and Global Corporate Social Engagement." *Third World Quarterly* 32, no. 3 (April 2011): 531–49.

Heintz, James. *Globalization, Economic Policy and Employment: Poverty and Gender Implications*. Geneva: ILO, 2006.

Hickel, Jason. "DeGrowth: A Theory of Radical Abundance." *Real-World Economics Review* 87 (2019): 54–68.

Hickel, Jason. *The Divide: A Brief Guide to Global Inequality and Its Solutions*. London: William Heinemann, 2017.

Hickel, Jason. "Is Global Inequality Getting Better or Worse? A Critique of the World Bank's Convergence Narrative." *Third World Quarterly* 38, no. 10 (October 3, 2017): 2208–22.

Hilton, Rodney, ed. *The Transition from Feudalism to Capitalism*. Reprint. London: Verso, 1985 [1976].

Himmelweit, Susan. "The Discovery of 'Unpaid Work': The Social Consequences of the Expansion of 'Work.'" *Feminist Economics* 1, no. 2 (July 1995): 1–19.

Hirshman, Linda R. *Get to Work: A Manifesto for Women of the World*. New York: Viking, 2006.

Hobsbawm, Eric. *Industry and Empire: The Birth of the Industrial Revolution*. New York: Penguin, 1999 [1969].

Hochschild, Arlie R., and Ann Machung. *The Second Shift*. New York: Morrow, William, and Co., 1990.

Hoskyns, Catherine, and Shirin M. Rai. "Recasting the Global Political Economy: Counting Women's Unpaid Work." *New Political Economy* 12, no. 3 (September 2007): 297–317.

Hozic, Aida A., and Jacqui True, eds. *Scandalous Economics: Gender and the Politics of Financial Crises*. Oxford Studies in Gender and International Relations. New York: Oxford University Press, 2016.

Hudson, Michael. *The Bubble and Beyond: Ficticious Capital, Debt Deflation and the Global Crisis*. Dresden: Islet-Verl, 2012.

Hudson, Michael H. *The Monster: How a Gang of Predatory Lenders and Wall Street Bankers Fleeced America—and Spawned a Global Crisis*. New York: Henry Holt, 2010.2

Humphries, Jane. "Economics, Gender, and Equal Opportunities." In *The Economics of Equal Opportunities*, edited by Jane Humphries and Jill Rubery, 55–79. Manchester: Equal Employment Opportunities Commission, 1995.

Humphries, Jane. "Enclosures, Common Rights, and Women: The Proletarianization of Families in the Late Eighteenth and Early Nineteenth Centuries." *Journal of Economic History* 50 (March 1990): 17–42.

Humphries, Jane. "Female Headed Households in Early Industrial Britain: The Vanguard of the Proletariat?" *Labor History Review* 63 (Spring 1998): 31–65.

Jacobsen, Joyce. *The Economics of Gender*. Malden, MA: Blackwell, 1998.

Joseph, Miranda. *Debt to Society: Accounting for Life under Capitalism*. Minneapolis: University of Minnesota Press, 2014.

Kabeer, Naila. "Gender Equality, Economic Growth, and Women's Agency: The 'Endless Variety' and 'Monotonous Similarity' of Patriarchal Constraints." *Feminist Economics* 22, no. 1 (January 2, 2016): 295–321.

Karim, Lamia. "Disposable Bodies: Garment Factory Catastrophe and Feminist Practices in Bangladesh." *Anthropology Now* 6, no. 1 (April 2014): 52–63. https://doi.org/1 0.1080/19492901.2013.11728417.

Karim, Lamia. *Microfinance and Its Discontents: Women in Debt in Bangladesh*. Minneapolis: University of Minnesota Press, 2011.

Kempadoo, Kamala, and Jo Doezema, ed. *Global Sex Workers: Rights, Resistance, and Redefinition*. New York and London: Routledge, 1998.

Keynes, John Maynard. *The General Theory of Employment, Interest, and Money*. New York: Harcourt, Brace, Jovanovich, 1964 [1936].

King, Mary C. "Black Women's Labor Market Status: Occupational Segregation in the United States and Great Britain." *Review of Black Political Economy* 24 (Summer 1995): 23–40.

Koonz, Claudia. *Mothers in the Fatherland: Women, the Family, and Nazi Politics*. New York: St. Martin's Press, 1988.

Kuiper, Edith, and Drucilla K. Barker, eds. *Feminist Economics and the World Bank*. New York and London: Routledge, 2006.

Kuiper, Edith, Jolande Sap, Susan Feiner, Notburga Ott, and Zafris Tzannatos, eds. *Out of the Margin: Feminist Perspectives on Economics*. New York and London: Routledge, 1995.

Kukreja, Sunil. "The Two Faces of Development." In *Introduction to International Politi-*

cal Economy, 2nd ed., edited by David N. Balaam and Michael Veseth, 320–45. Upper Saddle River, NJ: Prentice Hall, 2001.

Kunz, Rahel. "Remittances in the Global Political Economy." In *Handbook on the International Political Economy of Gender*, edited by Juanita Elias and Adrienne Roberts, 265–80. Cheltenham, UK: Edward Elgar, 2018.

Kuttner, Robert. *Everything for Sale: The Virtues and Limits of Markets*. New York: Knopf, 1997.

Kuttner, Robert. "The Market for Labor." In *Everything for Sale: The Virtues and Limits of Markets*, 68–109. Chicago: University of Chicago Press, 1999.

Lazzarato, Maurice. *The Making of Indebted Man*. Translated by Joshua David Jordan. Cambridge: Semiotext(e), 2012.

Lekakis, Joseph N., and Maria Kousis. "Economic Crisis, Troika and the Environment in Greece." *South European Society and Politics* 18, no. 3 (September 2013): 305–31.

Levanon, Asaf, Paula England, and Paul Allison. "Occupational Feminization and Pay: Assessing Causal Dynamics Using 1950–2000 U.S. Census Data." *Social Forces* 88, no. 2 (December 2009): 865–9.

Lister, Ruth. *Feminist Perspectives*. London: Macmillan, 1997.

Longino, Helen. *Science as Social Knowledge: Values and Objectivity in Scientific Inquiry*. Princeton: Princeton University Press, 1990.

Madison, Bernice. "Social Services for Families and Children in the Soviet Union Since 1967." *Slavic Review* 31, no. 4 (1972): 831–52.

Manalansan, Martin F. "Queering the Chain of Care Paradigm." *Scholar and Feminist Online* 16, no. 3 (2008).

Marx, Karl. *Capital Vol. 1*. London: Verso, 1990 [1867].

Marx, Karl, and Friedrich Engels. *The Communist Manifesto*. Reprint. London: Verso, 1998 [1848].

Michener, Jamila, and Margaret Teresa Brower. "What's Policy Got to Do With It?: Race, Gender and Economic Inequality in the United States." *Daedelus* 149, no. 1 (2020): 100–118.

Milanović, Branko. *Global Inequality: A New Approach for the Age of Globalization*. Cambridge, MA: Harvard University Press, 2016.

Mincer, Jacob, and Solomon Polachek. "An Exchange: The Theory of Human Capital and the Earnings of Women: Women's Earnings Reexamined" *Journal of Human Resources* 13, no. 1 (1978): 118–34.

Mintz, Sidney W. *Sweetness and Power: The Place of Sugar in Modern History*. New York: Penguin Books, 1986.

Moeller, Kathryn. *The Gender Effect: Capitalism, Feminism, and the Corporate Politics of Development*. Oakland: University of California Press, 2018.

Mohanty, Chandra. "One Third/Two-Thirds Worlds." In *Beyond Borders: Thinking Critically about Global Issues*, edited by Paula S. Rothenberg, 41–43. New York: Worth Publishers, 2006.

Mohanty, Chandra. "Under Western Eyes: Feminist Scholarship and Colonial Discourses." *Feminist Review* 30 (Autumn 1988): 61–88.

Morgan, Robin, ed. *Sisterhood Is Global: The International Women's Movement Anthology*. Garden City, NY: Anchor Press/Doubleday, 1984.

Molyneux, Maxine. "Beyond the Domestic Labor Debate." *New Left Review* 116 (1979): 3–27.

Mueller, Adele. *Peasants and Professionals: The Social Organization of Women in Development Knowledge*. Toronto: University of Toronto Press, 1987.

Nakano, Evelyn Glenn. *Forced to Care: Coercion and Caregiving in America*. Cambridge, MA: Harvard University Press, 2010.

Nelson, Julie A. "Feminism and Economics." *Journal of Economic Perspectives* 9, no. 2 (1995): 131–48.

Nelson, Julie A. *Feminism, Objectivity, and Economics*. New York: Routledge, 1996.

Nelson, Julie A. *Gender and Risk-Taking: Economics, Evidence and Why the Answer Matters*. London and New York: Routledge, 2017.

Nelson, Lynn Hankinson. *Who Knows: from Quine to a Feminist Empiricism*. Philadelphia: Temple University Press, 1994.

O'Connell Davidson, J. "Troubling Freedom: Migration, Debt, and Modern Slavery." *Migration Studies* 1, no. 2 (July 2013): 176–95.

Orloff, Ann Schola. "Gender and the Social Rights of Citizenship." *American Sociological Review* 58 (1993): 303–28.

Ott, Notburga. "Fertility and Division of Work in the Family: A Game Theoretic Model of Household Decisions." In *Out of the Margin: Feminist Perspectives on Economics*, edited by Edith Kuiper and Jolande Sap, 80–99. New York and London: Routledge, 1995.

Pearce, Diana M. "The Feminization of Poverty: Women, Work, and Welfare." *Urban and Social Change Review* 11 (1978): 28–36.

Pearson, Ruth. "'Nimble Fingers' Revisited: Reflection on Women and the Third World Industrialization in the Late Twentieth Century." In *Feminist Visions of Development: Gender Analysis and Policy*, edited by Cecile Jackson and Ruth Pearson, 171–88. London and New York: Routledge, 1998.

Pearson, Ruth, and Diane Elson. "Transcending the Impact of the Financial Crisis in the United Kingdom: Towards Plan F—a Feminist Economic Strategy." *Feminist Review* 109, no. 1 (February 2015): 8–30.

Peterson, V. Spike. *A Critical Rewriting of Global Political Economy: Integrating Reproductive, Productive and Virtual Economies*, New York: Routledge, 2003.

Peterson, V. Spike. "Rethinking Theory: Inequalities, Informalization and Feminist Quandaries." *International Feminist Journal of Politics* 14, no. 1 (March 2012): 5–35.

Pettifor, Ann. *The Production of Money: How to Break the Power of Bankers*. London: Verso, 2017.

Pettit, Becky, and Jennifer Hook. "The Structure of Women's Employment in Comparative Perspective." *Social Forces* 84, no. 2 (2005): 779–801.

Pietrykowski, Bruce. "The Return to Caring Skills: Gender, Class, and Occupational Wages in the US." *Feminist Economics* 23, no. 4 (2017): 32–61.

Pietrykowski, Bruce. *Work*. Cambridge, MA: Polity Press, 2019.

Polachek, Solomon. "Human Capital and Gender Earning Gap: A Response of Feminist Critiques." In *Out of the Margin: Feminist Perspectives on Economics*, edited by Edith Kuiper and Jolande Sap, 61–89. London and New York: Routledge, 1995.

Polanyi, Karl. *The Great Transformation: The Political and Economic Origins of Our Time*. 2nd Beacon Paperback ed. Boston: Beacon Press, 2001.

Pritchett, Lant. "Divergence, Big Time." *Journal of Economic Perspectives* 11, no. 3 (August 1997): 3–17.

Prügl, Elizabeth. "'Lehman Brothers and Sisters:': Revisiting Gender and Myth After the

Financial Crisis." In *Scandalous Economics: Gender and the Politics of Financial Crises*, edited by Aida A. Hozic and Jaqui True, 21–40. New York: Oxford University Press, 2016.

Pujol, Michèle A. *Feminism and Anti-Feminism in Early Economic Thought*. Aldershot: Edward Elgar, 1992.

Pyle, Jean L. "Sex, Maids, and Export Processing: Risks and Reasons for Gendered Global Production Networks." *International Journal of Politics, Culture, and Society* 15 (September 2001): 55–76.

Pyle, Jean L. "Women, the Family, and Economic Restructuring: The Singapore Model." *Review of Social Economy* 55 (Summer 1997): 215–23.

Rai, Shirin M., Catherine Hoskyns, and Dania Thomas. "Depletion: The Cost of Social Reproduction." *International Feminist Journal of Politics* 16, no. 1 (2014): 86–105.

Rajan, Raghuram. *Fault Lines: How Hidden Fractures Still Threaten the World Economy*. Princeton: Princeton University Press, 2011.

Razavi, Shahra. *Gendered Poverty and Well-Being*. Malden, MA: Blackwell, 2000.

Roberts, Adrienne. "Financing Social Reproduction: The Gendered Relations of Debt and Mortgage Finance in Twenty-First-Century America." *New Political Economy* 18, no. 1 (February 2013): 21–42.

Roberts, Adrienne. "The Political Economy of 'Transnational Business Feminism.'" *International Feminist Journal of Politics* 17, no. 2 (2015): 209–31.

Roberts, Adrienne. "Privatizing Social Reproduction: The Primitive Accumulation of Water in an Era of Neoliberalism." *Antipode* 40, no. 4 (September 2008): 535–60.

Rosenberg-Smith, Carroll. *Disorderly Conduct: Visions of Gender in Victorian America*. Oxford: Oxford University Press, 1986.

Rossi, Alice S., ed. *The Feminist Papers: From Adams to de Beauvoir*. New York: Columbia University Press, 1973.

Sainsbury, Diane. *Gender, Equality, and Welfare States*. Cambridge, MA: Cambridge University Press, 1996.

Sainsbury, Diane. "Gender and Social Democratic Welfare States." In *Gender and Welfare State Regimes*, edited by Diane Sainsbury, 75–116. Oxford: Oxford University Press, 1999.

Salzinger, Leslie. *Genders in Production: Making Workers in Mexico's Global Factories*. Berkeley: University of California Press, 2003.

Salzinger, Leslie. "A Maid by Any Other Name: The Transformation of 'Dirty Work' by Central American Immigrants." In *Ethnography Unbound: Power and Resistance in the Modern Metropolis*, edited by Michael Burawoy, 139–52. Berkeley: University of California Press, 1991.

Sanday-Reeves, Peggy. "The Socio-Cultural Context of Rape." *Journal of Social Issues* 37 (1981): 5–27.

Sassen, Saskia. *Globalization and Its Discontents: Essays on the New Mobility of People and Money*. New York: New Press, 1998.

Sassen, Saskia. "Women's Burden: Counter-Geographies of Globalization and the Feminization of Survival." *Journal of International Affairs* 53, no. 2 (2000): 503–24.

Schiebinger, Londa. *Nature's Body*. Boston: Beacon Press, 1995.

Schor, Juliet B., and Andrew K. Jorgenson. "Is It Too Late for Growth?" *Review of Radical Political Economics* 51, no. 2 (June 2019): 320–29.

Scott, Joan. "Gender: A Useful Category of Historical Analysis." *American Historical Review* 91 (December 1986): 1053–75.

Seager, Joni. *The State of Women in the World Atlas.* New York: Penguin Reference, 2000.

Seguino, Stephanie. "The Global Economic Crisis, Its Gender and Ethnic Implications, and Policy Responses." *Gender & Development* 18, no. 2 (July 2010): 179–99.

Seguino, Stephanie. "Global Trends in Gender Equality." *Journal of African Development* 18 (2016): 1–30.

Sen, Amartya. *Development as Freedom.* New York: Knopf, 1999.

Smith, Adam. *An Inquiry into the Nature and Causes of the Wealth of Nations.* Chicago: University of Chicago Press, 1976 [1776].

Standing, Guy. "Care Work: Overcoming Insecurity and Neglect." In *Care Work: The Quest for Security,* edited by Mary Daly, 15–31. Geneva: International Labour Office, 2001.

Standing, Guy. "Global Feminization through Flexible Labor: A Theme Revisited." *World Development* 27, no. 3 (1999): 583–602.

Standing, Guy. *A Precariat Charter: From Denizens to Citizens.* London and New York: Bloomsbury, 2014.

Stark, Agneta. "Warm Hands in a Cold Age–on the Need of a New World Order of Care." *Feminist Economics* 11, no. 2 (2005): 7–36.

Staveren, I. van. "The Lehman Sisters Hypothesis." *Cambridge Journal of Economics* 38, no. 5 (September 1, 2014): 995–1014.

Strassmann, Diana. "Not a Free Market: The Rhetoric of Disciplinary Authority in Economics." In *Beyond Economic Man: Feminist Theory and Economics,* 54–68. Chicago: University of Chicago Press, 1993.

Strauss, Kendra. "Accumulation and Dispossession: Lifting the Veil on the Subprime Mortgage Crisis." *Antipode* 14, no.1 (2009): 10–14.

Strober, Myra H., and Carolyn L. Arnold. "The Dynamics of Occupational Segregation among Bank Tellers." In *Gender in the Workplace,* edited by Clair Brown and Joseph Pechman, 107–58. Washington, DC: Brookings Institution, 1987.

Trydegård, Gun-Britt. "Care Work in Changing Welfare States: Nordic Care Workers' Experiences." *European Journal of Ageing* 9, no. 2 (2012): 119–29.

Vasile, Marian. "The Gender of Silk." *Journal of Research in Gender Studies* 31, no. 1 (2013): 102–7.

Waring, Marilyn. *If Women Counted: A New Feminist Economics.* New York: Harper Collins, 1988.

Weeks, Kathi. *The Problem with Work: Feminism, Marxism, Antiwork Politics, and Postwork Imaginaries.* Durham: Duke University Press, 2011.

Wellhausen, Rachel L. "Recent Trends in Investor–State Dispute Settlement." *Journal of International Dispute Settlement* 7, no. 1 (March 1, 2016): 117–35.

Williams, Joan. *Unbending Gender: Why Family and Work Conflict and What to Do about It.* New York: Oxford University Press, 2001.

Williams, Rhonda. "Race, Deconstruction, and the Emergent Agenda of Feminist Economic Theory." In *Beyond Economic Man: Feminist Theory and Economics,* edited by Marianne A. Ferber and Julie A. Nelson, 144–52. Chicago: University of Chicago Press, 1993.

Williams, Rhonda M., and William E. Spriggs. "How Does It Feel to Be Free?: Reflections on Black-White Economic Inequality in the Era of 'Color-Blind' Law." *Review of Black Political Economy* 27, no. 1 (June 1999): 9–21.

Women's Environment and Development Organization (WEDO). "Gender, Climate

Change and Human Security: Lessons from Senegal." In *The Women, Gender and Development Reader*, 317–26. London: Zed Books, 2011.

Yalom, Marilyn. *A History of the Wife*. New York: HarperCollins, 2001.

Yi, Yun-Ae. "Margaret G. Reid: Life and Achievements." *Feminist Economics* 2, no. 3 (November 1996): 17–36.

Zein-Elabdin, Eiman O., and S. Charusheela, eds. *Postcolonialism Meets Economics*. London and New York: Routledge, 2003.

Index

The page numbers in italics indicate tables.